WOKE,
INC.

WOKE, INC.

INSIDE CORPORATE AMERICA'S SOCIAL JUSTICE SCAM

Vivek Ramaswamy

CENTER
STREET

NEW YORK   NASHVILLE

Center Street
Hachette Book Group
1290 Avenue of the Americas, New York, NY 10104
centerstreet.com
twitter.com/centerstreet

Originally published in hardcover and ebook by Center Street in August 2021
First Trade Paperback Edition: August 2023

Center Street is a division of Hachette Book Group, Inc. The Center Street name and logo are trademarks of Hachette Book Group, Inc.

The publisher is not responsible for websites (or their content) that are not owned by the publisher.

The Hachette Speakers Bureau provides a wide range of authors for speaking events. To find out more, go to hachettespeakersbureau.com or email HachetteSpeakers@hbgusa.com.

Center Street books may be purchased in bulk for business, educational, or promotional use. For information, please contact your local bookseller or the Hachette Book Group Special Markets Department at special.markets@hbgusa.com.

Library of Congress Cataloging-in-Publication Data has been applied for.

ISBNs: 9781546090793 (trade paperback), 9781546059820 (ebook)

Printed in the United States of America

LSC-C

Printing 2, 2023

TO MY SON KARTHIK, AND TO HIS GENERATION.

CONTENTS

INTRODUCTION

The Woke-Industrial Complex

M Y NAME IS VIVEK RAMASWAMY, and I am a traitor to my class.

I'm going to make some controversial claims in this book, so it's important you know a bit about me first. My parents immigrated from India forty years ago to southwest Ohio where I was born. They weren't rich. I went to a racially diverse public school with kids who came from difficult backgrounds. After I got roughed up in eighth grade by another kid, my parents sent me to a Jesuit high school where I was the only Hindu student and graduated as valedictorian in 2003. I then went to Harvard to study molecular biology and finished near the top of my class. Rather than becoming an academic scientist, I joined a large hedge fund in 2007 and started investing in biotech. A few years later I became the youngest partner at the firm.

In 2010, I had an itch to study law, so I went to Yale while keeping my job at the fund. After law school, I started a biotech company called Roivant Sciences. My goal was to challenge big pharma's bureaucracy with a new business model—which proved to be easier said than done. I started by developing a drug for Alzheimer's disease that resulted in the largest biotech IPO in history at the time, though a few years later that drug failed spectacularly. Failure hurt, and I was chastened by it. Thankfully the company went on to develop important drugs for other diseases that helped patients in the end. I've also co-founded a few tech companies along the way, one that I sold in 2009 and another of which is fast-growing today, and now I'm philanthropically active in a number of nonprofit ventures. I know how the elite business world works—and elite academia and philanthropy too—because I've seen it firsthand.

I used to think corporate bureaucracy was bad because it's inefficient. That's true, but it's not the biggest problem. Rather, there's a new invisible force at work in the highest ranks of corporate America, one far more nefarious. It's the defining scam of our time—one that robs you of not only your money but your voice and your identity.

The con works like a magic trick, summed up well by Michael Caine's character in the opening monologue in Christopher Nolan's movie *The Prestige*:

> Every great magic trick consists of three parts or acts. The first part is called The Pledge. The magician shows you something ordinary: a deck of cards, a bird or a man. . . . The second act is called The Turn. The magician takes the ordinary something and makes it do something extraordinary. But you wouldn't clap yet. Because making something disappear isn't enough; you have to bring it back. That's why every magic trick has a third act, the hardest part, the part we call The Prestige.[1]

Financial success in twenty-first-century America involves the same simple steps. First, the Pledge: you find an ordinary market where ordinary people sell ordinary things. The simpler, the better. Second, the Turn: you find an arbitrage in that market and squeeze the hell out of it. An arbitrage refers to the opportunity to buy something for one price and instantly sell it for a higher price to someone else.

If this were a book about how to get rich quick, I'd expound on these first two steps. But the point of this book is to expose the dirty little secret underlying the third step of corporate America's act, its Prestige. Here's how it works: *pretend like you care about something other than profit and power, precisely to gain more of each.*

All great magicians master the art of distraction—flashing lights, smoke, beautiful women on stage. Today's captains of industry do it by promoting progressive social values. Their tactics are far more dangerous for America than those of the older robber barons: their do-good smoke screen expands not only their market power but their power over every other facet of our lives.

As a young twenty-first-century capitalist myself, the thing I was supposed to do was shut up and play along: wear hipster clothes, lead via practiced vulnerability, applaud diversity and inclusion, and muse on how to make the world a better place at conferences in fancy ski towns. Not a bad gig.

The most important part of the trick was to stay mum about it. Now I'm violating the code by pulling back the curtain and showing you what's really going on in corporate boardrooms across America.

Why am I defecting? I'm fed up with corporate America's game of pretending to care about justice in order to make money. It is quietly wreaking havoc on American democracy. It demands that a small group of investors and CEOs determine what's good for society rather than our democracy at large. This new trend has created a major cultural shift in America. It's not just ruining companies. It's polarizing our politics. It's dividing our country to a breaking point. Worst of all, it's concentrating the power to determine American values in the hands of a small group of capitalists rather than in the hands of the American citizenry at large, which is where the dialogue about social values belongs. That's not America, but a distortion of it.

Wokeness has remade American capitalism in its own image. Talk of being "woke" has morphed into a kind of catchall term for progressive identity politics today. The phrase "stay woke" was used from time to time by black[2] civil rights activists over the last few decades, but it really took off only recently, when black protestors made it a catchphrase in the Ferguson protests in response to a police officer fatally shooting Michael Brown.[3]

These days, white progressives have appropriated "stay woke" as a general-purpose term that refers to being aware of all identity-based injustices. So while "stay woke" started as a remark black people would say to remind each other to be alert to racism, it would now be perfectly normal for white coastal suburbanites to say it to remind each other to watch out for possible microaggressions against, say, transgender people—for example, accidentally calling someone by their pre-transition name. In woke terminology, that forbidden practice would be called "deadnaming," and "microaggression" means a small offense that causes a lot of harm when done widely. If someone committed a microaggression against black transgender people, we enter the world of "intersectionality," where identity politics is applied to someone who has intersecting minority identities and its rules get complicated. Being woke means waking up to these invisible power structures that govern the social universe.

Lost? You aren't alone. Basically, being woke means obsessing about race, gender, and sexual orientation. Maybe climate change too. That's the best definition I can give. Today more and more people are becoming woke, even though generations of civil rights leaders have taught us *not* to focus on race or gender. And now capitalism is trying to stay woke too.

Once corporations discovered wokeness, the inevitable happened: they used it to make money.

Consider Fearless Girl, a statue of a young girl that suddenly appeared one day in New York City to stare down the iconic statue of the Wall Street bull. It was apparently a challenge for Wall Street to promote gender diversity: the placard at Fearless Girl's feet said, "Know the power of women in leadership. SHE makes a difference." Feminists cheered. The trick? "SHE" referred not only to Fearless Girl but to the Nasdaq-listed exchange-traded fund (ETF) that her commissioners, State Street Global Advisors, wanted people to buy. State Street was battling a lawsuit from female employees saying it paid them less than their male peers in the firm. Instead of paying women equally, State Street made a statue for them. Fearless Girl was a line item in an advertising budget.

But it's not enough to spend money on a PR trick. No capitalist would applaud yet. You have to bring the money back. For its final act, its Prestige, State Street is suing the statue's creator, Kristen Visbal, saying that by making three unauthorized reproductions of Fearless Girl Visbal damaged State Street's global campaign in support of female leadership and gender diversity. A master class on the trick itself. Some feminists still adore Fearless Girl. I doubt many of them know about her ETF or the fees State Street charges on it. She now stands guard across from the New York Stock Exchange. Yes, SHE makes a difference—to the bottom line.

An essential part of corporate wokeness is this jujitsu-like move where big business has figured out that it can make money by critiquing itself. First, you start praising gender diversity. Next, you criticize Wall Street's lack of it, even though you're Wall Street. Finally, Wall Street somehow gets to be the leader in the fight against big corporations. It gets to become its own watchman and, even better, get paid to do it.

Sincere liberals get tricked into adulation by their love of woke causes. Conservatives are duped into submission as they fall back on slogans they memorized decades ago—something like "the market can do no wrong"—failing to recognize that the free market they had in mind doesn't actually exist today. And poof! Both sides are blinded to the gradual rise of a twenty-first-century Leviathan far more powerful than what even Thomas Hobbes imagined almost four centuries ago.

This new woke-industrial Leviathan gains its power by dividing us as a people. When corporations tell us what social values we're supposed to adopt, they take America as a whole and divide us into tribes. That makes it easier for them to make a buck, but it also coaxes us into adopting new identities based on skin-deep characteristics and flimsy social causes that supplant our deeper *shared* identity as Americans.

Corporations win. Woke activists win. Celebrities win. Even the Chinese Communist Party finds a way to win (more on that later). But the losers of this game are the American people, our hollowed-out institutions, and American democracy itself. The subversion of America by this new form of capitalism isn't just a bug; as they say in Silicon Valley, it's a feature.

This is a book that exposes exactly how this disaster unfolded and tells us what we can do to stop it. I'm not a journalist reporting on my research findings. This is the stuff I've encountered firsthand over the last 15 years in academia and in business. I've seen how the game is played. Now I'm taking you behind the curtain to show you how it works.

In the early chapters of this book, I reveal how the woke-industrial complex fleeces you of your money. Later, I expose how big business, corrupt politicians at home, and autocratic dictators abroad collude to rob you of your voice and your vote in our democracy. Under the banner of "stakeholder capitalism," CEOs and large investors work with ideological activists to implement radical agendas that they could never pass in Congress. Finally, I reveal how these actors consummate the most pernicious heist of all: they steal our shared American identity. Woke culture posits a new theory of who you are as a person, one that reduces you to the characteristics you inherit at birth and denies your status as a free agent in the world. And it deploys powerful corporations to propagate this new theory with the full force of modern capitalism behind it.

The antidote isn't to fight wokeness directly. It can't be, because that's a losing battle. You'll be canceled before you even stand a chance. The true solution is to gradually rebuild a vision for shared American identity that is so deep and so powerful that it dilutes wokeism to irrelevance, one that no longer leaves us susceptible to being divided by corporate elites for their own gain. The modern woke-industrial complex preys on our innermost insecurities about who we really are as individuals and as a people, by mixing morality with commercialism. That might make us better consumers in the short run, but it leaves us worse off as citizens in the end.

Banning bad corporate behavior isn't the ultimate answer. Rather, the answer is to do the hard work of rediscovering who we really are.

Earlier this year, writing this book forced me to rediscover who I was.

On January 6, 2021, an angry mob of rioters stormed the US Capitol as Congress convened to certify the results of the 2020 presidential election. It was a disgrace, and it was a stain on our history. When I watched it, I was ashamed of our nation. It made me want to be a better American.

But I grew even more worried about what happened after the Capitol riot. In the ensuing days, Silicon Valley closed ranks to cancel the accounts of not only the people who participated in that riot but everyday conservatives across the country. Social media companies, payment processing companies, home rental companies, and many more acted in unison. It was a Soviet-style ideological purge, happening in plain sight, right here in America, except the censorship czar wasn't big government. It wasn't private enterprise either. Rather it was a new beast altogether, a frightening hybrid of the two.

As a citizen, I couldn't stomach it. I argued in *The Wall Street Journal*, along with my former law professor, that companies like Twitter and Facebook are legally bound by the First Amendment and that they break the law when they engage in selective political censorship.[4] That's because Big Tech companies, unlike ordinary publishers, are the beneficiaries of a special federal law that protects them in certain ways but also obligates them to abide by the Constitution.

I couldn't anticipate what followed. Two advisors to my company resigned immediately. "Please immediately remove my name from all internal and public materials reporting or implying an association with Roivant or any of its subsidiary and affiliated entities," one of them wrote. "I am submitting my resignation, effective immediately," another wrote to me. "I was raised to value social justice causes and efforts for the greater good above all others." A third advisor texted me saying, "I am profoundly disappointed . . . your comments on right wing media have been deeply troubling."

It wasn't just my advisors. Close friends called me to say how disappointed they were. One of them pleaded with me on the phone: "My friends have made money by investing in your company. Don't ruin it for them." One of my former executives, her eyes filled with tears, said, "Vivek, I had such high hopes for you. What happened?" Many of my employees were upset too, even as some of them privately emailed me to say they agreed with me.

Yet there was a peculiarity about it too. Eight months earlier, my advisors and friends were impatient with me for a different reason. Following the tragic death of George Floyd at the hands of a police officer in the spring of 2020, they pressured me to do more to address systemic racism. They felt I hadn't done enough to condemn it. Apparently, being a CEO required me to speak out about politics sometimes, yet other times it required me to stay silent.

As CEO, I needed to effectively run a business focused on developing medicines without getting intertwined in political matters. Yet as a citizen, I felt compelled to speak out about the perils of woke capitalism. I tried my best to avoid using my company as a platform to foist my views onto others. But eventually I had to admit that I couldn't do justice to either while trying to do both at once.

So in the end I decided to practice what I preached. It wasn't easy, but in January 2021, I stepped down as CEO of my own company, seven years after I founded it, and gave the job to the person who was most qualified to do it—our longtime CFO, whose political perspectives couldn't be more different from my own. He's liberal. He's also brilliant. On the day I appointed him, I said that he would speak for the company going forward, and I meant it.

There was a certain irony to the decision that lingered with me. When left-leaning CEOs like Marc Benioff write books about their views on business and politics, it doesn't hurt their companies at all. Rather, it seems to help them. But my situation was different. At the company townhall explaining my decision to step down, I said that it was important to separate my personal voice as a citizen from the voice of the company in order to protect the company. No one was confused.

I do think there's a double standard at play in America, but ultimately I didn't step aside because I feared a firestorm. I did it because my own beliefs told me I had to keep business and politics apart.

A good barometer for the health of any democracy is the percentage of people who are willing to say what they actually believe in public. As a nation, we're doing pretty poorly on that metric right now, and the only way to fix it is to start talking openly again. I wasn't free to do that as a CEO, but now I am as an ordinary citizen. I hope some of you will find what I have to say worthwhile.

CHAPTER 1

The Goldman Rule

I N ONE OF MY FAVORITE EPISODES of *South Park*, two sleazy salesmen try to sell shoddy vacation condos in the glitzy ski town of "Asspen" to the lower middle-class residents of South Park. Their sales pitch is simple: "Try saying it, 'I've got a little place in Asspen.' Rolls off the tongue nicely, doesn't it?" Eventually, the residents open up their checkbooks.[1]

This is exactly what happened when recruiters from Goldman Sachs used to show up on Ivy League campuses in the early 2000s. You didn't join Goldman as a summer intern for the $1,500-per week-paycheck, though that wasn't bad. Or for the possibility of a $65,000-a-year full-time offer for a 100-plus-hour-a-week job. You did it for the privilege of saying: "I work at Goldman Sachs." There was something intoxicating about working at the most elite financial institution in America. For analysts who worked for Goldman in its day, the rush you got from saying you worked there was the equivalent of how today's graduates feel when they say they work for a "social impact fund" or a "cleantech startup in the Valley."

In the spring of 2006, I was a 20-year-old junior at Harvard College, and I fell for the trick. I joined Goldman Sachs that summer as an intern.

By the end of June, I knew that I had made a terrible mistake. People walked around Goldman Sachs with polished black leather shoes, pressed shirts, and Hugo Boss ties. I was selected to work in the firm's then-prestigious investment division, where the essence of the job wasn't so different from what my boss at a hedge fund had explained to me the prior year: to turn a pile of money into an even bigger pile of money. Yet at Goldman, we carried out that mission in a more genteel way. The managing directors at Goldman—the bosses at the top of the food chain—wore cheap digital watches with black rubber wrist straps, prominently juxtaposed against their expensive tailor-made dress shirts. It was an unspoken Goldman tradition.

One of the many vice presidents who worked in the cubicle diagonally across from mine would make a small scene every time he needed to use the restroom, dashing out and walking fast to and from his desk, just to show everyone how busy he was. I was the only one with a direct view of his computer screen; he was usually surfing different news sites on the web. Six weeks into the internship, I hadn't learned a single thing—save for the polite suggestion from my superiors that I wear nicer shoes to the office.

The hallmark event at Goldman Sachs the summer I worked there wasn't a poker tournament on a lavish boat cruise followed by a debauched night of clubbing, as it had been at the more edgy firm where I'd worked the prior summer. Rather, it was "service day"—a day that involved dressing up in a T-shirt and shorts and then dedicating time to serving the community. Back in 2006, that involved planting trees in a garden in Harlem. The co-head of the group at the time was supposed to lead the way.

I welcomed the prospect of a full day spent at a park away from Goldman's cloistered offices. Yet when I showed up at the park in Harlem, very few of my colleagues seemed interested in . . . well, planting trees. The full-time analysts shared office gossip with the summer analysts. The vice presidents one-upped each other with war stories about investment deals. And, of course, the head of the group was nowhere to be found.

It was supposed to be an all-day activity, yet after an hour I noticed that very little service had actually been performed. As if on cue, the co-head of the group showed up an hour late—wearing a slim-fit suit and a pair of Gucci boots. The chatter among the rest of the team died down, as we awaited what he had to say.

"Alright, guys," he said with a somber expression, as though he were going to discipline the team. A moment of tension hung in the air. And then he broke the ice: "Let's take some pictures and get out of here!" The entire group burst into laughter. Within minutes we had vacated the premises. No trees had been planted. Within a half hour, the entire group was seated comfortably at a nearby bar that was well prepared for our arrival—pitchers of beer ready on the tables and all.

I turned to one of the younger associates sitting next to me at the bar. I remarked that if we wanted to have a "social day," then we should've just called it that instead of "service day."

He laughed and demurred: "Look, just do what the boss says." Then he quipped back: "You ever heard of the Golden Rule?"

"Treat others like you want to be treated," I replied.

"Wrong," he said. *"He who has the gold makes the rules."*

I called it "the Goldman Rule." I learned something valuable that summer after all.

NEARLY A DECADE and a half after I learned that whoever has the gold makes the rules, the Goldman Rule had only grown in importance. In January 2020, at the World Economic Forum in Davos, Goldman Sachs CEO David Solomon declared that Goldman would refuse to take companies public unless they had at least one "diverse" member on their board. Goldman didn't specify who counted as "diverse," other than to say that it had a "focus on women." The bank just said that "this decision is rooted first and foremost in our conviction that companies with diverse leadership perform better" and that board diversity "reduces the risk of groupthink."

Personally, I believe the best way to achieve diversity of thought on a corporate board is to simply screen board candidates for the diversity of their thoughts, not the diversity of their genetically inherited attributes. But that wasn't what bothered me most about Goldman's announcement. The bigger problem was that its edict wasn't about diversity at all. It was about corporate opportunism: seizing an already popular social value and prominently emblazoning it with the Goldman Sachs logo. This was just its latest version of pretending to plant trees in Harlem.

The timing of Goldman's announcement was telling. In the prior year, approximately half the open board seats at S&P 500 companies went to women. In July 2019, the last remaining all-male board in the S&P 500 appointed a woman. In other words, every single company in the S&P 500 was already abiding by Goldman's diversity standard long before Goldman issued its proclamation.

Goldman's announcement was hardly a profile in courage; it was just an ideal way to attract praise without taking any real risk. Another great risk-adjusted return for Goldman Sachs.

Goldman's timing was also impeccable in another way. Its diversity quota proclamation stole the headlines from a much less flattering event: Goldman had just agreed to pay $5 billion in fines to governments around the world for its role in a scheme stealing billions from the Malaysian people.[2] In what has become known as the 1MDB scandal, Goldman paid more than $1 billion in bribes to win work raising money for the 1Malaysia Development Berhad Fund, which was supposedly meant to fund public development projects. In actuality, Goldman turned a willfully blind eye as corrupt Malaysian officials immediately turned the fund into their own private piggy bank, buying art and jewelry. Some of that money literally ended up funding *The Wolf of Wall Street*.[3]

Goldman's effort to change the narrative didn't go unnoticed. As one Redditor on the now-infamous forum WallStreetBets observed, "They want to make sure that any IPO they bring to market has a brown or black person on the board of the company they are IPOing, but are perfectly okay with ripping off millions of Malaysians by engineering a slush fund for an oil tycoon's jewelry collection and private jet."[4,5] Well, yes. Welcome to the woke-industrial complex.

Large banks like Goldman Sachs are particularly adept at playing the woke capitalist game. But in reality, by 2020 it was the prevailing business model in corporate America. Stakeholder capitalism—the trendy idea that companies should serve not just their shareholders but also other interests and society at large—was no longer simply on the rise. It had been crowned as the governing philosophy for big business in America.

At the end of 2018, the Business Roundtable, the top lobbying group for America's largest corporations, overturned a 22-year-old policy statement that said a corporation's paramount purpose is to serve its shareholders. In its place, its 181 members signed and issued a commitment to lead their companies for the benefit of all stakeholders—not only shareholders, but customers, suppliers, employees, and communities. "Multi-stakeholder capitalism is the answer to addressing our challenges holistically," Walmart CEO and Business Roundtable Chairman Doug McMillon said.[6]

In the years that followed, the Business Roundtable's CEO members dutifully recited their new catechism. "We uniquely appreciate the new definition of a corporation and the critical mindset it represents for business," said Beth Ford, CEO of Land O'Lakes. "The role of business is larger than the already high calling of providing value to those who buy our products and services," said Scott Stephenson, CEO of Verisk Analytics. "Verisk is an inclusive workplace that values diversity and perspectives." Of course, "diversity and perspectives" is different from a diversity *of* perspectives.[7] Larry Fink, CEO of BlackRock, the world's largest investment firm, issued an open letter to CEOs describing a "Sustainability Accounting Standards Board" that would tackle issues ranging from labor practices to workforce diversity to climate change. Scores of others followed.

If the turn of the decade was a tipping point, then the murder of George Floyd, a black man, at the hands of a white police officer in May 2020 broke the dam. Companies ranging from Apple to Uber to Novartis issued lengthy statements in support of the Black Lives Matter (BLM) movement. In a surprising about-face, L'Oréal rehired a model it had fired for her comments about "the racial violence of white people." Well-respected companies like Coca-Cola implemented corporate programs teaching employees "to be less white" and that "to be less white is to be less oppressive, be less arrogant, be less certain, be less defensive, be more humble" and that "white people are socialized to feel that they are inherently superior because they are white."[8] Starbucks said it would mandate anti-bias training for executives and tie their compensation to increasing minority representation in its workforce.

In 2021, the new trend became unstoppable. In response to Georgia's new voting rules this year, Delta's CEO declared that "the final bill is unacceptable and does not match Delta's values," failing to explain why Americans should care whether a voting law matches the values of an airline company.[9] Coca-Cola's CEO added: "Our focus is now on supporting federal legislation that protects voting access and addresses voter suppression across the country," a statement that sounded more like that of a Super PAC than a soft drink manufacturer.[10] Biotech industry leaders called on CEOs to "actively consider alternatives to investing within states that have enacted voter suppression laws" and to encourage "alternative venues for conferences and major meetings."[11] Hundreds of other companies issued similar statements.

Fifteen years ago, stakeholder capitalism might have represented a challenge to the system. Today, it *is* the system—and its tolerance for dissent is vanishing. Al Gore recently declared that stakeholder capitalism is "the proven model for business" and that corporate executives who fail to act accordingly could be sued for violating their fiduciary duties.[12] Marc Benioff, billionaire founder of Salesforce.com, proclaimed that shareholder capitalism is "dead."[13] Politicians on both sides, from Elizabeth Warren to Marco Rubio, have jumped on the bandwagon. Today the case is basically closed. In 2018, *New York Times* columnist Ross Douthat called this trend "woke capitalism."[14] I call it "Wokenomics"—a new economic model that infuses woke values into big business.

In late 2020, on the 50th anniversary of Milton Friedman's famous 1970 defense of shareholder capitalism, a few economists made a meek last-ditch attempt to resist this trend by defending "the Friedman Doctrine." But their arguments were at best persuasive only to other economists accustomed to speaking in the parlance of economic efficiency, lacking the moral sheen of the other side. For example, Harvard economist Greg Mankiw argued in *The New York Times* that corporate executives are unlikely to be well equipped with the necessary skills to serve society and that there is no "metric" to determine how well executives are serving society as a whole.[15] University of Chicago economist Steven Kaplan cited the US auto industry in the 1960s and 1970s as a cautionary tale about stakeholder capitalism: by treating their unions and employees as partners and stakeholders, US automakers significantly underperformed Japanese competitors.[16]

These economists miss the main point. The real problem with stakeholder capitalism isn't that it's inefficient. The deeper threat is this: it's the Goldman Rule in action. *The guys with the gold get to make the rules.* Not just market rules, but moral rules too.

Speaking as a former CEO myself, I'm deeply concerned that this new model of capitalism demands a dangerous expansion of corporate power that threatens to subvert American democracy. For corporations to advance social causes, they must first define which causes to prioritize and what position to take. Yet that isn't a business judgment; it's a moral one. America was founded on the idea that we make our most important value judgments through our democratic process, where each citizen's voice is weighted equally, rather than by a small group of elites in private. Debates about our social values belong in the civic sphere, not in the corner offices of corporate America.

I'd love to hear Larry Fink's favorite stock picks, but as a citizen I don't particularly care for his views on racial justice or environmentalism. Democratically elected officeholders and other public leaders, not CEOs and portfolio managers, should lead the debate about what values define America. Business leaders are supposed to decide how much to spend on a manufacturing plant or whether to invest in one piece of technology or another—not whether a minimum wage is more important for society than full employment or whether reducing America's carbon footprint is more important than the geopolitical consequences of doing so. CEOs are no better suited to make these decisions than an average politician is to, say, make the R&D decisions of a pharma company.

To be clear, that doesn't mean that citizens, including CEOs, should refrain from speaking up strictly in their *personal* capacities. Corporations may not be people, but CEOs definitely are, and it's a good thing when citizens personally engage on civic issues. But there's a difference between speaking up as a citizen and using your company's market power to foist your views onto society while avoiding the rigors of public debate in our democracy. That's exactly what Larry Fink does when BlackRock issues social mandates about what companies it will or won't invest in or what Jack Dorsey does when Twitter consistently censors certain political viewpoints rather than others. When companies use their market power to make moral rules, they effectively *prevent* those other citizens from having the same say in our democracy.

Curiously, today the most ardent supporters of stakeholder capitalism are liberal. Many progressives who love stakeholder capitalism abhor the Supreme Court's 2010 ruling in *Citizens United v. Federal Election Commission* because it permits corporations to donate to political campaigns and influence electoral outcomes. Al Gore, one of the principal proponents of stakeholder capitalism, has described this ruling as "obscene" and proposed overturning it through a constitutional amendment.[17] Joe Biden, Hillary Clinton, and Barack Obama have all made similar comments.

Yet stakeholder capitalism is *Citizens United* on steroids. It not only permits corporations to influence our democracy, it *demands* that they do that by advancing whatever social values they choose. Ironically, those who most vehemently proclaim that "corporations aren't people" are the ones who now demand that corporations act more like, well, people.

Advocates of stakeholder capitalism say it's totally consistent to oppose corporate contributions to political campaigns while still demanding that corporate leaders pursue social agendas that are good for society at large. Yet this argument ignores *why* it's bad for corporations to influence elections in the first place. It's not just the election that matters, but what the election symbolizes: the idea that every person's vote counts equally in our democracy. *That's* what's special about an election. *That's* what makes capitalist influence over elections so troubling—because when dollars mix with votes, everyone's vote no longer counts equally. When they pick which politicians to support, they're just pursuing their self-interest, and it's no different when they pick which "social goals" to prioritize too. Either Al Gore doesn't understand that, or else his new business interests as an ESG investor make that an inconvenient truth.

The damage to democracy is further-reaching. The heart of our democracy isn't just about casting a ballot in November. Rather, it's about preserving democratic norms in everyday life, including free speech and open debate. When companies make political proclamations, employees who personally disagree with the company's position face a stark choice: speak up freely and risk your career, or keep your job while keeping your head down. That isn't how America is supposed to work, yet that is a reality for many Americans today.

Even worse, partisan politics is now infecting spheres of our lives that were previously apolitical. Our social fabric depends on preserving certain spaces as apolitical sanctuaries, especially in an increasingly divided polity like ours. Until earlier this year, Major League Baseball used to offer one of those rare sanctuaries: fans were bound together by their love of baseball—whether black or white, Democrat or Republican. Thanks to the MLB's dramatic protest of Georgia's new voting rules earlier this year, that sanctuary has vanished.

Democracy loses twice: corporate influence pollutes the public debate about moral questions, and social solidarity is eroded as apolitical institutions slowly disappear. Stakeholder capitalism poisons democracy, partisan politics poisons capitalism, and in the end we are left with neither capitalism nor democracy.

In practice, liberals love stakeholder capitalism only insofar as companies advance social goals that they personally find appealing. Most liberals dislike the Supreme Court's ruling in *Burwell v. Hobby Lobby Stores* for permitting a corporation to limit health insurance coverage of certain contraceptives for its employees. But they cheered when Goldman Sachs issued its diversity edict for American companies that want to pursue an IPO. At core, Goldman's diversity edict is *Hobby Lobby* on steroids too. Hobby Lobby is a family-owned arts and crafts store whose policy applies to its own employees, whereas Goldman's quota system applies effectively to every public company in America. If liberals dislike *Hobby Lobby* on principled grounds, they should shudder at the raw societal power exercised by behemoths like Goldman Sachs.

Wokenomics is crony capitalism 2.0, and here's how it works: big business uses progressive-friendly values to deflect attention from its own monolithic pursuit of profit and power. Crony capitalism 1.0 was straightforward by comparison: corporations simply had to make campaign contributions to legislators in return for favorable legislative treatment. Here's an example: big Wall Street banks hire lobbyists to exert influence in Washington, and in return they get favorable regulations that codify their status as gatekeepers who enjoy oligopoly status in taking companies public. The regulations are so complex and onerous that they prevent upstart competitors from getting in on the action, keeping the oligopoly intact. Championship-level players of this game like Goldman Sachs top it off with a flourish, by lending their executives to serve as US treasury secretaries (Steve Mnuchin under President Trump, Hank Paulson under President George W. Bush, and so on). And it pays off in the end: winners like Goldman Sachs get bailouts in tough times like 2008, while less adroit competitors like Lehman Brothers are hung out to dry by Hank Paulson. That much is simple enough.

But crony capitalism 2.0 is far trickier. It uses a different playbook from that used by version 1.0—one that's designed to escape public notice. In January 2020, when David Solomon first issued Goldman's diversity proclamation at the World Economic Forum in Davos, it was at a time when Bernie Sanders and Elizabeth Warren, two of the biggest critics of the US government's 2008 bailout of Goldman Sachs, were presidential frontrunners. Having supplicated to the swamp uni-party of crony Republicans and centrist Democrats for decades, the moment had arrived for Goldman

Sachs to begin placating the identity-politics-obsessed far left, just as that wing of the Democratic party had begun to accrue greater political power. Their new CEO is woker than woke, and he's a DJ on the side too. That's how the 2020 edition of crony capitalism looks; Hank Paulson is outmoded by comparison.

TO BE SURE, many CEOs who promote stakeholder capitalism do it genuinely. Ken Frazier, the former chairman and CEO of Merck, is a pharma industry leader I greatly admire for his company's accomplishments in the treatment of cancer and other diseases. In 2020, he publicly declared that it's important for businesses like Merck to "stabilize society" amid rising economic inequity and racial injustice, saying it was time for "industry to step up to the plate." In a public interview in October 2020, he said: "What makes me worry ultimately is when people don't believe in our institutions, they don't believe in our system, they don't believe there's fundamental fairness, then I think our society begins to come apart."[18] Earlier in 2021, Ken was one of corporate America's most powerful voices against Georgia's new voting rules.[19]

Having met Ken myself, I can attest that he truly believes these things. He's an authentic leader; several employees at my company who used to work for Merck truly revere him. Merck is also a fundamentally different company from Goldman Sachs: its employee base is motivated by improving patient care rather than by the number of green pieces of paper that end up in their bank account at the end of bonus season. Personally, I don't necessarily think that one of those is inherently better than the other, though they are fundamentally different.

But Ken misses the point that his own acts, however well

intentioned, may actually *contribute* to the public's loss of faith in our system. Many Americans no longer believe in our institutions precisely because CEOs and other leaders use their institutional seats of power to crowd out the voices of ordinary Americans. When CEOs tell people what they're supposed to think about moral questions, then people stop believing that their own opinions really matter. In other words, they stop believing in the system.

Ken and I debated this issue in an email exchange last year. He quoted George Merck, his company's founder, who said that "medicine is for the people, not for the profits," and asked me whether rejecting stakeholder capitalism means putting profits ahead of patients.

My answer was no. In the long run, the only way for a pharmaceutical company to be successful is by serving patients first. But putting patients first also means putting them ahead of fashionable social causes. It means that we don't care if the scientist who discovers a cure to COVID-19 is white or black or a man or a woman. It means that we don't care if the manufacturing and distribution process that delivers cures most quickly to patients is carbon neutral.

Ken may self-identify as liberal, but his view actually reflects *conservative* European social thought, which was skeptical of democracy and convinced that well-meaning elites should work together for the common good, as long as the common good could be defined by them. In the Old World, that often meant some combination of political leaders, business and labor elites, and the church working together to define and implement social goals. But America was supposed to offer a different vision: citizens defining the common good through the democratic process—publicly through open debate and privately at the ballot box—without elite intervention.

That's what makes America great. That's what makes America itself.

But today, with the advent of Wokenomics, we are slowly receding back to the pre-American Old World model on the global stage. Even the Vatican is getting in on the act. In December 2020, Pope Francis issued an implicit endorsement of stakeholder capitalism by launching a "Council for Inclusive Capitalism" in partnership with the Vatican. The council "boasts over $10.5 trillion in assets under management, companies with over $2.1 trillion of market capitalization, and 200 million workers in over 163 countries."[20] This council endorses not only equality of opportunity but also "Equitable Outcomes" and "Fairness Across Generations on the Environment." There's a page on its website dystopically titled "Our Guardians," which includes a creepy-looking photo of billionaires like Marc Benioff of Salesforce, large corporate CEOs from Wall Street to big pharma, and descendants of the Rothschild banking family in Europe surrounding the Pope and making a pledge to "change capitalism for good."[21] The American vision of separating church from state, and democracy from capitalism, has been supplanted by this new global vision of mixing them all with one another—leaving us with none of them in the end.

In 2019, I attended a closed-door forum hosted by J.P. Morgan for a select group of startup company founders. It was the first time I'd been invited to join their ranks, so I attended with curiosity. Jamie Dimon, CEO of J.P. Morgan, spoke to the audience during dinner. Another CEO asked him: "Would you ever consider running for president?" Dimon didn't miss a beat: "I would love to *be* president. I just don't like the idea of *running* for president." The audience laughed—not because it was obviously outlandish, but because it was obviously true.

Dimon couldn't have better summarized the motives of many CEOs who embrace stakeholder capitalism: it allows them to exercise quasi-political power without having to go through the hassle of getting elected. Yet that hassle is part and parcel of democracy itself.

Jamie Dimon probably won't ever get to be president. But by being CEO of one of the largest banks, in today's world he still gets the social platform that he craves. Following George Floyd's death last summer, Dimon broadcast a video of himself dramatically kneeling in his office to demonstrate his solidarity with the protesters in the street. He was widely praised for doing so. I couldn't help but be amused. In a prior century, the founder of J.P. Morgan— John Pierpont Morgan—had once famously stated: "I owe the public nothing." He was hated in his day. Jamie Dimon wasn't quite as rich as John Pierpont Morgan, but he had learned that if you claim to owe the public everything, you will in fact owe it nothing.

Many Americans have justifiably lost faith in government yet still recognize that we need to solve important social problems. If government has failed us, then someone else needs to step up. And if that's big business, then so be it, right?

I think not. Admittedly, our democracy today is a far cry from the ideal that our Founding Fathers envisioned. But we owe it to ourselves to do the messy work of fixing our democracy from within rather than delegating that hard work to self-interested corporate leaders. Our democracy is messy for the same reason that it is beautiful: we often disagree with our fellow citizens about our most pressing social questions. Our mechanism for dealing with those disagreements is through public debate in our civic institutions, not corporate fiats issued from the mountaintops of Davos.

The crux of our concern about capitalism shouldn't be that companies serve their shareholders exclusively. That's just what capitalism is. Rather, our concern should be that capitalism has begun to pollute our democracy through the influence of dollars on our political system—and it's done so in more ways than one. The right answer isn't to force democracy and capitalism to share the same bed.

What we really need is social distancing between the two . . . to prevent each from infecting the other.

IN PRINCIPLE, "STAKEHOLDER capitalism" can mean one of two things. It could mean that corporations should affirmatively take steps toward addressing important societal issues like climate change, racism, and workers' rights. That's the bandwagon that most companies are jumping on these days—committing capital to fight climate change, making donations to BLM, conducting mandatory training sessions for employees on how to be "anti-racist," and so forth. That's where my criticism in this book is focused. This trend has taken corporate America by storm in recent years and threatens to subvert the integrity of American democracy.

But there's a more sympathetic version of the same idea that refers to something much simpler—namely, the idea that executives should just account for the negative externalities, or unintended consequences, of their actions before making important business decisions. That just means they should avoid hurting people. We all have a basic moral duty not to hurt others, and we don't lose it when we band together and start calling ourselves corporations, the argument goes.

Think of a tobacco company that might face a choice about whether to include an ingredient that makes its product more addictive, in a way that leaves both consumers and society worse off. If a company knows that its product will harm people but there's no technical legal prohibition on selling it, the "negative-externality" folks argue that the company should still exercise restraint even though the profit-maximizing course of action is to sell as much of the product as possible.

I acknowledge that's a hard case. In theory, it raises a dilemma for my argument. But in actuality this kind of case rarely arises in the real world: most corporate actions that are known to harm people are either illegal or likely to hurt the company's reputation—and profits—in the long run. During my seven years as a biopharmaceutical CEO, I never once had to make that kind of choice: our company's commitment to long-term value meant that it was never in our interest to harm people. We made medicines, not cigarettes.

Regardless of where you land on those hard cases, my point is this: a tobacco company's decision to include ingredients that are less addictive in its cigarettes is fundamentally different from that same company writing a check to BLM or mandating anti-racist employee training about how "to be less white." The ordinary duty not to hurt people doesn't require corporations to reshape the world into their vision of utopia.

Many sincere woke activists resist that distinction—and that's the root of our disagreement. According to their view, *capitalism itself* systematically rewards, say, white people over black people. That inequity is a negative externality of the very capitalist system that makes corporations possible, according to them. So any company that benefits from America's capitalist system is therefore contributing to systemic racism—and is *obligated* to fix it. According to this view, Marlboro should write a check to BLM for the *exact same reason* that it's obligated to include less addictive ingredients in its cigarettes.

The sometimes-blurry line between actively doing good and merely avoiding doing harm is one of those iconic debates in moral philosophy, and it reveals an important point about my disagreement with sincere woke capitalists. Our dispute comes down to this: they think they're morally obliged to minimize the harm that they already do just by "being capitalists," whereas I think they're overstepping their authority by trying to affirmatively enact their own conception of the good by using their market power. I think they're trying too hard to save the world; they think they're just trying not to make it worse.

But they are making it worse. Even if they're right that the American system harms some groups, the burden of remedying that harm falls on the American people, and the American people should decide what to do about it democratically. It is not a CEO's duty to shoulder America's responsibilities; in reality, that just causes new problems. I believe even honest woke capitalists fail to see how much additional harm they do to American democracy when business elites tell ordinary Americans what causes they're supposed to prioritize. In my view, this represents a *new* negative externality that must be weighed by any corporate leader who actually wants to do the right thing.

So that's my disagreement with sincere woke capitalists. But my bigger beef is with the *insincere* woke capitalists. Here's what the sincere guys miss: when they create a system in which business leaders decide moral questions, they open the floodgates for all their unscrupulous colleagues to abuse that newfound power. And there are far more CEOs who are eager to grab money and power in the name of justice than there are CEOs who are agnostic to money and power and care only about justice.

Under the guise of doing good, the corporate con artists hide all of the bad things that they do every day. Coca-Cola fuels an epidemic of diabetes and obesity among black Americans through the products it sells. The hard business decision for the company to debate is whether to change the ingredients in a bottle of Coke. But instead of grappling with that question, Coca-Cola executives implement anti-racism training that teaches their employees "to be less white," and they pay a small fortune to well-heeled diversity consultants who peddle that nonsense. That's the Goldman playbook. It's not by accident; it's by design.

So the "I'm just trying not to hurt anyone" version of stakeholder capitalism inadvertently provides intellectual cover for the real poison at the heart of modern Wokenomics. In the real world, very few American companies are able to harm people over the long run while still making sustainable profits—because the public holds them accountable over time, through both market mechanisms and democratic accountability. But now the rise of woke capitalism creates a decoy that *prevents* those corrective mechanisms from working as they should. It's the equivalent of tampering with a smoke detector in the airplane lavatory—which is a federal crime because it risks hurting people.

Some of my fellow CEOs make thoughtful arguments in response. I recently caught up with Nick Green, a former college classmate of mine, who leads Thrive Market, a very successful healthy lifestyle company in California. We're good friends (we even invested in each other's companies), but we disagree about stakeholder capitalism. Nick argues that stakeholder capitalism "works" because consumers are demanding more of companies. Consumers want to buy things from companies who share their values. And often that means supporting social causes that their consumers care about. What's wrong if companies just do what consumers want them to do? Isn't that what capitalism is all about?

Nick is a great CEO. He built a thriving enterprise from scratch. Each dollar that I invested in his company a few years ago is now worth nearly a hundred. So if he has something to say about building great companies, then he has my attention.

After reflecting on Nick's comments, I realized that practitioners of stakeholder capitalism come in a few different forms, each of which raises unique issues. First, there are woke *executives*, who use their positions as corporate managers to advance a particular social agenda. This is fraught with principal-agent conflicts. An agent is supposed to represent a principal. For example, a lawyer is an agent, and his client is the principal. A principal-agent conflict arises when the agent has different interests from the principal—for example, if the lawyer stands to make more money if the client loses her case. In the case of a company, the principal is the company's shareholder base, and the CEO is the agent. Often, the CEO has an interest in using the company to maintain his personal brand, often at the expense of the company's shareholders. Here, the main victims are the company's shareholders.

That's distinct from the phenomenon of woke *investors*, who demand that otherwise humdrum CEOs use their companies to advance certain pet social causes favored by the investors themselves. This isn't the agent betraying the interests of the principal, but the principal (a shareholder) demanding exactly what the agent (the CEO) should do. Effectively, this is what ESG investing is all about. But it's not just ESG investors who play this game. Sometimes these activist investors include sovereign nations and autocratic dictatorships like China who have their own ideas about what causes to advance.

Woke executives and woke investors raise distinct problems that I address later in the book, but at core they're both examples of this form of paternalism. In both cases, it's about business elites telling ordinary Americans what they're supposed to do and how they're supposed to think. Each presents an equal affront to American democracy. My critique is mostly directed at this top-down elitism.

But my friend Nick is talking about a third, distinct phenomenon in which woke *consumers* are the ones who demand that companies drive social change. That's what I call "woke consumerism." That isn't a top-down phenomenon. It's a grassroots, bottom-up demand that consumers make upon companies. For example, in 2020 many consumers boycotted Goya Foods following its CEO's praise of President Trump. This isn't a new trend; back in 2012, consumers turned on Chick-fil-A after its CEO made anti-same-sex marriage comments. That's different from top-down elitism, and it raises unique issues of its own. Woke consumerism is real. It divides us as a people and weaponizes buying power to stifle authentic debate. And there's no easy fix, since we live in a free country and people still get to do what they want.

Fundamentally, it's a cultural problem that demands a cultural solution, one that neither business nor law can provide. But woke consumerism is not nearly as big of a phenomenon as CEOs and investors claim. The idea that "consumers are demanding it and we're just giving them what they want" is often just a hollow excuse to justify top-down power-grabbing by influential executives and investors. Very few retail "mom-and-pop" investors in the stock market choose a BlackRock mutual fund over one from Fidelity based on the social values it adopts. They make their choices on the basis of investment performance, fees, or the warm smile of a financial broker.

In reality, companies like BlackRock, and in particular their leaders, are using social causes as a way of assuming their place in a moral pantheon. And in the process, they're quietly dropping hints to consumers to take the bait and make purchasing decisions on the basis of moral qualia rather than product attributes alone. And many consumers then do it, especially when they're feeling lost and hungry for a purpose, as so many Americans do today. It's like the equivalent of Virginia Slims targeting insecure teenagers with catchy cigarette ads in the 1990s. Woke consumerism is born when woke companies prey on the insecurities and vulnerabilities of their customers by deflecting our focus away from the price and quality of their products. As it turns out, morality makes for a great marketing tactic. Just ask Fearless Girl. SHE will tell you what to buy.

BEFORE THE 2008 financial crisis, "capitalist excess" took the form of lavish spending on oft-inappropriate entertainment: strip clubs, "dwarf-tossing" from private yachts, chartered jets to the Super Bowl, and so on, all funded by the corporate Amex card.

I had a front-row seat to capitalist excess during my first corporate internship—one that I did in 2005, the year before my internship at Goldman Sachs. That summer I worked at a hedge fund called Amaranth. The little-known investment firm had held a campus recruiting event at Harvard in the fall of 2004, and I'd shown up because the company had offered a free dinner at a fancy restaurant. Amaranth had hired a team of doctors and scientists who professionally evaluated biotech stocks. It sounded pretty cool to me, so I decided to give it a try.

The most valuable lesson I learned that summer was to understand the essence of what it meant to pursue pure wealth for its own sake. The firm's founder, Nick Maounis, graciously spent time with the summer interns during lunch sessions. He explained with disarming clarity that the purpose of a hedge fund was "to turn a pile of money into an even bigger pile of money" and "to get paid a lot for doing that." It sounded simple. Even honest. I asked him: "What's the main goal of your career?" He thought about it deeply in silence and then answered: "To be a billionaire. And also to own a sports team."

Sadly, Maounis never achieved either goal because Amaranth famously imploded the following year. It used complicated tactics to corner the market for natural gas, which proved to be a profitable strategy in the short run, but the house of cards came tumbling down when the market turned sharply against it. Maounis still left the whole situation a wealthy man because hedge fund managers lock in gains on an annual basis, and even if they lose everyone else's money, they usually still get to walk away with a good chunk of what they made during the good years. As one colleague explained to me, it wasn't all that surprising or even that unfair. Every job has its perks. If you're a nurse, you go home with a few extra latex gloves. If you're in finance, you go home with a few extra bucks.* His take was cynical, but there was something self-evident about it too.

But I later heard that even Amaranth's lavish offices and opulent antics weren't entirely funded from Nick Maounis's pocket.

---

* On Wall Street, a "buck" is the colloquial term of art for a million dollars. Not a joke.

Rather, the firm had reportedly pioneered a new model of expense accounting in which client funds could be billed for the expenses of the management company. That's messy business.

These behaviors were fraught with problems. The most obvious is naked self-dealing. Corporate executives were able to use the company piggy bank to fund their own lifestyles and tastes. This kind of thing often led to prosecution. Tyco's storied CEO Dennis Kozlowski went to jail for "looting" over $600 million from his company to pay for lavish parties, fancy art, and an opulent Manhattan apartment.[22] His behavior was different only in degree, not in kind, from his peers in that era.

Yet self-dealing wasn't the biggest problem. Some of these behaviors were questionable; others made for reasonable business strategies to drive profit. By appealing to base and primal human instincts, these companies were able to compete with their peers to attract talented traders, woo lucrative clients, and ultimately do what successful companies do best: make money.

Ordinary Americans winced at these stories of capitalist excess not because CEOs and star traders failed to obtain board or shareholder consent for their behaviors. Rather, ordinary Americans winced because the acts were inherently odious: paying to have sex with women or to watch little people being "tossed" is in no way virtuous. For example, Kozlowski was convicted only after his jury viewed a video of one particularly opulent toga-themed corporate party in the Mediterranean. The party itself was not a crime, but there was something about its ethos that made the jury want to convict Kozlowski of the more mundane accounting-related charges.

At the time of my summer internship in 2006, forward-thinking firms like Goldman Sachs were already getting ahead of the curve. Wayne Gretzky would've been proud: they weren't just skating to where the puck was, they were skating to where the puck was *going*. While their more uncouth peers at less esteemed places like Amaranth continued to entertain themselves and their clients with frivolous perks, Goldman had embarked on its metamorphosis into a company in pursuit of a nobler kind of indulgence: "corporate social responsibility."

Today, progressive social values like "going green" and "being diverse" have become, counterintuitively, the modern equivalents of strippers and dwarf-tossing. They are patronized and tipped by the same corporate chieftains who indulge their fancies, all while those corporate chieftains accrete greater wealth and power for themselves along the way.

Consider CEO Adam Neumann, the long-haired star CEO of the once-darling "decacorn" WeWork.[23] Adam became the Dennis Kozlowski of the 2010s. He built a decent real estate leasing business, yet he described the mission of his company as "elevating global consciousness." He trumpeted social values like diversity, all the while throwing multimillion-dollar parties featuring pop stars, purchasing a $60 million corporate jet for trips to the Maldives (burning the same carbon-based fuel as every other corporate jet), and appending an ice bath and sauna to his lavish office. I met him for the first time in early 2017 via one of his smaller US investors. While in public he waxed eloquent about social values like diversity, in private he bragged that the "beauty of hiring female executives" was that "they have other shit to do at home, so they go home early." How progressive.

Yet this version of corporate social responsibility is ultimately a scam—not on shareholders, who often profit from it, but on the American public as a whole. It's a new form of capitalist excess.

And it's even more insidious than its precursor in the decade before. Ordinary Americans may be put off by stripping or dwarf-tossing, but they instinctively *like* the idea of companies pursuing noble social values. That's exactly what allows a new class of corporate fraudsters to escape accountability from shareholders, competitors, customers, and the government all at once.

The real con job on society wasn't perpetrated by the lavish capitalists of the pre-2008 decade, but by the *nouveau* capitalists who got ahead by pretending to care about justice.

In 2019, Amazon laudably challenged Walmart to set a $15 minimum wage for its employees. The trick? Jeff Bezos had not suddenly discovered a newfound generosity for workers; rather, he was co-opting a popular social value to undermine his longtime foe Walmart when its profitability was vulnerable.

Amazon continued its act in 2020 when it pledged to donate $10 million to groups focused on aiding black communities. "We stand in solidarity with our Black employees, customers, and partners," it intoned.[24] The trick? Making you forget about the media firestorm just a few months earlier when Amazon fired several workers who dared to speak up on social media about working conditions at Amazon's warehouses. Many of them were black. Behind closed doors, Amazon executives planned to brand one of its fired black employees, Christian Smalls, as dumb and inarticulate.[25] But at least they capitalized "Black."

That very same month, Nike acted in synchrony, pledging "a $40 million commitment over the next four years to support the Black community in the U.S."[26] This followed Nike's widely aired commercial featuring former NFL quarterback Colin Kaepernick, who kneeled during the national anthem in protest of social injustice. The trick? Distracting you from Nike's practice of employing child labor in sweatshops across southeast Asia or marketing $200 sneakers to inner-city black kids who can't afford to buy books for school.

Right-wing CEOs are hardly blameless: they've started to simply imitate their progressive counterparts for their own private gain. MyPillow CEO Mike Lindell has achieved near folk-hero status in conservative circles, and he's often swarmed by fans at political conferences. Yet he marshals his political brand to sell more pillows and bedding—even though pillows have nothing to do with politics. So it's difficult to view his widely publicized comments about election fraud and his "prayers" that Trump use military force to retain power in January 2021 as being entirely separate from his own commercial agenda.[27]

The Chinese have gotten in on the act too. During the COVID-19 pandemic, one state-affiliated Chinese company charitably "donated" drones to local US law enforcement agencies to help enforce social distancing and contact tracing during the national lockdown. The trick? Free surveillance.

The victims of pre-2008 capitalist excess were the cash-strapped strippers and little people and, arguably, in certain cases, the shareholders and clients who were shortchanged a few bucks to pay for lavish entertainment. In 2008, the American taxpayers found themselves on the hook when corporate excesses were "fixed" with a bailout. But today, the victim is America's entire system of democratic governance. The perpetrators of pre-2008 capitalist sins were innocently naive by today's standards. Their actions were so glaring that they invited scrutiny, which in turn empowered society to hold the bad actors accountable, either through investor skepticism in the case of Maounis (where nearly all of his investors pulled their money out of the fund) or through the courts in the case of

Kozlowski (where he was convicted of fraud for duping sharehold-ers into funding his lavish personal lifestyle). It turns out that the American system works pretty well when the American public knows exactly what to expect.

Bill McGlashan partnered with one of the largest private equity firms in the world, TPG, to launch the world's largest "impact investing" fund, but he charged lucrative fees while doing it, and in his personal life he was discreetly bribing college admissions offi-cials to advantage his own children over less affluent, more merito-rious applicants. If greed and nepotism weren't pretty, then "social responsibility" offered the right brand of makeup.

Once the American public becomes "woke" to this new trend of self-interest masquerading as morality, our citizens and con-sumers will be able to see through the charade of corporate virtue-signaling. When Amazon issues a public challenge to Walmart to pay workers $15 per hour, we can simply chuckle to ourselves that Jeff Bezos is just doing what he does best: undermining his compet-itors when they're most vulnerable.

Most importantly, we can return the power to implement our social values back to American democracy where it belongs rather than allowing it to remain in the hands of corporate chieftains who are really just trying to make a buck and accrue more power. As a society we should allow and even *embrace* the corporate pursuit of financial self-interest above all. The only thing we should ask in return is this: keep it naked, instead of dressing it up as altruism. America might be better off in the end if Goldman Sachs executives just wear their Rolexes to work after all instead of preaching about diversity and pretending to plant trees.

CHAPTER 2

How I Became a Capitalist

THIS NEW WOKE VERSION OF capitalism isn't the capitalism I fell in love with. In fact, I hardly recognize it. I fell in love with capitalism when I was very young, when I had to spend months at a time apart from it, in a small village in India called Vadakanchery. But I also learned to be wary of it.

If there was one thing my dad wanted to teach me when I was a child, it was where we came from as a family. One thing he mandated during our childhood was that we spend several weeks every summer in the village where he'd been raised.

My father was one of seven children who grew up in the same house, along with more than twenty other relatives. His siblings, who lived in Ohio and neighboring Indiana, went back to Vadakanchery for the summer too. So every summer in the late 1980s and early 1990s, a cadre of elementary school-age kids from the Midwest would land in Vadakanchery for a few weeks. That often meant my dad had to floor his bank account in order to afford the international trip for our family of four.

It was worth it to him.

My father's childhood home in India couldn't have been more different from my hometown in Evendale, Ohio. It was a complex of three-and-a-half interconnected houses, including my grandparents' home. There was a veranda out in front with clotheslines where our clothes were washed and dried. The air was so moist that droplets of water would stick to our skin.

The ambient soundtrack of life in Vadakanchery included a cacophony of our cows mooing outside and rickshaws blaring their horns as they passed. The scent of incense hung in the air from the candles that burned in the morning and evening in our prayer room. There was no dishwasher, so we often ate meals served on large banana leaves instead of plates, using our hands. The toilets appeared to be holes in the ground that we squatted over; to flush them, we filled up a cup of water and poured it down the hole as many times as it took. We used to boil water and let it cool to have something to drink. Air-conditioning was only a dream, and we got a bad stomach flu at least once per trip.

But we also learned that there's more to life than being comfortable. We heard stories about my dad from family elders that he had never told us. We visited the same village school where my dad first learned English. We learned to pray at the local temple.

My cousins and I used to play hide-and-seek throughout the complex. Sometimes we'd try a makeshift version of baseball on the front veranda, where the clothes were drying and swaying in the wind, blocking our view. The service ladies didn't seem to mind that we changed their laundry schedule, but my dad definitely did—the games were even more challenging because we had to hide from him. He was irked we were being dumb American kids instead of absorbing traditional values. But we brought a new version of baseball to Vadakanchery; avoiding my dad was just part of the game.

On the surface, the absence of first-world comforts was the most striking difference. But as we grew accustomed to life in India's boonies, we found it was kind of fun. The more remarkable differences were cultural. There were some ways they were immediately visible: we usually walked around inside and outside without shirts, like most of the adult men, we visited the local temples by foot in the morning and evening, and so on. At my father's behest, we spent quite a lot of the day praying, just like the other Brahmins in the village. The prayers I still say today are the ones I learned in Vadakanchery.

But the strangest differences weren't visible to the untrained eye. My grandmother, whom we called Ammai, had lived in that house since she'd moved there with her three sisters in the 1940s. They weren't especially wealthy, but by birth they were all Brahmins, the traditional caste of priests and teachers, the protectors of knowledge and understanding, the scholars. We Brahmins were the highest caste, though not the richest or most powerful. The holiest of us are called sannyasins and are supposed to beg for their food. Kings were below us. Richest were some Vaishyas, the commercial class, but they were only of the third caste, just above Shudras, the service caste.

A Brahmin's obligation to pursue knowledge didn't come attached to money or political power. It came from his birth status. In the world of Grandma Ammai's village, it was most honorable to understand the world well, so it was obvious that Brahmins would be the highest caste.

Our status as Brahmins didn't even really correspond to our jobs. My grandfather was a farm manager, my dad was an engineer, and his older brother became a doctor. But they visited the temple morning and evening, lived modestly, observed customs, and passed on their traditions to future generations. As Brahmin men, we wore a *poonal*, a sacred string, across our bodies starting around age 8. Most Kerala temples required men to remove their shirts before entry, and you knew who was Brahmin and who wasn't based on who had a *poonal*.

We had people who supported the house by providing domestic help. They weren't technically my cousins, but we treated them like relatives in many ways. For example, the old lady who cleaned the home lived only a few houses down from my grandparents. We used to be scared of her as kids. She would scold us as though we were her own kids. We somehow always knew we were supposed to bow at her feet, just as we did to our grandparents.

As kids, we didn't process the fact that these people who provided service to our family were in the lower caste while we were the highest. But my family and hers knew the difference. Neither family would allow their kids to marry into the other. Money wasn't the reason for her family's difference in caste from ours. In fact, the money was entirely irrelevant.

If the villagers thought of the principles of India's caste system at all, they thought of them more as values than rules. Out of those values came beliefs, like the facts that only Brahmins could enter through the front door foyer and that lower-caste people ought to go down the alleyway and enter through the side door, past the cow. Only Brahmins enter the prayer room and kitchen at certain times of day. While these sound like rules and restrictions to an American ear, to the villagers, they were just facts associated with a proper understanding of the world.

I asked my father and the other elders why we Brahmins lived in different spaces and ways than the others in the village. I never got a straight answer. Kids like the son of the lady who served us could go on to get educated and make more money, but they would still be part of a different community. Seeing how much this system revolved around honor and status helped me understand how much the American system revolved around wealth. And while my father always taught me to never over-prioritize the pursuit of wealth over virtue, it seemed to me that the pursuit of wealth equally by all was still preferable to a system of honor based on birth.

That's when I began to fall in love with capitalism. Sure, in America it was possible for people to blindly pursue wealth above more virtuous callings in life. But because money gave some people access to status, America was a place where anyone could achieve any status no matter their birth, something that seemed fundamentally different from the world order of Vadakanchery in the 1990s.

That seemed pretty cool to me.

A S IT TURNS out, there's nothing superior about Brahmins and certainly nothing superior about them marrying each other. Not even their sense of humor is superior; they only seemed funnier to each other because the caste system had them hang out together. It's not even true that knowledge is better than power, wealth, or service. But all of those domains can be part of a good life, and to enable that diversity, you have to allow people from different groups to associate with each other freely. Sometimes, you even have to let them marry each other.

Historically, the caste system—certainly the British-influenced form of it—wanted to keep all groups and their provinces separate. That proved to be a convenient way for the British to pit different groups against one another and consolidate power. But the British didn't make it up from scratch. Even according to the ancient system, everything had to be kept pure. No doubt there was something beautiful about that purity, but there was even more beauty in what it missed.

As a child, I understood that the American system saw the world in a radically different light. The American dream is to have it all—knowledge, power, money, and service, in no particular order, and as much of each as you want—because America offers the hope that they can all fit together in one life. Here, knowledge is power, and so is wealth, and power gives you the ability to serve others. Service should give you power, too, especially in an efficient market. Work hard, do well at one or two things, get paid, and the money can help you get the rest. Anything that even *might* be good, America tries to offer you. Hang out with who you want, say what you want, pray with who you want, if you want, marry who you want. You and only you decide what it means to have it all.

The contrast between capitalism and the caste system was striking. Living in Kerala every summer as a kid made me miss America. Capitalism was the first ideal I really loved, the first time I'd ever loved a system. Capitalism brought people together; the caste system kept them apart.

My dad's a liberal, and he argues that American capitalism creates a new caste system based on wealth. That's hard to deny. But that's not the goal of capitalism—certainly not the pure form of it that I fell in love with as a kid. Capitalism is supposed to be just an economic system, not a social system. And the caste system is supposed to be the opposite—a social system, not an economic system. Paradoxically, that means they both share one fundamental precept in common: *the size of your bank account has nothing to do with your moral worth.*

Yet over the next 30 years, it was actually American-style

capitalism that slowly bound the wounds opened by caste. People now regularly marry across caste lines. There's no rule about who can and can't enter a house through the front door. The lower-caste guy who works at Domino's now delivers to our home in the village, and my family tips him to show their appreciation, just as we do in America. When you eat out at Pizza Hut, you ring a large bronze bell to say thank you when you leave—funny enough, the exact same kind of sacred bronze bell that we used to ring when we left the village temple.

By allowing Indians to share goods and services with each other freely, capitalism gradually allowed them to marry whomever they wanted to as well. Capitalism, an economic system, fixed these problems with caste, a social system: with the free exchange of money and services, people could choose their own relationships with each other. No matter what caste you were born into, you could work hard, get paid, work your way up, and end up meeting a lot of different people. From there, you could find out what others needed from you and get what you needed in return. An efficient market actually rewards figuring out exactly what other groups of people want and need. So people naturally stopped segregating themselves. In capitalism, people make good money figuring out how to efficiently distribute food. There's no honor code that requires you to beg.

MORE THAN THIRTY years have passed since the first time I visited Vadakanchery. As the years aged me, they changed Vadakanchery, too. After my wife and I got married, I took her on a trip to Vadakanchery to show her that village I remembered from my childhood summers.

But that village was long gone. Vadakanchery and I were both more mature, in some ways, and we each had a couple of new flaws. It was still a village near verdant rice paddies, but the house now had air-conditioning. The soundtrack still included cows mooing, but cars had replaced the noisy rickshaws. The road was paved. There were fridges and cold bottled water in them. There were toilets that you could sit on and flush.

Today, there's hardly a caste system left.* People regularly marry across caste lines. I don't think the pizza or air-conditioning caused it. But it was unmistakably the same force that brought pizza and air-conditioning to India that had also eroded the caste system. Capitalism was one of those rare forces more powerful than birth status. And it had spread to India. Not just to the cities, but out to the boonies, all the way to Vadakanchery.

Not everything is better. It's still 100 degrees in Kerala, and the moisture in the air still sticks to your skin. There seem to be more mosquitoes than ever, and they still love American blood. The caste system's gone, but there are new problems.

Many of the problems with capitalism are well known—for example, the unequal distribution of wealth based in part on how successful people are in the game of commercial enterprise. But the biggest problem with capitalism isn't just that it enables some people to buy more things than others.

Rather, the great danger of capitalism rests in its inherently expansive quality. Capitalism has an uncanny ability to organize our society's commercial affairs better than we could've ever imagined, but it has an equally uncanny ability to extend far beyond

---

* The main vestige of the caste system that's left is the government-enforced quota system that demands that colleges, businesses, and other institutions reserve a certain number of seats for "scheduled castes"—descendants of lower castes—a system that fuels toxic identity politics in India.

commercial life. Like light, it will reach as far as it possibly can unless we purposefully contain its scope. Even though it is an economic system, it has the power to reorder social systems too.

Our family experienced this firsthand. As consumerism extended its reach all the way from America to Vadakanchery, it quickly supplanted the historical norms of the village. While free enterprise had nearly eradicated the caste system, it also had the effect of pulling apart our once tight-knit extended family.

My grandmother, whom we called Ammai, had lived in that house in Vadakanchery since the 1940s, alongside her older sister Perisammai. I don't think any of them ever paid attention to who paid for which expense. It was just something that happened. It was a Brahmin virtue to live simply, so spending money was little more than an afterthought.

But everything changed in 2006, when my great aunt Perisammai passed away. She was the matriarch of the family and one of those rare figures who could, it seemed, contain the otherwise inevitable spread of light from one space to another. But she could only do it for so long.

She was in the prayer room, lighting the candles on each of the lamps, as she had done for countless decades. One day, the flame on one of the candles lit the back of her sari, setting it ablaze. She suffered full-body third-degree burns and passed away several days later.

Over the next decade, things changed dramatically in Vadakanchery. The house itself was better. There was the new refrigerator. The bathrooms had been redone with those Western-style toilets. When my cousins and I visited India, we got sick less frequently.

I learned that Sree, Perisammai's granddaughter and my second cousin, was responsible for those improvements. She had emigrated from India to Europe and married into a wealthy family. She used that newfound wealth to modernize her childhood home, where the rest of the clan still lived, including my own grandmother.

Yet there were other changes beneath the surface too. Years after Perisammai passed away, we heard that Sree's side of the family had requested that Ammai move out of the house and join her own children in America.

That would've been unthinkable a decade earlier. The biggest difference was the death of my great aunt Perisammai, whose sheer presence loomed large enough to bind a sprawling family together. But it would be naïve to think that the spread of capitalism had nothing to do with it. Yes, it brought air-conditioning and bottled water to our family home in Vadakanchery. But it also brought with it a new consciousness about who paid for what. My dad's side of the family was doing fine in America by that time and could have borne the costs too, but the real problem wasn't the money itself. It was the new *consciousness* of money within the family.

Eventually Ammai came to America, an immigrant like her children. Like all immigrants, she was searching for a better life, but in a different way. She had had a good life in Vadakanchery, and now she had come to America to make one here. She has, in many ways. Sree's side of the family was ultimately right that it would be good for Ammai and her kids to be together. She has thirteen grandkids and ten great-grandkids, and she visits them all, doing the rounds through Ohio, Indiana, Michigan, and Kentucky. She spends weeks at a time in each place and turns it into some kind of social hub that the rest of the family drops in on.

When I see Ammai watching her grandkids play or sitting on someone's front porch in the American Midwest watching a sunset, I think about how she used to sit on her front veranda in

Vadakanchery and how she'd watch us play baseball as the clothes dried and the light faded. I think about how money can change family relationships and about how there are still some things money can't buy. Maybe that's the moral of my family's story.

That's when I first learned that capitalism often shows up where it's not supposed to, an uninvited guest in a life. Like light, it travels everywhere constantly, in all directions. Like light, it can grow things. But sometimes the light of the candle becomes a fire that sets the whole thing ablaze.

Liberals know that capitalism sometimes hurts people, but they frame the issue poorly. They're too focused on how capitalism harms certain groups rather than focusing on how capitalism sometimes harms everyone by infecting other social systems, like family life or even social values. Capitalism hurts all of us when it undermines democracy through the influence of lobbyists or corporate-social fiats. It hurts all of us when it co-opts sincerely held values like faith or feminism to quietly make money.

John Rawls is one of those all-time great philosophers, who, if he were alive today, would still be looking in the wrong place for the dangers of capitalism. He argued that justice was a matter of fairness and that in a system agreed to by all under fair conditions, all would agree that whoever was left with the short end of the stick should still do as well as possible. So Rawls would wonder who the worst off were in American capitalism. He'd want to make sure they were still doing pretty well and that they weren't being exploited by the rest of us.

Who are the worst off, then? Who has fared poorly in America, and who are the people who have been given the least chance to do well? Is it the unemployed? Is it the homeless or the disabled? The elderly or maybe the poor? Are people of color the worst off?

Which people of color? Women? Jobless white men in the Rust Belt? Wounded veterans? Wayfaring beggars? The mentally ill? Do the worst off of all stand at the intersections of these groups? Is that what "intersectionality" means?

It's a common question about capitalism and one that I've struggled with too. To me the question "Who are the worst off?" is actually the wrong question to ask because it's nearly impossible to answer. There are many good things in life and many ways to lack them, and there's no fact of the matter about whether a poor white man is or isn't worse off than a rich black woman. Today, like the British in colonial India, we unnecessarily pit groups against each other when we ask who the worst off are instead of asking how capitalism sometimes complicates things for everyone.

Grandma Ammai probably wouldn't be counted among the worst off. She's made a good life here. We're a bit more distant from the other side of the family than we used to be, but we've made amends with them. As for our side of the family, we're closer than ever. Ammai visits Vadakanchery for a couple of months a year, escaping Ohio's cold winters for Kerala's warmth. She's not the worst off, but I still wish the spread of capitalism to Vadakanchery had treated her better.

I used to be angry at Sree. I thought of the way I'd appreciated the fridge, the toilets, and the stoves and never knew they would come with a cost. But they had come at an actual cost: someone had to, quite literally, pay for them. Meanwhile my side of the family was sitting blissfully unaware in American suburbia, acting like Vadakanchery was still in the idyllic 1990s and like money didn't matter to us Brahmins.

Over time I came to think my side of the family was in the wrong too. Capitalism had come to India, even to Kerala, and it brought changes we didn't expect. It changed the norms. I was mad at Sree because I thought she was violating Vadakanchery's old norms. But in reality that code had changed long ago. My dad and his siblings in the American Midwest just hadn't woken up to the reality that Vadakanchery in 2015 was fundamentally different from Vadakanchery in the 1990s.

In the new capitalist world, unlike in the old system, it was normal to expect that children would give financial support to their own parents. Sree had been fixing up the house that her dad lived in. She'd been doing that for years, mixing her sweat and labor with it, making it more and more a product of her efforts. In the new system, it was perfectly normal for her side of the family to feel like they should be the ones living in the house.

Back in the '90s, the fact that my grandmother Ammai had lived in the house for so long would've been a powerful justification for her to continue to stay there. Tradition trumped capitalism. But in modern Vadakanchery, the relevant fact is who invested in the home. So who really owns the house? Nowadays the answer is no different in Vadakanchery than in Ohio: *whoever paid for it.*

CAPITALISM DIDN'T JUST reorder the caste system in India. It changed religion too. In the '90s, we used to make pilgrimages to temples across India. We would wait in line with other devotees, often for a day or longer, waiting our turn for a few seconds before the deity. We used to get our heads shaved to the scalp while waiting in line. Like any spoiled American brat, I dutifully whined about it to my parents. Secretly, it was fun.

When my family visited India again in 2011, we didn't do that anymore. When we visited the big temples, we made a donation at the front and avoided waiting in line with the other devotees. We took a private car instead of a rickety bus. Our pilgrimages became more . . . efficient.

At Tirupati, a sort of Hindu mecca in southern India, there's a ticket-based system. Everyone gets in if they wait long enough. But if you pay, you can shorten the wait. If you pay a lot, you can skip the line altogether. And if you pay a ton, you get to do a special ritual right in front of the deity. You just select your ticket at the kiosk.

That's what's supposed to happen at Disney World, not a temple. It betrayed my understanding of what prayer was supposed to be about.

What's the moral of the story? I learned two lessons.

First, capitalism doesn't have an on/off switch. Capitalism eroded the caste system in India, but it also dissolved the subtle bonds that held my Vadakanchery family together for generations. My dad no longer has to run his bank account to zero to make a family trip to India, but capitalism had also caused my parents to worry in the 1990s, when my dad, who under Jack Welch's ruthless tenure at General Electric, faced layoff risks every day while raising two kids in a foreign land. Those realities were inseparable from one another.

Capitalism thrives on individualism and picks apart institutions built on collective identity. Maybe that's a good thing when it tears down institutions like caste. But it also tears down other communal institutions that are worth preserving.

And that's my second lesson: I love capitalism, but I love other things too. Like family. And religion. And democracy. In order to save those things, we need to protect them from being infected by capitalism. I shouldn't be able to buy a FastPass at Tirupati any more than I should be able to buy extra votes in a democracy.

Yet that's exactly what stakeholder capitalism is about.

Stakeholder capitalism pretends to be a milder form of capitalism, but it's actually capitalism gone wild: it encourages capitalism's winners to wield greater power in our democracy. Ordinary Americans who vote at the ballot box each November are like the poor devotees who wait in the long line at the temple. Meanwhile, CEOs and investors issuing moral fiats from Davos are the rich devotees who get to cut the line.

Liberals think the answer is to change capitalism by putting words like "stakeholder" or "conscious" or "environmental, social, and governance" in front of it. For their part, classical conservatives think the answer is to ignore the problem and recite a Milton Friedman or Ronald Reagan quote, failing to recognize that—as Dorothy might have said to Toto—we're not in 1980 anymore. Instead we're in a postmodern Oz where the Wizard is no longer just big government. It's a new hybrid of big business and big government; of capitalism and democracy.

Abraham Lincoln said eight score years ago: "The dogmas of the quiet past are inadequate to the stormy present . . . we must think anew." We would do well to heed his wisdom. The solution to today's new dilemma isn't to change capitalism, as Democrats try to. But neither is it to ignore the inherently invasive qualities of capitalism, as many Republicans are prone to do. Rather it's to prevent capitalism from changing everything else, by building protective walls around the things that we cherish most, like democracy.

America was built on the idea of separating powers between different institutional spheres to protect people. Our Constitution ordains a separation of power between the executive, legislative, and judicial branches; between federal and state government;

between church and state. As Americans, we now need to separate the powers of capitalism from the workings of democracy. To keep them alive, we need to keep them apart.

In order to do that, we must first understand what the modern corporation is supposed to be—and what it's not.

CHAPTER 3

What's the Purpose of a Corporation?

URING MY TENURE AS A CEO, there was nothing that more dramatically revealed the struggle for the soul of corporate America than what happened in the aftermath of George Floyd's horrific death. It was another tragedy in an already-tragic year. Floyd was a black man who died in May 2020 at the hands of police in Minneapolis during his arrest for using a counterfeit $20 bill to buy a pack of cigarettes. The nation erupted in protests and riots across America's streets. It was painful to read about in the news, and it was even more painful to watch the video of how he died. The offending officer, Derek Chauvin, was later convicted of second-degree unintentional murder and other charges.

Notwithstanding the sad news, I quickly returned to focusing on my work in leading Roivant—including all that we were doing to address the ongoing pandemic and the issues that I thought we were well positioned to solve. The murder of George Floyd was tragic, but it was also tragic that thousands of people of all races died of diseases every day that could be better treated by a broken health-care system, one that regularly fails to deliver lifesaving medicines quickly. And I was in the privileged position of leading a company that developed medicines for exactly those people—including medicines that the broken pharma industry had failed to even develop for the people who needed them most. I thought that the best way for our company to do *our* part to improve all lives, including black lives, was to return to our work of saving lives rather than protesting on the streets—namely, by developing medicines for patients who needed them.

As it turns out, we were among the few companies that had prioritized new therapies for uterine fibroids and endometriosis, diseases that disproportionately impact African American women. The pharma industry had historically ignored these diseases, in an almost systematic way. Was that evidence of systemic racism or evidence of companies ignoring diseases that affected populations that were disproportionately covered by Medicaid, which offered much poorer reimbursement for new drugs than private health insurance did? Either way, I was certain that we were doing the right thing by working on those therapies for the millions of women who needed them. Just as we were among the few companies working on a gene therapy to literally *cure* sickle cell disease, a disease that almost exclusively impacts dark-skinned people because of genetic factors.

As I watched videos of stirring and occasionally violent social protests across the country, I couldn't help but wonder whether three months of quarantine and lockdown were a main driver of the pent-up frustration. Sure, there were underlying social issues that our society needed to address, but did looting stores really make a positive difference? Were mass protests in the middle of a pandemic that was killing a lot of black people really a good way to save black lives?

But those nuances didn't stop media outlets from reporting a singular black-and-white narrative. And it didn't stop corporations from pouncing on the opportunity to achieve their own ends.

High-profile CEOs like Tim Cook of Apple and Dara Khosrowshahi of Uber rushed to issue staid statements of solidarity. Khosrowshahi stated that Uber was donating millions to fight racism and that "Uber stands in solidarity with the Black community and with peaceful protests against the injustice and racism that have plagued our nation for too long."[1] The company announced that it would promote black-owned businesses on its ride-sharing app and tie executive pay to "diversity goals." Lastly, Khosrowshahi wrote, "Let me speak clearly and unequivocally: Black Lives Matter." In the weeks later, he pledged that Uber would be an "anti-racist company." Meanwhile, at the exact same time, he was aggressively lobbying California to pass Proposition 22, which permits Uber to classify its drivers as independent contractors rather than as employees. Uber said it would go out of business if it had to reclassify drivers as employees, pleading unprofitability even as it doled out millions to BLM. I don't know what exactly it means to be anti-racist, and Khosrowshahi's dual actions certainly didn't help clarify it for me.

Uber and Apple were hardly alone. Countless other companies did the exact same thing, down to the exact words they chose. It was as though they had all hired the same PR consultant to copy and paste the same text for different clients.

The pressure to publicly support BLM started to weigh heavily on me personally. My peers pressured me to be courageous enough to do the same thing that, well, everyone else was doing. Of course I believed that black lives mattered. But I definitely didn't believe in the stated goals of the Black Lives Matter organization—for example, "disrupting the nuclear family structure." Wouldn't that harm black families?

So I chose to take a different approach and sent the following email to the company:

Dear Roivant team,

I enjoyed seeing all of you at the townhall on Friday. I just wanted to offer a brief comment on the tumultuous period in our world and in particular in the United States in recent days. The last few months have tested us. The COVID-19 pandemic disrupted our lives. A staggering forty million Americans lost their jobs, and many others continue to live in fear of both the virus and its economic consequences. On top of that, the events of the last week have been particularly painful, especially the tragic death of George Floyd. As you probably know well, cities are erupting in protests—including New York City, as well as other cities where some of you are located. My main reason for writing is to ask all of you to stay safe during these difficult times, and to let you know that as a company we are here for you, both physically and mentally. Please talk to any of Roivant's senior leaders, including me, at any time—and you can also reach out to the HR team (cc'd) to access our health resources during this challenging period. Personally, I am at a loss for words as I am still processing these recent events. In the meantime, I am proud to continue our own work on developing important new medicines for patients who need them. Even if our efforts won't cure all of our society's ills, curing diseases and treating patients are among those rare things that everyone can agree is strictly good for our world.

I read it over a couple of times before sending it, and I was convinced that it struck the right balance between exhibiting empathy for our employees while avoiding using my company as a vehicle for foisting social views onto them. I thought it fit the culture of Roivant—a company whose very name centered on improving the "ROI" (return on investment) of pharmaceutical research and development above all else.

But I misread the situation . . . badly. We had spent years recruiting top students from Ivy League universities, inviting them to join the pharmaceutical industry rather than finance or consulting or Silicon Valley, in part with the pitch that they could actually save lives by joining us. That helped us attract brilliant people who were motivated not just by money but by the inherent social value of our company's work in developing much-needed medicines. I was proud of that fact. But that also meant we had attracted an entire class to our workforce that was hungry for a cause—and hungry to work at a company that would take up the causes they cared about.

The day after I sent the company-wide email, I started getting text messages from my trusted senior managers. My email had, apparently, "missed the moment." It was "tone-deaf." I had revealed my "privilege."

Foolishly, I ignored the brewing tide, hoping that it would naturally subside. We were due to have a townhall later that week, and I decided to use it as an occasion to try to focus the company on our near-term strategy for developing a treatment for COVID-19 and on stemming the impact of the virus on our other ongoing clinical trials.

But within minutes after sharing our progress on COVID-19 initiatives, employees began asking questions like "What is Roivant doing to address systemic racism across its many subsidiaries?" "Are we going to revisit our recruiting practices?" I personally reject the narrative of systemic racism, so I listened and didn't say much in response, trying to sound empathetic whenever I could.

My senior colleagues told me I came across as uncharacteristically aloof that day, maybe even dismissive—and, worst of all, inauthentic. In retrospect, I failed as a leader that day: I had let my own personal views get in the way of connecting with my employees at a time when they had an important issue on their minds. That was on me.

Some of my younger employees were understandably upset with me, so they convened a meeting of a committee they had formed called the Roivant Social Responsibility Committee. They issued demands, similar to demands that were popping up at companies all over the country. They wanted more regular townhalls to address social issues, a "Chief Diversity Officer," a company task force to meet on issues of diversity, and a change to our campus recruiting practices. They were earnest in their demands and sincere in communicating them.

Part of my job as CEO was to make sure my employees were comfortable in their workplace. But part of my job was also to make sure we were productive in developing medicines without getting sidetracked. I met with senior leaders across the company and discussed how to handle the situation. Nothing that I said seemed to help. Employees wanted me to denounce systemic racism and express solidarity with Black Lives Matter, and fundamentally I didn't want to do that. Morale waned, and some employees were uneasy.

Later that week, I had a regularly scheduled conference call with Roivant's board of directors. I looked forward to a sanctuary where I could focus on doing what I thought I was supposed to do: develop medicines and deliver value to shareholders. No better place to discuss the latter, I thought, than a forum with the largest of those very shareholders. We needed to make important decisions on a transaction that we were weighing, and I had prepared a list of potential drug prospects and deals to discuss with the board.

Yet I was blindsided by a question from one of my investors who had in the past been most focused on making sure that we were minimizing our cash burn. What, he asked, were we doing as a company to examine whether we too were perpetuating systemic racism?

There was something curious to me about corporate America's fixation on the BLM movement, even as other obvious injustices continued to abound. I was personally appalled by China's persecution of its Uighur population in what Beijing calls Xinjiang and the Uighurs call East Turkestan. That too was happening during those same months and was no less relevant to a global business like ours, especially considering that we were still actively doing business in China. Yet none of my employees or directors expressed concern to me about these human rights violations. Meanwhile, I wanted to make the world better by developing medicines while leaving it to public officials to address problems like inequality at home or human rights abuses abroad.

The problem with tackling these broader issues as a CEO, I felt, wasn't simply that it would distract us from our mission of developing medicines. Even more importantly, it was that I might actually make the world *worse* by using my position as the CEO to foist my own views onto our democracy. The murder of George Floyd was an issue that we as Americans needed to sort through *together* as citizens, through the judicial system and otherwise, without elite corporate intervention.

I also felt uncomfortable being inauthentic with my employees. Personally, while I believe racism exists and should be eliminated, I don't believe in "systemic racism." In fact, I don't even know what it means: to me, it sounds like a catchall phrase designed to allow political leaders to escape accountability for solving real-world problems like poverty and failure in education. So I didn't want to publicly denounce something that I didn't believe in—or, at the very least, that I didn't fully understand.

At the same time, my senior team at Roivant convinced me that I needed to do *something* to address the concerns of our employees. So I declared that Juneteenth would be a holiday and a day for reflection at our company, an action I felt had inherent value, especially in a difficult COVID-19 year when people might have appreciated a day to reflect on what was happening in their lives and in the world.

I kept my promise and canceled all of my meetings that day and instead spent Juneteenth doing my own reflection. Where did this notion that CEOs were supposed to pursue social ends come from in the first place? If my employees and even some of my investors believed in this new philosophy, then why was I so hesitant to get on board? Was I wrong? Why was I hopelessly clinging to the antiquated ideal of maximizing shareholder value?

As it turns out, the answer wasn't so simple.

THE MILTON FRIEDMAN–APPROVED account of the corporation goes something like this. DJ, my barber since childhood in Sharonville, Ohio, started a barber shop because it was his dream to run a business and to drive a Corvette to work. In order to do this, he needed enough money to buy that Corvette. So he opened a shop, hung a shingle, and started to cut people's hair. Eventually, there were more people waiting to get their hair cut than he had time to handle himself, so he hired two employees. DJ still runs his shop in Sharonville. So far, so good.

Suppose he wants to expand his business by opening branches in other townships. First, DJ would need to hire people to operate those stores, and he wouldn't be able to manage them directly anymore. That means DJ might need to hire a professional manager to oversee the operation. But entrusting people with what you've created is a risky proposition. DJ owns the business; the people he'd hire, no matter how good they were, would just be hired hands. Those hired managers would be accountable for certain results and would be paid to deliver those results, but it would be impossible to fully police their every action to make sure they were truly acting in DJ's interest at all times. That's what business school professors call "the separation of ownership and control": the guys who run businesses often aren't the ones who own it.

There's a second problem too: as soon as DJ expands his business, he exposes himself to the risk of getting sued out of existence. When he's operating just one store, he can personally make sure that customers don't slip and fall because someone forgot to clean the hair on the ground. But DJ can't do that on his own if he were to expand to two locations, or five, or a hundred.

The reality is that nearly every major business ends up with some disgruntled customers and employees over time. It would be a pretty frightening prospect for an entrepreneur like DJ if people could sue him *personally* every time they got upset with one of his shops. The wrong lawsuit could wipe out his entire personal savings: if the damages in a given case were high enough, he might have to sell his Corvette and his house and still not have enough to pay up.

If people like DJ face a risk, even a small one, of personal bankruptcy every time they want to scale their business, very few people would do it. Certainly, fewer people would do it than is optimal for society overall. We would have fewer places to shop, and we'd have fewer opportunities to find employment. The only people who would be able to do it are those who already have enough assets to withstand the risk of liability.

The invention of the modern corporation solved both of these problems in one fell swoop. A "corporation" is nothing more than a legal invention, a bunch of words written on a piece of paper. Those words on paper accomplish two basic things.

First, corporate law creates an obligation owed by managers to the owners of a business. That obligation is known as a fiduciary duty—the highest form of trusted obligation that one person can legally owe another. It's the same obligation your lawyer owes you when you entrust him to write and administer your will. Likewise, it's the obligation that an executive or director owes to the shareholders, or owners, of a corporation.

So if you run DJ's business for him, you owe the highest standard of care to DJ as the *owner* of the business: you have a legal duty to put DJ's interests above all else. In fact, if you fall short of fulfilling your legal obligation, DJ can actually sue *you*—not the corporation, but *you as a person*—for betraying your fiduciary obligation. The corporate shield from liability protects DJ as the owner from outside claims, but it does *not* protect DJ's managers from being directly sued by DJ himself. Poof . . . a nice win for DJ.

Many businesses—like Roivant, for example—are more complicated than DJ's because they have more than one owner. These owners each hold "shares" in the corporation, so we call them "shareholders." Publicly traded companies have thousands of shareholders at any given time, and who owns the company changes every day, even every second. When DJ is the sole owner of his business, it's relatively easy for him to directly communicate to his managers what he wants to see—on matters of profitability and workplace culture to the social values that matter to him. But what if there are thousands of owners, each of whom may have different views on those questions?

Enter the "board of directors." Because shareholders are often disparate geographically, diverse in their views, and unknown to one another, they elect a board of directors to look after their affairs by representing their *collective* point of view. The board then becomes the so-called *fiduciary* of those shareholders: they owe the shareholders the highest level of care, just as DJ's externally hired managers owed him that duty.

What if shareholders have different views on what the board should do? Corporate law in most jurisdictions deals with this problem in a simple way: it demands that the board make decisions to maximize *overall* shareholder value. In simple terms, this means maximizing profits. Delaware is the state where most American companies are incorporated, and in 2015 Delaware's Chief Justice Leo Strine summed it up well when he said that Delaware law "reveals that . . . directors must make stockholder welfare their sole end."[2] Not their main end, but their *sole* end.

Sure, there's room for valid debate about what time horizon matters. That's usually where most debates about stakeholder capitalism get hung up. Proponents of stakeholder capitalism say that the classical model is too focused on the short term. Should the board focus on short-term profits or long-term profits? That's a fine question, but one that is *internal* to classical capitalism. Milton

Friedman's most faithful disciples still disagree with one another about the answer.

But the key point is that the decision centers on what most maximizes *profits*—rather than the myriad other important questions on which individual people could actually have a wide range of personal opinions. The members of a corporation's board are indeed people. But corporations *aren't* literally people. Unlike people, corporations as entities have a view on one thing and one thing alone: profits.

So, that's the first important thing that corporate law does: it creates a fiduciary duty owed by the directors and officers of a corporation to their shareholders. That's an important protection specifically reserved to shareholders.

But the second piece of the puzzle is even more important: it gives shareholders *limited legal liability*. That is, corporate law creates a legal barrier that prevents anyone wronged by a corporation from holding an owner of that corporation personally liable. In effect, it creates an artificial shield that protects business owners like DJ from being sued. This is arguably the most important feature of the corporation: it's a legal shield that was created to bear liability so individual people didn't have to.

A customer falls and hits his head while in the store? The customer can sue and collect damages from the corporation, but not from any of its owners individually. In other words, the customer can sue DJ's Barber Shop, but not DJ the person. So DJ still gets to keep his Corvette and house no matter how badly the lawsuits against his shop go. That's the real victory for owners like DJ.

Of course, the real story isn't about DJ at all. Like most small businesses, DJ is the sole owner of his company. The real reason that limited shareholder liability is so important is that it empowers entrepreneurs to raise outside capital from third-party investors to build businesses that they could never have possibly built on their own. Take shipping, for example. Shipping is incredibly capital-intensive and risky. If an investor puts $100 into a shipping venture and stands to lose his house if things go south, he's not going to put up the $100. But with limited liability, the $100 investor risks only his $100. *That's* really what limited liability is all about—enabling the $100 investor to back a risky shipping project, or a railroad, or a steel mill. Or in today's world, a clinical trial, a new piece of software, or a 5G network. You might be able to build a chain of barber shops or restaurants without taking on outside investors, but you simply *can't* build a major pharma company, telecommunications company, or shipping company without taking on serious outside investment. And no investor would put up capital to fund any of those ventures in the absence of limited liability.

The invention of the limited liability corporation unleashed the massive aggregation of capital that drove the unprecedented economic revolutions of the last two centuries. *The Economist* called it "one of man's greatest inventions," and many economic historians believe that it sat at the heart of the Industrial Revolution, as well as the internet and biotech revolutions in more recent years.[3] And they're right: we probably wouldn't have the iPhone, the cure to hepatitis C, or electric cars without the invention of limited liability. The investors who were asked to put up the capital to fund Apple, Gilead, or Tesla simply wouldn't have done so if they had borne personal liability for the losses of the company in the event that it failed.

Limited liability is nothing short of a man-made superpower. It was a legal invention created to defy the basic principle by which ordinary people live—namely, that you bear the consequences of your action. With the birth of the corporation, we as a society intentionally created a gargantuan exception to that otherwise ordinary principle.

Predictably, that is exactly what gave rise to the titanic corporate behemoths that have become so familiar today. Entrepreneurs amassed unlimited capital from investors who bore nothing more than the risk of losing that capital and built businesses of previously unimagined size and scope.

This isn't at all a modern surprise. From the very birth of the corporation, people rightly worried about the power that monstrous corporate behemoths could wield. Take the Dutch East India Company. It wielded not only financial power, but state-like political power as well. Like modern corporations, the Dutch East India Company received special privileges—in its case, to access trade routes across vast swaths of territories. According to British corporate historians Leonardo Davoudi, Christopher McKenna, and Rowena Olegario, chartered companies in the Old World waged wars with their own private armies and fleets, built forts and infrastructure, conquered territories, negotiated treaties, and, in the case of the Dutch East India Company, even minted their own corporate currency.[4] I heard echoes of the Dutch East India Company's voice in Mark Zuckerberg's statement in 2020 that he wanted Facebook to launch its own cryptocurrency.

At the same time, the Dutch East India Company also pursued philanthropic causes back at home, like donating funds to relieve poverty, build hospitals, and establish schools. And they were assiduous about noting those charitable activities in the company minutes. It wasn't just a matter of generating good PR; it was fundamentally to "assuage core cultural concerns of the era and demonstrate their dedication to improving their societies."[5] The philanthropic activities of the Dutch East India Company and its exercise of state-like political power were two sides of the same coin. In many ways, it was the Silicon Valley of its era.

Here's the good news: the people who invented the American corporation in the eighteenth century weren't fools. They knew exactly what they were doing. They were well aware that limited shareholder liability was effectively a necessity to spawn unprecedented economic growth, but they also knew that it would create a monster that could eventually supplant democracy itself.

So they crafted a clever solution . . . one that already existed, actually. Counterintuitively, *it was actually the legal mandate to maximize shareholder value*. To protect against corporations becoming behemoth monsters, corporations needed to be restricted to their purposes. They needed to be kept in their lane. Maximizing shareholder value wasn't about unleashing corporate greed, or rewarding shareholders, or even about unlocking greater economic productivity. Rather, it was about *reining in corporate power*—by preventing an abuse of the corporate form to aggregate undue power and social influence and limiting corporations to focus on the humdrum activity of selling goods and services.

Twentieth-century proponents of classical capitalism like Milton Friedman completely missed that point. They only knew one mantra: maximize productivity and the size of the economic pie. They correctly noted that limited shareholder liability was an incentive for entrepreneurs and investors to pursue risky new projects. But they wrongly assumed that the mandate for corporate boards to maximize shareholder value was just another incentive to take risks. Limited shareholder liability was the incentive to do that. By contrast, the mandate to focus on profits, rather than on social or moral issues, was the *demand* that society made in return to ensure that powerful corporations didn't supplant the state itself.

THOUGHTFUL LIBERALS HAVE long argued that in return for the gift of limited liability, the state *ought* to have demanded something greater in return from companies.[6] That's effectively the idea that we now call "stakeholder capitalism"—the idea that businesses have at least *some* obligation to serve not just their shareholders but the interests of society at large. They argue that this was an implicit social contract at the birth of the modern corporation.

Professor Luigi Zingales, a well-respected economist at the University of Chicago, captures this debate aptly: "Historically we know that corporations were born as public institutions with a special privilege granted by the state. Even today, we do know that the privilege of limited liability, especially with respect to tort claims, is an extraordinary privilege granted by the state. So to what extent does this special privilege bring with it a special responsibility?"[7]

This is the most compelling case for stakeholder capitalism. Advocates of stakeholder capitalism correctly point out that corporations didn't exist in the state of nature. Rather, the corporation only exists because the state *permitted* it to exist. Society gave corporate shareholders the extraordinary gift of limited liability—a gift that no ordinary person enjoys. In return, those shareholders owe an implicit obligation back to society: their corporations ought to consider not only shareholder interests but broader societal interests when making decisions—employees, local communities, minority groups, the climate, and so on.

That was the unspoken grand bargain at the birth of the corporation, progressive advocates argue. Professor Thomas Jones of the

University of Washington in Seattle explains that "the corporation which acts in a responsible manner may simply be paying society back."[8] Stakeholderist-in-chief Larry Fink borrows this logic when he frequently proclaims that "companies need to earn their social license to operate every day."[9]

The shield of limited liability is what allows entrepreneurs to raise capital from outside investors who can bet on risky new ventures while limiting their losses to the amount of their investment. But it's also what allows the Sackler family to remain multibillionaires even as their wholly owned company, Purdue Pharma, goes bankrupt for having illegally marketed a painkiller that resulted in hundreds of thousands of deaths globally. It's what allows President Donald Trump to remain a billionaire even though many of his properties have defaulted on their debts over the years, including payments to contractors who were struggling to make ends meet. It was the dark side of the grand bargain that society struck to incentivize entrepreneurial innovation.

Classical capitalists have all but ignored this fundamental argument that corporations owe society concern for its welfare in return for its gift of limited liability. Milton Friedman evaded this issue in his famous and otherwise compelling 1970 essay. His free market disciples never addressed the point in the subsequent decades either. Free marketeers and classical capitalists reject out of hand the idea of an implicit social contract. Yet they fail to offer a compelling answer to what corporations owe society in return for the state-granted superpower of limited liability.

In doing so, they have missed a fundamental opportunity to defend shareholder primacy. A critical reason why state corporate law codified shareholder primacy wasn't simply to protect shareholders from management. It was to protect American democracy from both managers *and* shareholders. The creation of the limited-liability corporation was a potent tool to unlock not only productivity through the private sector but also potentially limitless corporate power that could infect other spheres of society beyond the marketplace for goods and services. By limiting the focus of corporate boards to shareholders' financial interests alone, corporate law is actually *confining* the sphere of influence of corporations. That protects our democracy and other civic institutions from corporate overreach.

This view is analogous to the approach that federal law takes to the formation of nonprofit corporations. In return for tax-exempt status, we demand that nonprofits confine their activities to the sphere of charitable causes. With for-profit corporations, we do precisely the reverse—not just to protect corporate shareholders but also to protect the rest of society from frighteningly expansive corporate power to influence every aspect of our lives.

History provides ample support for this view. In the eighteenth and nineteenth centuries, US corporations were created by government charters that limited them to specific purposes. This was derived from the British system created in the 1600s, when the monarch granted monopolies to groups of people to incentivize them to undertake certain ventures the government had an interest in. Alexander Hamilton, for instance, successfully argued for a federally chartered national bank, and in the 1800s the federal government granted charters to Union Pacific Railroad and others to create the transcontinental railroad.[10]

In the early nineteenth century, each US corporation had to receive a special charter from the legislature laying out its purpose. States granted charters to corporations to pursue very narrow purposes—for example, to build a bridge. Corporations were legally barred from going beyond the scope of their charters and could be sued for doing so. If a corporation were granted a charter to build a bridge and tried to build a general purpose road instead, it would lose all of the formal benefits of incorporation, including limited liability.

By the late 1800s, the US had shifted to a model of general incorporation, in which states granted charters to any corporation that met fixed statutory requirements. But the underlying statutory requirement to sharply limit the scope of corporate activities remained intact. In Massachusetts, for instance, a corporation "had to have a single, specific purpose set out in its charter, and the law generally held corporate actions unconnected to that purpose void," with only unanimous shareholder consent able to alter a corporation's charter-specified purpose.[11] This restriction became so fundamental that it came to bear the signifying hallmark of any truly important legal doctrine: a Latin name. It was called the *ultra vires* doctrine ("beyond the powers").

Today, almost all corporate charters allow corporations to conduct any lawful business, and the *ultra vires* doctrine has become a formality that only has serious legal consequences for nonprofit corporations and state-created ones like universities. But history teaches us a lot: for most of our nation's life, our law has held that corporations were granted their special legal protections as part of a package deal saying that their activities had to be *strictly limited* to the narrow purposes outlined in their charters. The general-form version of those charters today is the mandate to simply maximize shareholder value—and to avoid pursuing other activities that could result in a greater aggregation of corporate power than society intended.

Making the pursuit of profit the corporation's singular mission wasn't simply a matter of administrative convenience. It was a fundamentally new American invention. In the Old World European model—what is now termed classical "corporatism"—the role of the corporation was to serve as one among many societal institutions tasked with the betterment of the public at large. In Europe, business leaders were supposed to work with labor leaders, church officials, and politicians to determine and implement the common good. But in America, the job of corporate managers has been to maximize profits alone—leaving it to other institutions to look after broader societal goals.

The genius of the American vision was to separate the activities of innovators and entrepreneurs from those of other societal institutions, like church and state and local government. While the leaders of other institutions—including government—looked after the interests of society at large, American capitalists were legally obligated to look after only their own interests.

History supports this view, but so does common sense. Society gave corporations superpowers. Foremost among them was the gift of limited liability. In return, society demanded that companies use that power for only a narrow set of activities—namely, to make products and services—to prevent them from wielding too much power in our politics and other noncommercial spheres of our lives.

Advocates of classical capitalism like Milton Friedman wrongly assumed that *both* fundamental features of the corporation—limited shareholder liability and the mandate to maximize shareholder value—were strictly about incentivizing entrepreneurs and investors to unleash innovation. They ignored the way in which limited shareholder liability would create titanic corporate monsters with power heretofore unimagined, offering no coherent theory for how society should constrain the power of those monsters outside the marketplace.

By contrast, advocates of stakeholder capitalism were *correct* to acknowledge a social contract between shareholders and society in which shareholders owe something back to society in return for the great gift of limited liability. They were also correct to recognize that the social contract was one that demanded *restraint* from corporations. They erred only in surmising that this social contract was "implicit" and that corporate restraint was about tamping down the pure pursuit of profit. To the contrary: if limited liability was the *quid* from society, then the mandate to maximize shareholder value was the *quo* from corporations.

That was the true grand bargain. The requirement to maximize profits wasn't just about protecting shareholders, as Milton Friedman types had assumed. *It was about protecting the rest of society from a Frankensteinian corporate monster.* That's why we keep the monster trapped in the cage of capitalism: to protect democracy and other civic institutions from a monster that, once unleashed, would exercise more power than any business or person ever should. Just as society demands that nonprofits confine their activities to the sphere of charitable causes in return for tax-exempt status, with for-profit corporations society did precisely the reverse—not just to protect shareholders but to protect democracy and our other institutions.

And therein lies the solution to the true problem of expansive corporate power in the twenty-first century: limit the scope of limited shareholder liability itself. That might sound scary to business elites at first, but on inspection its effect is intuitive and even mundane. Institutional shareholders like BlackRock, one of the largest asset managers and proponents of stakeholder capitalism, should enjoy the benefit of the limited liability shield when their portfolio companies produce goods and services for profit. But if BlackRock uses the corporate shield to implement its own vision of "social responsibility" for society by using its portfolio companies as a vehicle for advancing that agenda, then aggrieved consumers, employees, and other stakeholders shouldn't just be limited to suing those corporations. They should be able to go after BlackRock directly—as well as any other social-activist shareholder of that corporation.

Let's get specific: suppose there's a big parade organized by a bunch of social activists around a particular cause—say, climate change. Right now, if a regular social activist drives a car in that parade and crashes into someone, she faces personal tort liability. She could be sued in court and lose everything she has. But now, suppose she's the owner of a company and sends one of her employees in the company car to do the same thing, and the exact same thing happens. Then she *can't* be sued: her personal assets are protected by limited liability. That gives her a shield that ordinary social activists don't get. That's the shield that woke shareholders like BlackRock or other ESG investors enjoy on a large scale today.

So I'm just proposing that we level the playing field and make those woke shareholders, like BlackRock or Al Gore's Generation Investment Management, bear the same liability as any ordinary social activist when they engage in ordinary social activism through the companies that they invest in. Limited shareholder liability was never meant to protect well-heeled woke investors from the consequences of their actions during PR stunts at woke parades. Yet that's precisely the privilege that these woke shareholders enjoy today—one that society never intended to provide when it created limited shareholder liability in the first place.

This solution may seem modest, but it would completely

reorder stakeholder capitalism. Today, BlackRock preaches about the need for corporations to meet the standards of its "Sustainability Accounting Standards Board," since as a shareholder it is protected from liability from anything that its portfolio companies do. Yet the corporate shield was created to incentivize capital formation for the pursuit of profit—not to use the corporate shield as a way of conducting a protected form of social activism. If BlackRock were to face tort liability for its social advocacy efforts—like an ordinary human social activist would—then its willingness to embrace those social causes would predictably change.

Of course, shareholders like BlackRock can avail themselves in court of the affirmative defense that their primary interest was simply the pursuit of profit itself rather than any social or charitable agenda. In that case, they would continue to benefit from the shield of limited liability—which exists precisely to protect for-profit corporate activities. But it would also reveal the true essence of stakeholder capitalism for the self-interested farce that it is, in a way that would enlighten consumers and citizens alike about the true motivations of today's newly woke capitalist class. It's the same motivation that Milton Friedman surmised all along: the pursuit of self-interest above all.

For those like me who believe the rise of Wokenomics represents a problem for democracy, the simple answer is to limit the scope of limited liability of the corporation to cover only the set of activities it was intended to cover. A corporation ought to be free to pursue activities that go beyond the pursuit of profit—America is a free country, after all—but to the extent that it does, its social-activist shareholders shouldn't receive any special protection from direct liability. There is no government regulatory action needed here. Just a simple legal fix—arguably a form of *deregulation*—that clarifies that the construct of limited liability is . . . well, limited.

I KEPT MY promise to my employees to engage in a day of reflection on Juneteenth. Though I was initially frustrated by the employee backlash, I learned something valuable from it. It forced me to think about how to build a better company. I began the day wondering where this social revolution had come from. But I ended the day by asking the question of how the social tumult in America could push Roivant to become the best version of itself.

A new week brought a new townhall and a new chance to engage with my socially conscious employees. I told my employees that I'd realized Roivant had indeed fallen short of its goals. One of our founding values was scrappiness—it might as well have been written in our corporate charter. "Think Big, Stay Scrappy," we often said. We weren't supposed to be one of those glossy big pharma companies. We were always supposed to be the young upstarts with chips on our shoulders. We were supposed to be hungry. And we needed to recruit fresh hires who saw themselves as underdogs too.

For years we had prioritized Ivy League schools in our campus recruiting process. Sure, there are plenty of scrappy kids at Harvard just as there are at state universities. But recruiting Ivy League grads wasn't *automatically* going to select for hunger and scrappiness.

There was another issue, too. As CEO, I often declared with pride that we valued diversity of thought and diversity of experience among our employee base. But if I'm being honest, we weren't actually doing very much to screen for diversity of thought or diversity of experience in our recruiting process, even though we declared that to be an important objective. At the prior week's townhall, one of my employees had been brave enough to publicly challenge me about that in front of the entire company, pointing to a campus recruiting process that was concentrated heavily on Ivy League universities. At the time, I had answered her question defensively, meekly pointing to the fact that colleges like Harvard and Yale already invested immense efforts to create diverse student bodies. But as a company, when did we simply take someone else's judgment as gospel without pressure-testing it ourselves? Especially about something that we said was important? Answer: we didn't. If anything, we prided ourselves on being contrarian.

So on that Zoom call the following week with my employees, I made a surprise announcement about a new hiring policy—one not only that would help keep Roivant scrappy but that respected our long-standing business principle that actions speak louder than words. I announced that we would prioritize recruiting a certain number of candidates who grew up in a family where the household income was below the 25th percentile. (Over the last year, Roivant has since expanded the program to be more inclusive by increasing the qualification threshold to below the 50th percentile.) If one of those employees joined our company and remained employed by us for four years, we would assume any outstanding student debt that they had, up to a total of $100,000. And we would implement that program without compromising on the other qualities we seek from our job candidates.

The announcement came as a shock to the entire company. To be sure, some employees thought that I'd once again "missed the moment," since the program made no mention of "fighting racism" or "standing with the Black community." But for many of my employees, it was exactly the kind of solution they'd been yearning for.

From my perspective, recruiting less economically privileged employees wasn't a means to the end of fighting racism *per se*. It wasn't even a means to the end of solving inequality. That was important work for American democracy to tackle. Rather, our new policy was just one small way to make Roivant a better company. As CEO, that was my own small way of making the world better too.

CHAPTER 4

The Rise of the Managerial Class

M Y EMPLOYEES AT ROIVANT WHO pushed me to "do more" as CEO were sincere in their desire for justice. But it's more often the case that high-powered executives are the ones pushing their own values on everyone else. While they may claim to be pursuing justice or responding to "stakeholders," when members of America's managerial class mix business and politics, it's usually about burnishing their own personal reputation and power.

To successfully merge business with politics, managerial elites must control both. As it turns out, the managerial class seized control of government long before it captured private industry. The year 2020 offered a case in point.

Shortly after 1 a.m. EST on the morning of Friday, October 2, 2020, the world learned via Twitter that President Trump had tested positive for COVID-19. Given President Trump's age and health, there was a very real chance that the president of the United

States might become incapacitated or even die on the eve of the presidential election.

President Trump was admitted to the Walter Reed National Military Medical Center in Washington, D.C., where he received an unconventional combination of medicines. One of them was an unapproved antibody cocktail from a biotech company called Regeneron. By Monday, President Trump had departed Walter Reed feeling healthy. In a widely publicized video later that week, President Trump voiced his opinion that the investigational therapy from Regeneron is what made the biggest difference in his recovery.

The idea isn't crazy. Regeneron's cocktail contained antibodies that were specifically engineered to bind to the virus responsible for the COVID-19 infection. Regeneron had used the same approach to successfully treat Ebola. The company's clinical trial had been promising. That's why President Trump's doctors made special arrangements for him to receive this therapy even though it wasn't yet approved by the US Food and Drug Administration (FDA).

If I'd had an elder family member who'd contracted the virus at the same time as President Trump, I'd have wanted them to receive the exact same treatment regimen as him. But here's the rub: there's no way that would've happened. I couldn't have accessed Regeneron's therapy for a family member. I was a well-connected biotech CEO and still wouldn't have stood a chance. Hundreds of thousands of hospitalized COVID-19 patients could simply forget about it. The reason? A three-letter answer: FDA.

Regeneron's antibody cocktail wasn't FDA approved at the time that President Trump received it. As it happens, President Trump belongs to the same golf club as Len Schleifer, the CEO of Regeneron. And President Trump was also the president. So he was in a unique position to make one phone call and immediately access an investigational therapy that no ordinary American could.

It's obvious that the president of the United States should get the best possible treatment. The problem was that everyone else couldn't—because of barriers erected *by the US government itself.*

That may sound puzzling. And it's particularly ironic to have been the case under President Trump's watch since he was the one to champion "Right to Try" legislation through Congress. The name of the law summarizes it well: it gives patients a right to try treatment options that aren't yet FDA approved.

Except it didn't, in the end. Here's a dark secret that most Americans don't know: no respectable biotech or pharma company *actually* makes its investigational therapies available to patients via "Right to Try." Companies simply refuse to engage with it.

The reason? Once again: the FDA. The agency absolutely *hates* the Right to Try law. If patients need to access drugs before they're approved, the FDA prefers a different program—the "expanded access" program that is overseen by the FDA—rather than Right to Try, which is not.* Maybe that's a reasonable perspective. But even if the FDA doesn't like Right to Try, it's still the law of the land, right? In name, yes. In reality, no.

The general rule of thumb in the pharma industry is this: you do what the FDA wants. Period. It's well known in the industry that if you indulge Right to Try, then you do so at your own peril. As the old adage in pharma goes, "FDA never forgets." Companies don't make money when making drugs available through Right to Try. But every year of delay in formal FDA approval to *sell* the drug

---

* As a side note, this is actually the program through which President Trump accessed Regeneron's antibody cocktail.

could be very costly. All it takes is a line-level bureaucrat citing some technicality as the reason for a delay. Measured against that risk, no rational company wants to alienate the FDA, even if that means giving a cold shoulder to Right to Try.

As if there were any doubt, the FDA makes its view known in no uncertain terms: "There is no evidence that either bill would meaningfully improve access for patients, but both would remove FDA from the process and create a dangerous precedent that would erode protections for vulnerable patients," a group of former FDA leaders wrote.[1] It was typical FDA: they hid behind the reasonable-sounding talking point that "there is no evidence" of expanding patient access through Right to Try. Yet the very reason why Right to Try doesn't expand patient access is precisely because companies don't want to take the risk of pissing off their bureaucratic regulator.

In sum, even though the American people went through the proper democratic process to pass Right to Try legislation, it's wholly futile. Why? Because the FDA's managerial class just doesn't like it. Congress passes laws, but it can't prevent administrative agencies from exercising soft power. When the FDA blows its dog whistle, the pharmaceutical industry listens very carefully.

This is the fourth branch of government in action. It's the real deep state—not a conspiratorial kind, but a much more mundane version. They teach us in high school that there are three branches of government: legislative, executive, and judicial. That's certainly what the Constitution says. Yet in real life, the fourth branch of government—the administrative state—is often more powerful than any of the other three. This alphabet soup of government agencies—SEC, FAA, FTC, HHS, FCC, and so on—runs the day-to-day affairs of the federal government, staffed by civil servants largely insulated from political accountability.

The reality is that most career staffers at the FDA genuinely care about protecting public health, just as most career staffers at the CIA genuinely care about protecting national security. That noble motivation guides their day-to-day actions, occasionally combined with a hunger for relevance and power. They usually make sound scientific judgments. Even when these staffers are wrong, they often have good reasons for wanting things to be done in a certain way.

But my chief complaint isn't that these technocrats are making the wrong judgments. It's that they use their technocratic authority to subvert the will of the American people. Right or wrong on the merits, that's an insult to democracy.

In 2016, political scientist Michael Lind observed that the greatest threat to Western democracy is its gradual decay under well-educated, well-mannered, and well-funded elites.[2] According to Lind, modern American government implicitly "transfers political power from national legislatures to executive agencies, transnational bureaucracies, and treaty organizations."[3] Congress's toothless Right to Try law is emblematic of the problem that Lind described.

But my focus goes beyond government. Today there's a "deep corporation" problem in the private sector as well. The perpetrators are the hired C-suite managers at large companies. Just like government bureaucrats, these executives often implicitly frustrate the will of a corporation's shareholders. Their main goal is to aggregate power for themselves in the name of serving their companies and society.

Similar to the three branches of government, there are three legs to the stool of any company: founders, investors, and employees. Founders start companies, investors fund companies, and employees work for companies. It's supposed to be simple. But as in government, especially at America's largest corporations, there's now an invisible fourth leg to the stool: the managerial class. The folks who sit in glass-walled corner offices in Manhattan skyscrapers or communal bean bags in Silicon Valley and use the company piggy bank to travel to Davos each January. They're high-paid bureaucrats charged with balancing the interests of founders, investors, and employees.

These managers often make handsome salaries, but they own much less of the company than founders and investors do. In general, they're not billionaires. And they're not playing the capitalist game just for money. They're playing for power.

Academics like Michael Jensen and Eugene Fama have commented at length about incentive misalignments between hired corporate managers and their shareholders. They wrote a famous paper in 1998 titled "Separation of Ownership and Control," which made the basic observation that managers own very little of firms yet wield day-to-day control of them.[4] And that in turn creates so-called "agency costs," an economic term referring to the value an entity loses when it outsources some of its decision-making to an entity with different interests.

But misalignments arising from differential ownership are only part of the story. In the real world, there's an even bigger issue: shareholders of public companies are generally anonymous, while CEOs and other corporate managers are personally well known. Unlike shareholders, managers have a personal reputation to maintain. Unlike a shareholder, a corporate manager's main asset isn't wealth. It's *social stature*. That's their ticket to wielding power, to getting hired to run another company in the future, to gaining a membership at a prestigious golf club, to getting appointed to a cushy job as an ambassador.

According to academics like Jensen and Fama, the role of a

corporation's board is to oversee CEOs and other managers to protect shareholders from their actions. Problem solved? Not quite. In the real world, most board members are themselves hired hands— in other words, themselves members of the managerial class.

These independent directors are well compensated for their services—often six-figure or even seven-figure sums for attending one half-day board meeting per quarter. There's a reason they call it "sitting" on a board. In practice, this class of "independent directors" is now populated by people who professionally serve in that capacity, some of whom become lifers in that role. Some are ex-politicians; some are ex-CEOs and ex-CFOs; others are retired partners of large law firms or accounting firms.

Regardless of their backgrounds, these repeat players in the game know where their bread is buttered. In practice, they aren't selected by public shareholders. Most often, they're selected by CEOs themselves. Every time I've personally been asked to join the board of a public company, it's almost always the CEO of that company who invites me to do it. (To date, I've always declined; personally, I find the idea of serving as another CEO's pawn about as appealing as a sharp poke in the eye.)

So in sum, independent directors get paid a lot of money to provide oversight of CEOs at public companies. Yet those CEOs are effectively the main ones who select and influence the people who will oversee them. Sounds like a racket? Welcome to the world of the managerial class.

The consequences aren't just bad for corporate shareholders. They're bad for America. Michael Lind correctly observed that "the most important managers are private and public bureaucrats who run large national and global corporations and exercise disproportionate influence in politics and society."[5] Political theorist James Burnham first wrote about this phenomenon in his 1941 best seller *The Managerial Revolution*. In 1946, George Orwell summarized Burnham's theory well:

> *Capitalism is disappearing, but Socialism is not replacing it. What is now arising is a new kind of planned, centralized society which will be neither capitalist, nor, in any accepted sense of the word, democratic. The rulers of this new society will be … business executives, technicians, bureaucrats, and soldiers, lumped together by Burnham, under the name of "managers." These people will eliminate the old capitalist class, crush the working class, and so organize society that all power and economic privilege remain in their own hands.*

One of the main motivations of hired CEOs is to maintain their personal reputation in order to open future doors for themselves. But that goes beyond future job opportunities or country club memberships; if it were just that, corporate shareholders might be the victims, but no one else. As Lind argues, the public, private, and nonprofit sectors in the modern West no longer have clear lines separating them. Rather, they are all populated by a common stock: "Diplomats become investment bankers, investment bankers become ambassadors, generals sit on corporate boards, and corporate executives sit on nonprofit boards." That enables what Lind calls "managerial dominance reinforced by lateral mobility at the top levels of society."[6]

That managerial dominance subverts the will of the American people. It renders our actual democracy impotent. Together, these bureaucrats crush the will of the shareholders they're supposed to represent, substituting democratic judgments with their own judgments—which are of course informed by their interest in preserving their own *personal* interests and reputations.

I N ADOPTING THE multi-stakeholder model, the corporate managerial class has pulled off the perfect con: CEOs can *do* whatever they want so long as they *say* they have everyone's best interests in mind. Wokenomics is a powerful weapon for CEOs, which they can readily deploy as a smoke screen to distract from greed, fraud, and malfeasance. It provides the perfect alibi: accountability to everyone is accountability to no one at all.

No man can serve two masters. Corporate executives know that better than anyone. They claim to serve both shareholders and stakeholders. But as you'll see, when they have to pick one master to serve, they serve themselves.

Consider the case of Volkswagen. Its managerial class claimed to serve everyone—its CEO trumpeted that under his leadership the company had become a good steward of the environment, a good servant to its customers, and a good investment for its shareholders. But that was all lip service. In the end, Volkswagen's executives really only helped themselves.

Volkswagen appeared to have achieved its well-publicized goal of becoming the world's leading automaker in early 2015. Global sales figures showed it beating Toyota for first place.[7] Volkswagen had been working toward this goal for a decade, with a particular focus on achieving massive sales growth in the US, the world's largest car market.

Volkswagen had previously been a small player in the US. It changed that with a prominent "clean diesel" marketing campaign, positioning its cars as environmentally friendly alternatives to hybrids like the Toyota Prius.[8] The PR campaign paid off. In September 2015, the Dow Jones Sustainability Index (DJSI) named Volkswagen the most sustainable automobile company in the world. It had earned a near-perfect score, with full marks for "codes of conduct, compliance and anti-corruption, as well as innovation management and climate change strategy."[9]

Volkswagen Chairman and CEO Martin Winterkorn had spearheaded Volkswagen's transformation from a middling automaker to the world's largest in just a few years at the helm. By 2014, Winterkorn had successfully steered Volkswagen to the top with his climate-conscious strategy. In an annual letter to shareholders, he said, "The automotive industry is currently experiencing fundamental change. Look no further than the increasingly stringent CO2 legislation or the rapid digitization of vehicles, plants and showrooms. This costs us a great deal of energy and money, too. But at Volkswagen, we do not see this transition as a threat, but rather as a tremendous opportunity—one that we must and will take advantage of."[10]

Winterkorn and Volkswagen did indeed take advantage of a tremendous opportunity. A week after their self-congratulatory press release, the US Environmental Protection Agency (EPA) issued a formal notice of violation to the German automaker alleging that Volkswagen had installed software, or "defeat devices," in its cars to circumvent EPA emissions standards.[11] EPA had discovered that nearly half a million Volkswagen diesel cars on American roads were emitting up to 40 times more toxic fumes than permitted by the Clean Air Act. EPA would later uncover that up to 590,000 cars were implicated.

Two days later, Volkswagen leadership publicly admitted to cheating on emissions tests and revealed that defeat devices were installed in 11 million cars around the world. The defeat devices allowed the cars to detect when they were being driven under test conditions and to change performance and anti-pollution controls to appear more environmentally compliant. Under normal circumstances requiring greater performance, the cars would go back to guzzling gas. The negative news sent Volkswagen's stock price tumbling 50 percent from its all-time high.[12] It was quietly cut from the DJSI.[13]

Volkswagen initially accused a group of rogue engineers of perpetuating the fraud, but over time it became clear that it was using them as scapegoats to shield top executives. In a July 2015 executive team meeting, Winterkorn was allegedly alerted to EPA and California Air Resources Board (CARB) refusals to permit the sale of Volkswagen model year 2016 diesel cars due to an emissions test anomaly. Winterkorn was reportedly very engaged in the technical aspects of the cheating. He directed underlings "to seek an informal meeting with a senior-ranking CARB official," according to a sentencing memo in a US criminal case against Volkswagen engineers. An FBI affidavit said that "rather than advocate for disclosure of the defeat device to U.S. regulators . . . executive management authorized its continued concealment." On orders from above, Volkswagen engineers lied to CARB officials. They eventually confessed, which triggered the EPA notice.[14]

Winterkorn ultimately took responsibility for overseeing the scandal and resigned shortly after Volkswagen's admission. But he denied any early knowledge of the defeat devices.[15]

Volkswagen itself was hit with fines from US and German authorities. And in September 2020, five years after Volkswagen's cheating admission, Winterkorn was ordered to face trial in Germany on charges of fraud. This followed an April 2019 indictment of Winterkorn and other Volkswagen senior executives. A German District Court said in a statement that there was a "substantial probability of conviction" based on the evidence provided in the indictment.[16]

Here's the key takeaway from the Volkswagen affair. Critics of Volkswagen often cite it as a paradigmatic example of the evils of *shareholder* capitalism. They say that if Volkswagen hadn't been so focused on short-term profits it wouldn't have cheated. But this crude conclusion belies a more subtle point: the scandal only happened in the first place because Volkswagen had gained market clout by advertising its supposedly "clean diesel" cars. Being the environmentalist golden boy was what made Volkswagen so successful selling snake oil for a decade.

If only what happened at Volkswagen had been an isolated incident. Unfortunately, it's just one example in a long and ongoing history of executive wrongdoing in the name of stakeholders. There's Wirecard, a German ESG darling that used its sterling reputation to cover up the fact that it committed massive fraud by generating $1.9 billion in fake transactions. There's Nikola, a supposed Tesla rival whose Executive Chairman Trevor Milton promised to save the planet with its hydrogen-powered vehicles, only to quickly unravel as he was, in a matter of days, accused of fraud and sexual abuse and investigated by the Department of Justice and the Securities and Exchange Commission. There's WeWork, a trendy, socially conscious, VC-backed hero that imploded under the weight of CEO Adam Neumann's voluminous self-dealing. The list goes on.

I could write an entire chronicle on each of these nefarious episodes, but that's not the point of this book. Just for fun, though, let's go through one more example. This time, I'll take you behind the curtain to show you how pharmaceutical companies use stakeholder capitalism as a smoke screen to continue doing business as usual.

In September 2015, Hillary Clinton famously tweeted, "Price gouging like this in the specialty drug market is outrageous. Tomorrow I'll lay out a plan to take it on,"[17] in response to a *New York Times* article detailing Martin Shkreli's exorbitant price increase of Daraprim by over 5,000 percent.[18] Clinton was the Democratic presidential front-runner, so her comments sent biotech markets into a tailspin.[19] Clinton's concerns were echoed by then Republican presidential candidate Donald Trump. The writing was on the wall for pharma companies—drug pricing would be a policy focus of any new administration, and the industry was losing in the court of public opinion.

So what did it do in response? In 2016, the pharma industry created an unofficial social contract to limit drug price increases to 10 percent per year. Allergan CEO Brent Saunders kicked it off by pledging to increase prices at most once per year and to do it by single digits. Other companies quickly fell in line. This created a new norm of all companies raising their prices by, of course, about 9.9 percent.

A price increase of 10 percent per year compounding each year adds up quickly—but slowly enough to escape the public's notice. The pharma industry's insight was that it could continue to raise prices, but it needed to do it in stages rather than all at once. Then the companies could condition the public to accept price increases as normal while also somehow making themselves seem socially responsible by "only" raising them 10 percent. If government regulators stepped in, drug prices would be restricted far more. As one article put it, "As rising drug prices continue to be a major cause for discord in the US, the self-regulation of price hikes could help the industry avoid regulatory reform. With rising drug prices more constrained in 2017 and 2018, the pharma industry may be on its way to dodging federal regulation."[20]

Stakeholder capitalism has created a world in which ordinary people not only expect but also *assume* that companies pursue not just their own interests but societal interests too. Yet when we make that assumption, we as consumers are less likely to question those companies' business decisions. Customer cynicism is a powerful force in the market too—one that any well-functioning market depends on—but also one that gets blunted by corporate stakeholderism.

Pharma companies know this. That's exactly what they have in mind when they make hollow declarations to help stave off climate change or make public commitments to cap the magnitude of annual price increases that they take. By acting like the good guys, as Wokenomics demands they do, pharma companies are actually able to get away with behavior that leaves society *worse* off in the end.

It's no accident that Allergan, the very company that kicked off the societal pledge to cap its annual price increases, was also the company that just a couple of years later tried to skirt the US patent regime by making a legally dubious deal with a Native American tribe as a gambit to enjoy prolonged immunity from generic competition. Allergan had sold the rights to a best-selling eye drug to the Saint Regis Mohawk Tribe, who were then going to claim sovereign immunity to dismiss a challenge to the patent from generic pharmaceutical manufacturers—a standard step in the process of how generic drugs reach the market when branded pharmaceutical patents expire. The tribe was going to lease the patent back to Allergan and get $15 million in annual royalties, which in turn would have allowed Allergan to still book hundreds of millions of dollars in added profits per year.[21] Hiding behind Native Americans was a daring legal move for the pharmaceutical giant, though the Supreme Court spoiled the fun by forbidding it.[22]

So even as Allergan was paying lip service to stakeholders by proposing some grand bargain limiting price hikes, it was brazenly bypassing the regular old deal between society and drug developers. The standard deal is that patents allow you to charge higher prices for a time to reward the resources the company spent on research and development, and in return, once the patent expires, society gets to make cheap generics and reap the benefits of the drug in perpetuity. Even as Allergan was pledging to limit price increases for the sake of stakeholders, it was trying to use the Mohawks' sovereign immunity as a legal shield to allow it to keep its patent and charge monopoly prices forever to those same stakeholders. It was hypocrisy of the highest degree. Allergan wanted to raise those prices 10 percent per year *forever* instead of letting the party end someday.

I believe that America is better off if we simply accept the system that we have for fostering pharmaceutical innovation. Sure, it needs some technical tweaks here and there, but broadly speaking, the system works for delivering lifesaving cures to people who need them. We should recognize that this means pharma companies will act in their self-interest by charging relatively high prices for their drugs while patent protected but make them available dirt cheap thereafter. If that happens, then we're all better off in the end. But when we demand that those same companies behave as societal benefactors by charging lower prices even while their drugs are on patent, then those same companies simply use that do-good smoke screen as a weapon to evade the market mechanisms we already have in place to check pharmaceutical prices.

Capitalism tends to work well when everyone knows what to

expect. The less clear those expectations are, the better the system works for the managerial class—but worse for society at large.

H OW DO WE end the tyranny of the corporate managerial class? Here's a thought: limit the scope of the business judgment rule (or the BJR, as it's often called). In practice, most examples of stakeholder capitalism in the real world start with a CEO who decides to use the company's corporate platform to solve a social problem. This often results in the CEO making bad business decisions that have negative externalities for democracy. Yet they are aided by the BJR, a corporate privilege that is *designed* to protect CEOs and corporate directors from being sued for bad business decisions that they make. There are good reasons for this legal doctrine, but today it applies far too broadly in a way that is toxic both for companies and for democracy.

Here's how it works: the BJR protects directors and officers of a corporation in the event that they are sued for violating their duty of care to a company. According to this rule, a court will uphold the decisions of a director as long as they are made (1) in good faith, (2) with care that a reasonably prudent person would use, and (3) with the reasonable belief that the director is acting in the best interests of the corporation. In practice, every corporate lawyer knows that the BJR means that an officer or director of a company is off the hook as a legal defendant in a case.

The general logic for the BJR is obvious—that qualified people would never want to serve as directors and officers if they risked being sued every time they made a business decision that looked bad in retrospect. It's supposed to apply to *business* decisions, not social decisions.

In practice, the only way for a plaintiff to pierce the BJR is this: if the plaintiff can prove that the director had a *conflict of interest* when making a decision, then the BJR doesn't apply. Today, we define conflicts of interest in exclusively *financial* terms. For example, if you serve on the board of a company, but that company is also a major customer of another company that you own, then that's a conflict of interest that disqualifies you from benefiting from the BJR. It makes sense that we shouldn't just take your "business judgment" at face value in that case.

But suppose you're a progressive ex-politician—one who might want to get appointed as secretary of Health and Human Services at some point during Biden's tenure as president—and you're on the board of a pharmaceutical company. I happen to know a few people who probably fit that description. Now suppose it comes to a decision on how you're supposed to price a drug. You obviously have a conflict of interest, even though it's not a strictly *financial* conflict of interest.

Therein lies the rub: in real life, not all conflicts of interest are financial—they show up in many forms and flavors. Not all human motivations are financial. In fact, most aren't.

That's what allows woke corporatism—the flavor of woke capitalism that's driven by hired CEOs and board members rather than the shareholders themselves—to thrive. A critical feature that distinguishes executives and independent directors—members of the "managerial class"—from shareholders is that the former have a reputation to maintain while the latter do not. *This is itself a conflict of interest*, even though it's not one that the law recognizes today.

To be clear, I'm not arguing that CEOs or directors should be legally *prohibited* from using corporate resources to support their own pet social causes. Sweeping government prohibitions designed to solve a narrow set of cases usually do more harm than good. Rather, my proposed solution is much more modest. I'm just saying CEOs and directors shouldn't be protected by the BJR if a shareholder sues them for doing so. Why? Because using the corporate dime needed to fund your favorite social causes is no less a conflict of interest than a classical *financial* conflict of interest.

The BJR was *never intended* to protect executives from liability for corporate actions that weren't motivated by maximizing profits for shareholders in the first place. Legal scholars almost universally agree that the only reason for the BJR is that executives and directors are supposed to be the stewards for protecting shareholder value. That's why it's called the *business* judgment rule, not the "social judgment rule."[23] The BJR makes little sense if it protects executives who act on their own whims and interests instead of maximizing shareholder value.

The very risk of bearing *personal* liability for a new class of "conflicts of interest" that didn't previously exist would have the effect of changing corporate behavior—in my opinion, strictly for the better. Executives will at least think twice about the shareholder-centric justification before writing a check to BLM or exhorting their customers to support Joe Biden or Donald Trump or whatever else it is that they feel an impulse to do from their seat of corporate power.

THE POWER OF the managerial class is now spreading like a plague to other spheres of our society. It afflicts governments, nonprofits, universities, and even hospitals. It's a cultural cancer that threatens to erode American identity in each of these institutions from within.

So far, I've discussed stakeholder *capitalism*, a game in which greedy executives play stakeholders and shareholders against each other to make sure that they're answerable to no one. That's my main focus in this book. But I would be remiss not to point out that stakeholder capitalism is only part of a broader phenomenon I call stakeholderism, in which institutions beyond for-profit corporations invoke amorphous "stakeholders" to justify expanding their original missions to suit their manager's personal desires.

This stakeholderism is perhaps nowhere more dangerous today than at universities where the next generation of elites is being educated right now. The core mission of a university is supposed to be education, and universities' relevant "stakeholders" were originally supposed to be their students, the ones who were paying them to be educated. But as socially conscious managers have gradually taken over the universities, they've expanded their conception of their stakeholders to include racial minorities, sexual minorities, future generations, the environment, and whatever other groups progressive activists say they should care about. So the students are still the stakeholders footing the bill, but their money is now paying to support nebulous, distant stakeholders like future generations, whose will liberal administrators get to represent.

A 2014 analysis found that from 1987 to 2012, the higher-education sector added more than half a million administrators. Their numbers have doubled relative to academic faculty. And the clout of these administrators has also grown alongside their numbers: as Philip Hamburger of Columbia Law School has argued, the balance of power at universities has increasingly shifted toward administrators, who increasingly control academic policy.[24] In his book *Restoring the Promise: Higher Education in America*, economist Richard Vedder calculates that if the ratio of campus bureaucrats to faculty had held steady since 1976, there would be 537,317 fewer administrators, saving universities $30.5 billion per year and allowing student tuition to decrease by 20 percent.[25] It's no wonder college costs so much these days.

Today university administrators are generally monolithic in their political perspectives, choking the free exchange of diverse ideas at universities. Samuel Abrams, visiting scholar at the American Enterprise Institute, found that liberal staff members outnumber their conservative counterparts by an astonishing ratio of 12 to 1. Yet ironically, the fastest growth in recent years has been in the area of "diversity" administrators.[26] Mark Perry, an economics professor at the University of Michigan-Flint, recently calculated that his university has nearly 100 diversity administrators, with a total cost of approximately $14 million per year, or $300 per enrolled student.[27]

Just as in corporations, the goals of these university administrators are misaligned with the goals of the principals—in this case, the university itself. The "diversity administrator" has a vested interest in perpetually preserving the perception of a "diversity problem"—or else their own job becomes superfluous.

Remember, Michael Lind framed the rise of the managerial class as part of a battle between elites and ordinary people, one the elites were winning. There's some truth to that account. But it's too low-resolution. Not all elites are the same. Both professors and university administrators are "elites." But their contributions, roles, and essential character are completely different from one another. Professors come up with new, wild, often controversial ideas. University administrators . . . well, "administer" things. In my view, zany professors are more likely to help the university realize its own essential purpose than any administrator.

The same goes for companies. Founders, investors, and hired C-suite managers are all "elites" in the grand scheme of things. But that entirely misses an important power struggle within the corporation itself, between the founder-shareholder class and the managerial class. To me, America is about empowering true innovators (like founders), true risk-takers (like investors), true thinkers (like professors), and true elected leaders over the bureaucratic intermediaries who are hired to "manage" them all.

So the real problem with the rise of the managerial class isn't simply that the "elites" are winning and "ordinary people" are losing. It's that the essential purpose of an institution—be it a company or a university—is less likely to be realized when it's led by a manager than when it's led by someone who embodies the essence of what that institution does.

That's where my view departs from Lind's. We both agree that the rise of the managerial class is a fundamental problem for America. But Lind views it as a battle between elites and ordinary people. By contrast, I view it as a battle between hired hands and those who embody the essence of an institution—like professors at universities, doctors at hospitals, or founders and shareholders at companies.

When viewed through my lens rather than Lind's, the relevance of all of this to "stakeholderism" becomes clear. Stakeholderism is the philosophy that posits that institutions should not only advance their essential purpose but also advance societal goals that go beyond the institution's essential purpose. On its face, that philosophy sounds benign enough. Sure, you could argue that a university is worse at educating students if its administration is also focused on, say, addressing climate change or fighting racism. But you could equally argue that engaging with those social questions makes the university better positioned to educate students on how to address important societal challenges. Reasonable minds can differ.

But that's not really what stakeholderism is about. At its core, it's a tool that empowers the managerial class and allows them to escape accountability for their failures to properly advance the essential purpose of an institution. It's what gives university administrators or charity administrators or hospital administrators or fancy New York City private school administrators greater power and insulation from the people they're supposed to be accountable to. And *that's* a critical part of the cultural cancer afflicting America today—not just the government, but companies, universities, museums, philanthropies, and even religious institutions.

If that's true for stakeholderism broadly, then it's most acute in the case of stakeholder capitalism. Here's why. The number-one rule of the game for any CEO to consolidate power is this: the more people you are accountable to, the more powerful you become. In my industry, that's why nearly every hired CEO wants to take their company public if given the choice. Why? As a private company, you're accountable to a small group of shareholders, often venture capitalists and private equity firms who are looking over your shoulder at every step of the way. But as a public company, you get to be accountable to thousands of shareholders, most of whom you'll never meet and most of whom will never meet each other. That means that even if one shareholder isn't happy with what you do, you can always claim that another one was. That's nearly impossible to do at a closely held private company.

If it's true that CEOs become less accountable by becoming accountable to more people, then stakeholder capitalism empowers the corporate managerial class to consummate their coup. By becoming accountable to literally everyone, they become accountable to no one. That's the heart of the problem of stakeholder capitalism: it's not about serving "stakeholders" rather than shareholders. It's about serving the managerial class itself.

With the rise of the managerial class, America is becoming less and less like itself and more like a bastardized version of the European model of social progress, where elite executives work hand in hand with the government to do what they think is best for society. Maybe this works for Europe; I'd say that America's history of innovation shows that our corporate focus on shareholder value works better, though that's an argument to be had elsewhere. My point is different: if America claims to be America, but quietly yet gradually moves toward the European model through the back door, we'll just become a worse version of Europe and a worse version of ourselves.

We could become a worse version of Japan, too. I've done a lot of business there, and I was surprised to find that in Japan, it often doesn't matter what the CEO of a company says: the managers at the company will in many cases do what they want because people can't be fired. They don't work for the CEO if the CEO can't actually fire them. Maybe that model works well for Japan. But our social culture is different, so our corporate culture must be as well.*

The main issue with the rise of the managerial class in the US is this: American employees harbor a self-interested greed that Japanese employees often do not. That self-interest is a fuel for good if channeled through a system like ours that was built on that premise but wouldn't work as well in the Japanese or European system. America's competitive advantage rests in harnessing our self-

---

* These observations are based on confidential conversations with executives, consultants, and investment bankers in Japan and are nonspecific to the pharma industry.

interested impulses toward building something greater than ourselves. But if we try to pretend that we're Japan, where ordinary people behave according to duty rather than self-interest, then when our people don't *actually* behave that way, the "new" American model will be worse than either the classical capitalist model, the European model, or the Japanese model and will be a broken version of all of them.

America's identity was always about the power of the people overcoming the managerial class—in our democracy and also culturally, in our universities, companies, and government. The rise of the managerial class is a disease afflicting the soul of our most important institutions. History teaches that what begins as an accountability crisis for individual companies, if left unchecked, becomes a crisis for the system as a whole.

CHAPTER 5

The ESG Bubble

E ARLIER THIS YEAR, I GOT a call from the House Financial Services Committee to testify as an expert about a seemingly abstruse issue: new SEC rules that would require US public
companies to regularly disclose so-called ESG factors. Congress
was weighing new laws to require companies to disclose not only
their financial metrics in their quarterly and annual reports but also
"environmental, social, and governance" factors as well—things
like racial and gender diversity in the workforce, climate change
impact, and so on.

As I listened to the Democratic congressmen and their witnesses
lay out their case for these new SEC rules, I had a flashback to my
own experience watching the 2008 financial crisis. In fact, my own
induction into the business world *began* with the 2008 financial crisis. No doubt that shaped my own cynicism of Wall Street from
early on.

In 2007, I joined a firm called QVT Financial right after I'd
graduated from Harvard. I was a young analyst on a biotech team

that represented, at least at the time, a tiny portion of the sprawling hedge fund. The people who ran the firm were physics majors from places like Harvard and Caltech who discovered that they could make more money trading complex securities than working in a lab. The firm's culture was distinct from its peers: it lacked the artifice of Goldman Sachs and the frivolity of Amaranth. Its leaders were among the smartest people I'd ever meet. They were obsessed with figuring out the truth and making contrarian bets—not just about stocks but about people too. If I'd been judged simply on my math skills, I doubt I'd have ever made it through the interview process; I owe a lot of my success to their willingness to take an early bet on me.

Dan Gold, the founder and CEO of QVT, sat at the center of the trading floor, flanked by multiple computer monitors and telephones. He was the fixed point around which the rest of the firm turned. The most important people sat closest to Dan, and the guy who sat to his right was Arthur Chu. In the same year that I joined QVT, Arthur and his team figured out something that very few people in the financial world recognized: there was a bubble in mortgage-backed securities in the United States. He and Dan made a series of complex bets that their prices would fall, and they were right, making QVT one of the most profitable hedge funds in the world in 2007 and earning it a mention in Michael Lewis's best seller *The Big Short*, despite Dan's request that Lewis not mention the company in the book.

The standard explanation for the subprime mortgage bubble was that predatory lenders were greedy sharks who took advantage of the opportunity to make home loans to individual borrowers who weren't very creditworthy. That's why they were called "subprime" mortgages. Prime mortgages were home loans made to people with reasonable creditworthiness. Subprime referred to everything else. Wall Street banks bundled up these different mortgages to reduce risk and then sold them to speculative investors. That bundle is what we call mortgage-backed securities.

But the unsatisfying thing about simply blaming greed for the 2008 financial crisis is that it fails to account for the fact that the greediest (and smartest) thing that someone could have done in 2005 and 2006 was to bet *against* those mortgages. In retrospect it should've been obvious that many of these subprime borrowers would default on their home loans, and that's exactly what happened. If Wall Street bankers were so greedy, then why did so many of them fail to capitalize on the opportunity?

The true culprit was upstream of that greed. Starting in the 1990s, the US government embarked on an ambitious policy to drive home ownership. The idea of owning a home was seen as the pinnacle of the American Dream—so the government decided to make that dream come true by creating special categories of loans to spur more home ownership, including among people whose incomes didn't support the value of the homes they went on to buy. That's where government swamp creatures like Fannie Mae and Freddie Mac came from: though they were technically created during the Great Depression, they took on a role of renewed importance under President Clinton.

The real question isn't why predatory lenders in the early 2000s lent money to a bunch of borrowers who had poor credit scores; it's why bad predatory lenders had all that money to give out in the first place. Answer: bad government policy.

That ought to be one of our key lessons from the 2008 financial crisis: *socially driven economic policy risks creating asset bubbles*. And when those bubbles burst, they end up hurting the very causes and people the original policy was intended to help. That's exactly what happened when the mortgage bubble burst in 2007, especially when that subsequently led to the failure of large financial institutions in 2008.

If you want to learn more about that whole phenomenon, read *The Big Short*, which provides a full account of the subprime mortgage bubble and the people who made money by boldly betting against it. In reality, the factors behind the 2008 financial crisis were multiple and complex. I can't sum it up in a few pages here, and my reason for bringing it up isn't to offer a history lesson. Rather, it's a warning.

It's exactly what I saw on display during the congressional hearing where I testified earlier this year. President Biden and his comrades in Congress were trying to tilt the scales of how today's investors allocate capital to promote a social agenda—except this time it was to foster "racial diversity" and "climate justice" rather than home ownership. It's distorting how investors allocate capital. And just like last time, I don't think it will end well.

FOR THE PURPOSES of argument, assume that when I refer to "ESG investing," I'm referring to the now-widespread practice of large investment funds who raise capital under the banner of investing in ESG-friendly companies and who then go on to invest in companies that successfully convince them that they are indeed ESG-friendly companies.

Let's start with first principles. In theory, if the market works according to its normal rules, these ESG investors ought to accept a systematically *lower* rate of return as part of the bargain for investing in companies that adhere to their principles. Accepting lower returns from ESG investing isn't just an unfortunate consequence of trying to do social good. To the contrary, it's precisely what you'd predict would happen if you traded off traditional investment factors for social ones. In fact, if you're an authentic ESG-oriented investor who cares about environmental and social goals, this is a desirable outcome—in fact the only way you can effect the changes that you want to see.

In demonstrating why, I'm going to borrow heavily from an argument made by Cliff Asness, founder of AQR Capital Management ("AQR" stands for "Applied Quantitative Research"), a successful global investment manager with around $150 billion in assets under management. Notably, AQR offers multiple ESG investment products. But the difference between AQR and other ESG investors is that AQR doesn't try to lure its clients with the false promise that applying virtue to investing will somehow make them more money.

Let's start with the common ESG investing practice of avoiding so-called "sin stocks." Sin stocks include companies with businesses in industries that are considered unethical, immoral, or unsavory. Historically, sin stocks included businesses in the alcohol, gambling, tobacco, and weapons sectors. Asness explains that investors who practice negative screening can't make more than investors who don't because negative screeners are subject to constraints that the others are not. In Asness's words, "constraints can never help you ex ante and only sometimes ex post through luck. Why? Because if they help they aren't constraints, they are what you want to do anyway."[1] In effect, when evaluated purely on return and risk, constrained investors should only expect to make less than or equal to the return of unconstrained investors.

What happens if a bunch of ESG investors don't want to own

sin stocks? Well, someone else must own them, even if they end up owning more than they'd otherwise want to. How does the market solve for this? Well, it gives buyers of sin stocks a lower price for the stock and therefore a higher expected return as the underlying company goes on to earn profits for shareholders in the future.

How can this be? Let's assume that, all else equal, nothing has fundamentally changed when an ESG investor chooses not to invest in or divests an existing position in a sin stock. So why is there then a lower price? If fundamentals haven't changed, then the firm's expected future cash flows remain the same. The lower price is the product of a higher discount rate. The higher discount rate is the result of less capital available to the company (or, in other words, less demand for the company's stock). The discount rate is a higher "cost of capital" to the company because it raises money at a lower price when it offers its shares, but that means a higher "expected return" to the sinner who buys them—paying less for shares that earn the same amount equals a higher expected return.

That doesn't necessarily mean ESG investing is pointless. It's just that, by design, it is *supposed* to be relatively less profitable. As Asness points out, this is precisely what ESG investors should want. By increasing "sinful" companies' cost of capital, they make each project they consider undertaking more expensive, so strictly fewer potential projects will be profitable. That means that by raising a sinful company's cost of capital, the ESG investor has won by making the company take on fewer of its sinful projects. But by the same token, when they force the company to sell its shares more cheaply, they also guarantee higher expected returns to the people still willing to buy them. And by constraining their own investment choices, the ESG investor lowers their own expected returns.

"It sucks that the virtuous have to accept a lower expected

return to do good, and perhaps sucks even more that they have to accept the sinful getting a higher one," says Asness, but he also says to "embrace the suck as without it there is no effect on the world, no good deed done at all. Perhaps this necessary sacrifice is why it's called 'virtue.'"[2]

In response, advocates of ESG investing and stakeholder capitalism might retort that the problem with classical capitalism is that it requires businesses to focus on short-term profits rather than long-term value—and that in the long run, analyses will prove that ESG-informed investment approaches are indeed more successful. Klaus Schwab in his recent book *Stakeholder Capitalism* echoes this refrain. Under a paradigm of stakeholder capitalism, "Companies do not have to stop pursuing profits for their shareholders," he says. All it takes is that "they shift to a long-term perspective."[3]

The question of why this simple truism deserves entire books, let alone a new global movement to reinvent capitalism, is a mystery. Even Milton Friedman believed that the pursuit of profits over the long run dominates short-term profit-seeking when you compare the two strategies over . . . well, the long run. It's pretty intuitive.

Suppose a company's stock price craters because it misses the quarterly earnings benchmark that analysts had set, but the company is actually destined to generate a lot more cash flow in the future. What happens? Some investors may foolishly sell their shares. That's what causes the stock price to crater. But that creates an opportunity for someone else to buy those shares at an even lower price and to make even more money over the long run. This happens every day. It's what made Warren Buffett a multibillionaire. Many other billionaires have made their fortunes following his formula. Individual investors mint small fortunes each year using similar strategies. There's even a name for this strategy. It's called "value investing."

Indeed big pharma's short-termism is what allowed me to start Roivant in 2014. It was always a head-scratcher for me that large pharma companies often had billions of dollars in their bank accounts yet felt such acute pressure to meet the quarterly earnings benchmarks set for them by some 30-year-old analyst at a Wall Street bank. CEOs of these pharma behemoths often feel compelled to make cuts to their R&D budgets to improve their profitability on paper in a given calendar year, even though the underlying research projects that involve making investments today may actually be far more profitable in the long run. This is the kind of woe that folks like Klaus Schwab lament in their hackneyed critiques of "short-termism."

Yet they miss the fact that even though *those particular corporations* who act according to short-term impulses may miss out on long-term profits, society overall *doesn't* miss out—because someone else just takes advantage of the business opportunity. As the rapper Macklemore eloquently says it, "One man's trash is another man's come-up." In the case of my company, I initially got the business off the ground by in-licensing drugs from pharma companies that were far more financially well heeled than my own but that nonetheless succumbed to short-term pressure to cut R&D projects. In some cases, they had invested tens or even hundreds of millions of dollars into a promising drug that they had to cut simply because it would've cost an extra few million dollars in their budget—*even though they had billions of dollars in their bank accounts and were worth hundreds of billions of dollars in their own right*. Why? Because Wall Street tends to focus on the profit line at the bottom of an income statement in a given year, turning a blind eye to how a company can deploy its balance sheet into investment that generates even more profits in the future, even if that comes at the expense of profitability in the near term.

Of course, that doesn't make any sense. It's one of many reasons why the efficient market hypothesis is a load of garbage. But the good news is that it's what allowed people like Warren Buffett to get rich and people like me to build successful companies. I was able to pay a small upfront payment—often just a few million dollars—for drugs that could be worth tens or hundreds of times more.

Why? Because my company was a private startup, we didn't have to obsess over quarterly earnings calls. It didn't matter if our annual income statement showed a loss in the early years, and my investors understood that. So we were able to buy drugs that larger companies had invented and had often invested fortunes in, paying literally pennies on the dollar relative to their true value. Drugs are risky, and some of them failed. But enough of them would go on to succeed to make the entire project a value-creating one—and on a scale measured in the billions.

Best of all, society benefits too: several of those drugs are now approved by the FDA for patients with important diseases, ranging from prostate cancer to overactive bladder. I can proudly say that those drugs would've never reached patients if they had stayed in the hands of companies that were oriented toward the short term (or, apparently, those whose CEOs didn't think that urology was a sufficiently sexy area for investment). Patients in the real world benefit today because my company was able to take advantage of a market inefficiency created by other pharma companies that care about pursuing short-run profits. At the same time, I was able to generate a lot of wealth for Roivant's shareholders, including myself, in the process. All stakeholders, including shareholders, benefit. That's how capitalism works in reality. Yes, it's true that some investors and companies think of the short run, and they often succeed by doing that with the mentality of a trader rather than a long-term owner. But when they sacrifice the pursuit of long-run value, that often creates an even juicier, *more* profitable opportunity for someone else.

Here's the punch line: that's not stakeholder capitalism. That's just capitalism. Brazen cost-cutting for one company creates a golden opportunity for another. Investors who follow the crowd and dump a stock because of a bad quarterly report create fertile inefficiencies for other investors to exploit. The logical approach to address the perils of short-termism isn't to reinvent the rules of global capitalism. It's to start a business or to invest capital in ways that capture those opportunities.

All told, this critique of "short-termism" ends up being a straw man that doesn't actually defeat the theoretical argument for why ESG investors should systematically underperform other investors.

That wraps up the theoretical debate. So how does this theory actually perform in practice?

If you ask most ESG proponents, they'd say that the empirical data decisively prove that the foregoing theory is bogus. Indeed the most popular argument for ESG investing is that it "works." In 2020, Al Gore boldly took this argument one step further. In a widely read *Wall Street Journal* editorial, he argued that "voluminous research has shown conclusively that businesses properly integrating ESG factors into their plans are typically more successful and profitable. As the value of this paradigm becomes widely recognized, investors who fail to take it into account may be at risk of violating their fiduciary duty to their clients."[4] According to Gore, it's no longer simply optional for corporate executives to practice ESG principles; they have an affirmative legal obligation to embrace them.

As an aside, take a look at the fine print in Gore's slippery reasoning. For example, note that he added the qualifier "properly" to his declaration, which leaves a lot of wiggle room. That is, if certain ESG stocks happen to underperform, Gore can simply say *those* businesses didn't implement ESG values "properly," just as someone in the opposite camp could say that underperforming pure-profit businesses didn't focus on pure profits "properly"—a classic case of the logical trap known as the No-True-Scotsman fallacy.*

On this count, Larry Fink is more polished than Gore. In a paper titled "A Fundamental Reshaping of Finance," Fink writes, "[Blackrock's] investment conviction is that sustainability—and climate-integrated portfolios can provide better risk-adjusted returns to investors."[5] Fink's comments were well crafted to elude criticism: he didn't say that ESG portfolios *will* provide better returns, but only that they *can*. That's harder to argue with, even though average mom-and-pop investors probably don't stop to make the distinction.

And Fink has ample quantitative support to back up his claims. In 2019, Savita Subramanian, head of US Equity and Quantitative Strategy and Global ESG Research at Bank of America, observed that US companies with high ESG rankings in the S&P 500 index outperformed their counterparts with lower ESG rankings by at least 3 percent each year for the preceding five years. Subramanian went so far as to argue that ESG metrics are the best measure for signaling future earnings risk—superior even to financial risk factors like the level of a company's leverage, or debt burden.[6]

---

* Here's how the No-True-Scotsman fallacy works. Suppose I say that no Scotsman wears red socks. You counter by pointing out that your friend Logan wears red socks. I then say, "Ah, yeah, but no *true* Scotsman wears red socks."

Harvard Business School professor George Serafeim, working in collaboration with Boston mutual fund manager State Street, observed that "during the market collapse" in the early stages of the COVID-19 pandemic, "firms experiencing more positive sentiment on their human capital, supply chain, and operational response to COVID-19 experienced higher institutional money flows" and less downside in share prices.[7]

Similar analyses abound. Morningstar found that sustainable index funds outperformed traditional index funds in the first quarter of 2020.[8] Hermes Investment Management observed in 2018 that companies with good or improving ESG characteristics outperform companies with poor or worsening characteristics.[9] Countless other reports come to similar conclusions.

So which one is right: the theoretical account or the empirical account? The answer is neither.

As for the empirical data, on closer inspection, it's mixed at best. Most of the "analyses" are contrived, cherry-picked, or circular. Take the analysis from Serafeim and State Street, for example. Their argument is both circular and conflating: they say that "firms experiencing more positive sentiment" were the ones that "experienced higher institutional money flows" and thus performed better in the stock market. Yet that argument fails to distinguish whether "ESG asset class outperformance"—even if it exists—is actually a function of improved underlying corporate performance or simply a function of an asset bubble driven by growing pools of capital chasing "socially conscious" investment opportunities. Serafeim's data set suggests it's the latter— that positive share price performance correlates with favorable news coverage. In other words, he's saying that the best reason for investing in ESG-oriented companies is that everyone else is doing it.

Further, it's even debatable whether ESG-oriented companies

actually do command higher stock prices or not. It depends on how you count. For example, in contrast to Bank of America, Credit Suisse observed that the Dow Jones Sustainability Index, which represents the top 10 percent of the world's most sustainable companies by market capitalization per industry in the S&P Global BMI, has underperformed the full S&P Global benchmark index by approximately 20 percent from 2010 to 2019. Institutional Investor observed that the median annualized return between 2010 and 2019 of ESG equity funds with a track record of at least 10 years and $100 million in assets was only 11.98 percent, while the S&P 500 had returned an annualized 13.56 percent. Volatility was identical across both indices, suggesting that ESG assets underperformed not only on an absolute basis but on a risk-adjusted basis as well.[10]

Many of the analyses in favor of ESG outperformance are cherry-picked. Fudge factors include which companies to include versus exclude, the relevant time horizon to examine, what benchmark indices to use, and so on. Those are fundamentally subjective decisions, often made by the very people who know what conclusion they wish to reach.

In sum, the existence of dueling data sets shouldn't surprise anyone—in this case, the "data" itself is a charade. Data doesn't mix well with self-interest or politics, and here it's blended with both. The so-called "empirical" exercises are in actuality agenda-driven all the way down. It's no accident that Savita Subramanian, the analyst at Bank of America who concluded that ESG stocks outperform, also headed up the "Global ESG Research" group. If she reached the opposite conclusion, she might be out of a job.

The same might go for Larry Fink: a cynic may rightly conclude that he just needed to find a new excuse for raising capital to actively manage under his mutual fund complex—and to justify higher fees than passive index funds like Vanguard charge their clients. Passive index funds were starting to take market share from the higher-fee mutual fund business, so the rise of ESG investing may well have saved the day for the likes of Fink.

At the end of the day, it's debatable whether ESG investment strategies have outperformed or underperformed conventional investment strategies. They're certainly not the slam dunk that Larry Fink and Al Gore would have you believe. On the other hand, there's no clear data set that clearly "proves" the theoretical argument that ESG should consistently underperform either. There are still many analyses that argue that ESG stocks have outperformed.

S O WHAT GIVES? One very real possibility is that we are in an ESG asset bubble that is ripe to crash—just like the housing bubble in 2008.

A true hallmark of many financial bubbles is the overflow of funds into a particular asset class. It's hard to argue that we're not seeing that in the ESG sector today. Morningstar estimates about $50 billion of capital flows into US sustainable open-end and exchange-traded funds in 2020—approximately 10 times more than in 2018 and 2.5 times more than in 2019.[11] According to the Forum for Sustainable and Responsible Investment's 2020 report, total US-domiciled assets under management employing ESG investing strategies increased 42 percent between 2018 and 2020, up to $17 trillion. This means that ESG-mandated assets now represent a staggering 33 percent of the $51.4 trillion US assets under professional management.[12] This composition is only expected to rise, ESG-mandated assets are projected to represent 50 percent of all managed assets in the US by 2025.[13] The point: there is *a lot* of money piling into ESG and sustainable investing right now. It's reminiscent of the amount of money that piled into home loans as a result of mandates in the years leading up to the 2008 financial crisis.

Good fundraising strategies don't always make for good investment strategies. Asset prices may rise in the short run because there are more dollars chasing them due to the expectation they'll keep rising. But that's the logic of a Ponzi scheme. It's what Burton Malkiel refers to as the "greater fool theory" in his book *A Random Walk Down Wall Street*. It's a self-fulfilling prophecy: as long as there's another buyer, the gravy train keeps running, yet it only lasts for so long.

Who wins this game? Just like in 2008, the answer is large financial institutions. Mutual fund complexes like BlackRock make money based on the totality of assets that they manage, not based on the actual investment performance of those assets. If you've ever invested in a mutual fund, you've probably noticed that they quote a fee for their product—often something like 1 percent. Know that they're referring to the fee that they charge on the money you hand over to them, *not on the actual gains that they generate*. In fact, mutual funds like BlackRock profit just the same whether they make money or they lose money. Just like during the pre-2008 housing bubble, the people who sold financial products stood to gain whether the underlying investment strategy performed well or not.

So is it time to short the growing ESG asset bubble and make a ton of money when the whole thing collapses—just like the smartest hedge funds did in 2007 when the housing bubble collapsed? If market logic were all that mattered, I'd bet my money on it.

But there's another relevant actor in the game: government.

Here's the issue: woke capitalists often win in the end because they use their do-good smoke screen to capture the government itself. Unfortunately, that often proves to be the most profitable strategy of all: it's modern crony capitalism, and it "works." The winning trade may not be to short ESG stocks but to short American democracy.

After BlackRock created its Sustainability Accounting Standards Board, the firm quietly secured its status as the main financial administrator of the economic stimulus package during the COVID-19 pandemic, effectively playing the role of the government—and probably made a pretty penny for doing it.

In January 2020, pharmaceutical giant AstraZeneca announced to much fanfare at (of course) the World Economic Forum in Davos a new investment commitment of $1 billion over ten years into environmental sustainability initiatives to fight climate change. Just a couple of months later, it received a $1.2 billion grant—not a loan, but a *grant*—from US taxpayers to subsidize its development of for-profit vaccines. Flushing $1 billion down the drain over ten years may be financially nonsensical, but it's a pretty good trade in return for getting $1.2 billion now. The list of examples goes on.

My point isn't that there was some explicit *quid pro quo* in these particular "exchanges." Almost certainly, there wasn't. Rather, it's that this new corporate practice of feigning wokeness *indirectly* wins favors in return from the government over the long run—favorable legislative treatment, lenient prosecutorial discretion, fiscal grants, and other forms of corporate welfare. During Republican administrations, big companies used to gain political advantage by lending their alumni to occupy powerful government positions. Even President Trump, a swamp drainer, filled the posts of Secretary of Treasury and Secretary of State with recent Goldman Sachs and Exxon Mobil executives. Now corporations have simply come up with a new trick tailored for Democrats: they lend corporate power as a tool to implement radical agendas that Democrats could never pass in Congress.

That's exactly what we are seeing in the early days of President Biden's tenure. He called climate change "the number one issue facing humanity" and outlined a plan to achieve net zero emissions by 2050 and other environmental initiatives, all building on the "Green New Deal," a flawed but ambitious resolution advanced by Congressional Democrats in 2019.[14] The original Green New Deal failed in a Republican-controlled Senate, and it's unlikely to do any better in a 50-50 split Senate that includes Joe Manchin.

Yet with the advent of the modern alliance between big government and big business, new laws may not be required at all: the Biden administration can simply use Wall Street's ESG apparatus to do it instead. Earlier this year, *Politico* reported that US climate envoy and former Secretary of State John Kerry "wants America's banks on board with the administration's climate goals" and that he was "leveraging his personal ties with Wall Street to persuade Citi, Wells Fargo, Bank of America, Morgan Stanley, Goldman Sachs, and JP Morgan Chase to create a U.S. net-zero banking alliance." The effort was reportedly aimed at "drawing pledges that could be announced for the administration's climate strategy rollout."[15]

Do we really want to live in a democracy where top government officials "leverage their personal ties" with the CEOs of big banks to accomplish what they can't get done in Congress? Banks are not charitable institutions. When they do favors for government officials, they expect something in return. The real question is this: What did America's banks get in return for agreeing to Kerry's climate-related demands?

I doubt we'll ever know, but the answer goes to the heart of why the likes of Larry Fink and Al Gore may have the last laugh in the end. Reducing carbon emissions, implementing racial diversity goals, and waxing eloquent about social justice don't inherently make them more profitable. That's just the dowry they pay in return for the protection of big government, consummating the marriage of America's newest power couple.

To be clear, it's not that I think furthering social causes is meritless. Some are definitely worthwhile. I'm just skeptical that an investment strategy centered on these narrow characteristics is likely to outperform in the long run or to substantively advance the cause in a way that's actually impactful. Even if some good comes out of it, that's outweighed by the negative consequences of the outsized political and social influence that these ESG-oriented investors and executives exercise.

There are better ways to further those same social causes. One way is through targeted and meaningful nonprofit endeavors. Another is through sound government policy with proper democratic accountability, including open public debate and the ability to be elected out of office if you do a poor job. As imperfect as these solutions may be, one thing is clear to me: mixing ancillary social causes with the pursuit of profit is a bad investment in every sense.

Here's another good way to advance a social cause: make a great product that happens to help the cause you care about. Don't just throw money at ESG funds; make an exceptional product that advances your goals. And sell a lot of it. That's the kind of business that shareholder capitalists and stakeholder capitalists can both get behind. Making a great product that happens to serve your social goals is an authentic form of stakeholder capitalism, like the kind that focuses on minimizing harm.*

Take a couple of causes that are near and dear to my heart. I'm

---

* I discussed this harm-minimizing kind of stakeholder capitalism at the end of Chapter 1.

a vegetarian, for religious reasons and moral ones. I think it's generally wrong to kill animals simply for culinary pleasure. I also consider myself to be an environmentalist—I care a lot about the quality of the air people breathe and the water people drink. The right way to advance these goals through a commercial enterprise isn't for a biotech CEO to use the company as a platform to advocate against pollution and killing animals. Rather, it's to start a company that creates products that accomplish those same goals.

And indeed several companies today are doing just that. Take UPSIDE Foods (formerly Memphis Meats), led by Uma Valeti, which grows meat from the ground up using the building blocks of life: cells. Rather than slaughtering animals, UPSIDE sources these cells from animals and cultivates the cells by feeding them essential nutrients. According to UPSIDE, meat can be made "healthier, safer, and more nutritious" through its process.[16]

I first met Uma at an event hosted by a large institutional investor, where one of the events involved test-driving race cars. (Yes, these are the kinds of things that CEOs do at fancy conferences in places like Los Angeles.) Uma and I drove a race car together, and we had a chance to chat during the ride while we weren't turning around hairpin bends.

At first when he started telling me about the mission-orientation of his company, I reflexively rolled my eyes. Blah-blah, I thought. But over the course of the conversation, two things became clear to me. First, he was a better race car driver than I was. Second, he was genuine and sincere about his actual desire to improve the world through his company's work. In his personal life, he converted to veganism, and it wasn't just for show. He believed in animal rights. And that was the very same reason he'd started UPSIDE Foods. By the end I believed him, and I hope he succeeds.

Similarly, Beyond Meat is a public company that specializes in plant-based protein products. Instead of using animal cells, Beyond Meat "sources proteins, fats, minerals, flavors and colors, and carbohydrates from plant-based sources like peas, beans, potatoes and brown rice" to produce its meat alternatives. Beyond Meat believes that "by shifting from animal to plant-based meat, [they] can positively impact four growing global issues: human health, climate change, constraints on natural resources, and animal welfare."[17] According to a comparative assessment, its "Beyond Burger" "generates 90% less greenhouse gas emissions, requires 46% less energy, has >99% less impact on water scarcity and 93% less impact on land use than a ¼ pound of U.S. beef."[18]

Personally, I'm not sure Beyond Meat and other brands like Impossible Foods will meet all their lofty goals.* Their stated connection to climate change in particular seems a bit tenuous to me, but the connection to animal welfare and environmental respect is straightforward. I applaud these companies for trying. They're inventing innovative, potentially world-changing technologies to advance causes that their founders personally care about. That's fundamentally different from a new-age tech company making glossy brochures about board diversity in a bid to make it into BlackRock's ESG portfolio.

Institutional investors should stop playing this game of shuffling money around and rewarding companies that they like and punishing ones they dislike based on factors that have nothing to do with commercial value. CEOs should stop playing the same game on the other side by making hollow proclamations that have nothing to do with their companies. If you want to improve the world through your business, there's a better way: make a great product that you believe in.

---

* In fact, Beyond Meat and competitors have been criticized for making "overly processed" products that are not as healthy as they claim to be. See, for instance, Kelsey Piper, "Meatless Meat Is Becoming Mainstream—and It's Sparking a Backlash," *Vox*, 7 Oct. 2019.

CHAPTER 6

An Arranged Marriage

W HEN PEOPLE LEARN MY MOM came here from India, one of the first questions they ask her is "Did you have an arranged marriage?" Today, I ask that question of corporations when they espouse woke causes.

I want to tell you about two arranged marriages in this chapter, one that worked and one that didn't. Let's start with the success story. My mom skips the extended story these days, but I like it, so I'm going to tell it. Don't worry, it'll all be about wokeness and capitalism in the end. That'll be the second arranged marriage, the failed one.

My mom Geetha and her sister were the apples of their parents' eyes. Her father was a traveling salesman, and her mother was a homemaker. My grandparents spent every moment of their lives striving to give their daughters the things they'd never had, including a proper education. Both children became doctors.

Thanks to a good test score, my mom got to skip undergrad and go straight to medical school at 16, both a blessing and a curse. She arrived there a shy, sheltered teenager who'd barely even spoken to any men outside her family. The first day, surrounded by a class full of older men, she stared at the ground the whole time and hoped no one would talk to her. Grandpa walked her to and from school every day to protect her from catcalls.

Years later, my mom graduated with excellent grades only to realize that her parents were off to their next mission: finding her a husband. She had never held hands with a man. She imagined herself as the star of a Bollywood movie, meeting the hero of her dreams and running around trees singing songs while dressed in a beautiful sari.

Parents end up being good matchmakers. They literally go down a checklist of compatibility: family background, cultural and religious values, dietary preferences, education, looks, and of course astrological compatibility. Maybe Grandpa really was just a genius at reading horoscopes.

He came home from one of his long trips one day brandishing a horoscope and a couple pictures of a potential groom, a PhD student in America whose face struck her as handsome but so serious. My dad, VG, passed all her parents' tests with flying colors. My mom dreamt of singing birds and beautiful saris.

My mom and her parents took a long trip to Vadakanchery to meet VG's family, though VG had already immigrated to America. My mom was swarmed by first, second, and third cousins. Everyone liked her, but VG's mother and aunts raised a serious concern: Was she tall enough? They had her stand next to a niece for comparison and held a friendly yet spirited debate. My mom and her parents went home a few hours later after a great visit, but that crucial question remained unanswered.

My mom came back to Vadakanchery a month later, and this

time VG was there. There were somehow even more cousins than before. VG walked into the room with a charming smile, and my mom decided that he was not overly serious after all.

After dinner, VG and my mom were led into a private room and seated in two chairs facing each other. It was crunch time. This was their chance to have a private moment and really get to know each other. All the adults followed them into the private room, and the children perched on the window sills outside to observe. VG really wanted to make sure she was okay going to America, a strange and foreign land. She was.

Things were going smoothly, perhaps too smoothly for one of VG's aunts, who interjected to make sure he knew my mom was only 5' 3", while he stood at 5' 11". VG hastily corrected her to point out that he was actually 5' 10". My mom laughed, along with everyone else. Maybe their meeting had been arranged, but that was really the moment he proposed and she accepted.

They got married twelve days later. On her wedding day, my mom held a man's hands for the first time, and that made it mean all the more to her.

T HAT WAS THIRTY-EIGHT years ago. They're still together. My mom and dad often say that trust is the foundation of their marriage: they each trusted the judgments of their parents to find each other, and that in turn gave them trust in each other. They weren't thinking about what each of them would get out of it; there was no *quid pro quo*.

That's the first arranged marriage I wanted to tell you about, and it turned out to be a good one. But now let's talk about a marriage of convenience, one that left both partners worse off than they started.

I refer to the unholy union of wokeness and capitalism, more of an arranged marriage than my parents' ever was. Circumstances forced wokeness and capitalism together, and they only stayed together so they could both gain money and power. But each secretly disdained the other.

The seeds of this unhappy marriage were sown decades ago, but wokeness hadn't even been born yet. Capitalism was coming of age.

This story begins with not a courtship but a rivalry. Our contemporary understanding of capitalism is influenced by a little-appreciated intellectual feud between Milton Friedman and Klaus Schwab. In September 1970, Friedman famously wrote in *The New York Times Magazine* that the social purpose of the corporation was to pursue profit. He argued that "the doctrine of 'social responsibility' " in business, if "taken seriously would extend the scope of the political mechanism to every human activity." He warned that its proponents were "preaching pure and unadulterated socialism," and "undermining the basis of a free society."[1]

Yet as Friedman argued for shareholder primacy, other prominent economists organized against him. In 1973, Schwab, the World Economic Forum executive chairman, wrote the "Davos Manifesto" calling for a new "Code of Ethics for Business Leaders." Executives were no longer simply to seek a return on investment for their shareholders, Schwab declared, but to "serve" their "workers and employees, as well as societies, and to harmonize the different interests of the stakeholders." Corporate executives and investors were beginning to redefine the very purpose of the corporation. The single largest driver of prosperity in American history, the corporation, was to be legally and structurally reimagined and rebuilt with an eye toward "social responsibility." The motivation of a corporation and its leaders would change to reconcile the disparate "interests of . . . stakeholders," as Schwab said in 1973.[2]

It was to be left to a class of capitalist leaders to decide just what that meant. So every January they met at a ski resort in Davos, Switzerland, to pontificate about "ethical capitalism."

Speaking of pontificating about ethical capitalism, Schwab just came out with a book on stakeholder capitalism, cunningly titled *Stakeholder Capitalism*. I was asked to review it for *The Wall Street Journal*. The first two-thirds of the book is Schwab's history of the world's economic system since World War II—the short of it is, things were good for a while, and then climate change and inequality became problems. In the last third, Schwab gets to the solution, which he presents in an updated Davos Manifesto. It's typical of Davos-think that his new manifesto asserts that a good company "serves society at large . . . as a steward of the environmental and material universe for future generations."[3] "Steward" means "unofficial king."

Schwab's idyllic vision of benevolent company-kings shepherding society toward prosperity strikes me as a very European way of thinking. Part of what it means to be American is to have no king.

Notwithstanding Davos, in America there was a broad bipartisan consensus favoring classical shareholder capitalism in the '80s, '90s, and early 2000s. The public debates about capitalism focused on whether government should interfere more or less in business (regulation), whether or not to redistribute wealth (taxation), and whether businesses wielded too much pricing power over consumers (antitrust).

Yet these narrow debates ignored the separate question of whether businesses exercised undue social, cultural, and political power. Regulations were designed to affect only market-oriented activities or to transfer wealth from those who had it to those who didn't. But regulations were mostly unconcerned about the question of corporate power beyond the market. It was a crucial lingering question, like my mom's height.

No one in America really debated finding a suitable partner for capitalism; part of the whole point of shareholder capitalism was that it was meant to exist on its own, with its own goals. American capitalism was independent. It didn't need a spouse.

But the 2008 financial crisis marked a critical turning point in public attitudes toward classical capitalism. The big banks controlled so much power in the financial market that they were deemed by the US government "too big to fail"—requiring a taxpayer-funded bailout of Wall Street itself. US Treasury Secretary Hank Paulson, who was CEO of Goldman Sachs before assuming his cabinet post, picked favorites. Shamefully, he chose to bail out Goldman Sachs, his alma mater, while letting certain of his less favorite rivals like Lehman Brothers go bankrupt without any assistance. To this day, neither Paulson nor other decision-makers have offered a satisfactory account for how they made the decision to bail out some large investment banks but not others. It was crony capitalism at its worst.

As for Paulson, the combination of his tenure at Goldman Sachs and his time as US Treasury Secretary left him a particularly wealthy man. Paulson had amassed a fortune in the form of a $700 million equity stake in Goldman Sachs, and ordinarily he would pay capital gains taxes when liquidating that equity. Yet because of a tax loophole reserved only for government-appointed officials, Paulson was able to take advantage of a provision that allowed him to sell his assets while deferring capital gains so long as the proceeds of his sales were reinvested in government-approved securities within 60 days. The purpose of this loophole was supposedly to avoid a conflict of interest. In reality, the ignominious choice Paulson made as US Treasury Secretary to advantage Goldman Sachs over others showed that the tax loophole didn't deter corruption. It invited it.

The public was understandably livid about having to support bankers who made more money than they did in good times yet who required a bailout from the public when things went bad. Public attitudes toward capitalism became jaded. Capitalism was equated with cronyism—and rightly so. The public came to expect something different from business leaders and government leaders alike.

That's when modern stakeholder capitalism really took off—the moment where the Klaus Schwab crowd overtook Milton Friedman in the fast lane. Meanwhile, in 2008, a former community organizer was elected president of the United States. For the first time in decades, a true political reordering of the power structure appeared possible, if not likely. Wall Street was overrun by the Occupy Wall Street movement. My hedge fund bosses in 2008 advised the new class's analysts that compensation would be chronically lower for years to come, and one of them warned that if we wanted to exit the finance world, "now is probably a good time."

A ND THEN SOMETHING curious happened.
        Consider what happened at an Occupy Wall Street protest in Richmond, Virginia, in October 2011. A group of protesters had gathered in Monroe Park at the "First General Assembly" of Occupy Wall Street—a movement that had grown in fewer than

three years to be something more than just a local affair in Lower Manhattan. One particular incident happened to be captured on video by an attendee.[4]

A white woman in her late 20s spoke to a sprawling audience in the park. She explained at the start of the rally how things were going to work. The leaders of the protest were going to start emulating a practice that had originated in New York City, "stacking" names, a list of people who were due to speak at the rally. But it came with a twist: the stack was to be administered as a "progressive stack." This means that if you're on the list, and you "come from a traditionally marginalized background," then you move up higher on the list.

But this was an Occupy Wall Street movement. Everyone there was protesting on behalf of those who were marginalized and against those who wielded disproportionate economic power—right?

The millennial white woman had an answer for that too. "Race, gender, or ethnicity—anything that is sufficiently marginalized you get bumped up the list. We want to hear what everyone has to say," she explained. There were a couple of distributed shouts of "Woohoo!" from the audience. But they were scattered, and most attendees listened with a tentative silence.

She continued with her explanation to the crowd: "Also, one of the things stressed at Occupy Wall Street now is Step Up, Step Back." There was a notable verbal emphasis when she said "Step Back." "This means people who have been privileged their entire lives—white men, maybe women even—people who have been privileged need to step up and step back."

The crowd murmured. After some uncomfortable silence, someone spoke up from the back. He didn't identify himself, but he was a white male. In response, he said: "Um, uh, I think it doesn't matter, you know, what their general background is because, you know, most of us are already part of the marginalized class of people." Some people in the crowd sounded "boos" in dissent, while others could be heard saying "yeah" in assent. Continuing, he said, "Your background doesn't matter because more people would get to speak anyway. And I think . . ." But then he was interrupted as more people began to object to what he had to say. He asked: "What?" He was confused why anyone had thought he said anything wrong. And then a speaker interrupted him from the stage. "We are talking about *privilege*. You have privilege over other people at certain levels. Some of us are far more marginalized than others. There are people who are way more marginalized than we are." This speaker from the stage was, of course, also a white man.

According to this new orthodoxy, the problem really wasn't corporate power—as Occupy Wall Street had presupposed. Rather, it was based on inherited disempowerment. Race and gender—the immutable and the visible—took the place of class-based struggle. Decades of critical theory at American universities gave the imprimatur of the academy and its supposed rigor to these new ideas.

In short, woke culture stole the show. Unlike Occupy Wall Street, "wokeness" called on its practitioners to wake up to the privileges that certain people (generally straight white men) are born with rather than inequalities arising from other factors— like, say, the exercise of corporate power. Wall Street didn't have to kill Occupy Wall Street from the outside. Instead, woke culture eroded it from within.

And so began Wall Street's love affair with wokeness. My mom often says that marriages are made in Heaven and simply arranged on Earth—by your parents, by a website, or by serendipity itself.

There's something beautiful, even metaphysical, about that idea. But the marriage of big business and woke culture was made in hell. It certainly wasn't born from love. It was arranged by necessity. Wokeness needed money. Wall Street needed a moral imprimatur. So Wall Street eagerly embraced the new identity-based hierarchy and used wokeness to shield itself from the harsh glare the financial crisis had shed on it. That was the dowry of this arranged marriage.

By adopting these new "woke" values, America's business leaders stumbled upon a once-in-a-generation opportunity to leap from heresy to sainthood. Corporations were no longer the oppressors. Instead, corporate power—if wielded in the right way—could actually empower the new disempowered classes who suffered not at the hands of evil corporations but instead at the hands of straight white men—the real culprits who had exploited their power not only since the birth of the corporation but throughout all of modern human history.

Enter woke capitalism—or, more elegantly, the "multi-stakeholder model" of the corporation. The corporation would no longer exist to serve just shareholders but the interests of society at large, including those who deserved the kind of special protections that the rest of society had failed to afford. Women. "People of color." LGBTQ people. Victims of climate change. The tailwinds for this new conception of capitalism could not have been better timed to serve the objectives of the new class of corporate titans who readily espoused this new model.

To be sure, the causes for the meteoric rise of wokeness in America are complex and plural in nature. Generational demographic trends surely played a role. By the early 2000s, as children of America's baby boomers entered adulthood, America was poised to witness the largest intergenerational wealth transfer in the nation's history. In the early twentieth century, Ludwig Von Mises summarized in his book *The Anti-Capitalistic Mentality* that the son of a self-made man has an opportunity to exceed his father's accomplishments in one of two ways. The first is to "beat his father on his own terms." That's hard and risky and unlikely to succeed. The second approach was to be morally superior to one's own father—a goal that is easier to achieve because moral superiority can be subjectively defined. According to Mises, anti-capitalism thus serves an important psychological need created by capitalism itself.[5]

So what happens when an entire generation stands to benefit from the economic spoils of their parents' work? Enter millennials—the children of baby boomers. For example, many of my peers at Harvard and at Yale grew up on the Upper East Side of Manhattan, attended Ethical Culture Fieldston School, and then matriculated at Ivy League colleges, often advantaged by their parents' alumni status. These were the kids who needed at once to benefit from their parentally endowed privileges while also being morally superior to their parents for recognizing those privileges. Becoming woke to genetically inherited attributes like "whiteness" fit the bill perfectly, since it allowed an entire generation to blame their forefathers for the sin they had inherited at birth. It wasn't quite their fault; it was someone else's sin that they were merely burdened with. When big business took up their causes, the woke movement—having already shunned their sinful parents—awkwardly embraced their new corporate patrons.

So, in a nutshell, here's how wokeness and capitalism shacked up: large corporations knocked up woke millennials. Together they birthed woke capitalism. And they put Occupy Wall Street up for adoption.

That trade couldn't have come at a better time for big business. On the back of the government scratching Wall Street's back with its corrupt bailout, it was corporate America's turn to return the favor. They did it by directly assuming the responsibilities of democratic government—especially the agendas of liberal politicians who might otherwise have harmfully regulated or penalized big business. Messy debates about racial inequality? Don't worry: we've got it covered. New policies to fight climate change? We'll take care of that too. Big business volunteered to take on the role of liberal government itself—crucially, on terms that were favorable to its own interests. That's what woke capitalism is all about. It's the hip new avatar of old-school crony capitalism.

Wall Street and Silicon Valley pounced on the opportunity. Capitalist elites were able to skillfully craft a new conception of social purpose—not as an alternative to capitalism but rather through capitalism itself. Al Gore—who famously "invented" the internet and then went on to "discover" climate change—had now made his greatest discovery of all: a new model for the corporation that existed to serve not just shareholders but also other societal stakeholders as well. And he raised a large-scale family of ESG (environmental, social, and governance-oriented) funds that turned him from an impecunious former civil servant into an investment titan worth hundreds of millions of dollars. Those who followed in his mold—riding what was to become a boom in the ESG "asset class" over the subsequent decade—were also handsomely rewarded. On the one hand, Gore advocated to repeal *Citizens United v. Federal Election Commission* because it allowed companies to influence government. On the other hand, he became a professional investor in companies that proposed to replace the work of government—and to get rich himself by doing it. Not a bad consolation prize for losing a presidential election.

W HAT MAKES AN arranged marriage work?

My mom and dad's marriage worked because people who knew and cared about them got them together after thinking hard about whether they'd be compatible. Each of their parents ran through an exhaustive checklist. The whole point of it all was to make sure that each of them would end up as happy as possible. And when the time came, the decision about whether to get married or not came down to whether they liked each other.

That's not how wokeness and capitalism came to be intertwined. The way I see it, corporations were the ones who arranged that marriage, and they arranged it mostly to take the heat off themselves after the financial crisis. Get people talking about identity politics and they'll stop talking about socialism and—perish the thought—communism. Robin DiAngelo, high-fee speaker and author of *White Fragility*, and other elite diversity consultants like her are no threat to big banks. But Karl Marx is. You can pay a diversity consultant good money to do the rounds giving bankers seminars on how whiteness is bad. It's much harder to buy off a principled Marxist, and bankers would not like the seminars they would give.

So corporations embraced wokeness to give themselves cover from the financial crisis and to direct anger toward white men instead of capitalism. Yes, big business is a problem, they'd say, but what do you expect when it's run by white men? We all know the patriarchy is the real problem, along with racism. Oh, now you want to say *systemic* racism is the problem? Yes, yes, very good.

Systemic racism and systemic patriarchy. We condemn them. Look, we will build a statue for you. Just don't say that systemic financial risk is a problem.

So corporations never truly loved wokeness, even as they embraced it and married it to capitalism. They always intended to use it. But wokeness never truly loved capitalism, either. There was nothing fundamentally woke about capitalism, no natural compatibility. When corporations started proclaiming that wokeness and capitalism were inseparable and offering money and status to anyone who could help spread that message, each side accepted the proposal not because there was any truth to it but because it was profitable.

I don't just mean that the marriage of wokeness and capitalism was profitable to the woke in monetary terms, though it was. I'd love to see Robin DiAngelo and Ibram Kendi disclose the speaking fees they've earned from preaching about white privilege and anti-racism to corporations. (It's definitely in the millions of dollars, the only question is how many.) But the main thing wokeness gets out of this marriage of convenience is that it gets to use every major company as a platform to blast its message to the universe. Money was not the only dowry that corporations offered. What they really promised wokeness was a megaphone to turbocharge its message and make it mainstream. By turning wokeness into the default ideology of business, they offered to make it the default everywhere. In exchange, corporations got to wear the protective cloak of wokeness's moral superiority. It was a cynical arrangement.

I gave a presentation on an early version of this book to a class at Harvard Law School. What one woman said stuck with me. I thought that pointing out the cynicism and hypocrisy behind Fearless Girl and her exchange-traded fund and her lawsuits would be enough to make people see that something was deeply wrong with what she represented. But this woman basically said, "So what? She still gave me hope. I was black and a woman and felt all the odds were against me and seeing Fearless Girl made me feel fearless too."

I can't say that woman was wrong to be inspired. But that's exactly the bargain that corporations offer you with woke capitalism: accept the way they profit from your ideals because they'll help spread them. The bargain did good things for her. I just wish it could've done them in a better way. And while the artificial connection of wokeness and capitalism may do some good for individuals, it's death for our democracy.

The wedding of wokeness to capitalism offers a tempting, individually rational choice that harms the nation as a whole by handing corporations social and political power. They don't truly have wokeness's best interests at heart, and the two systems aren't truly compatible. Wokeness and capitalism simply tolerate each other because each feels it can use the other. They will turn a blind eye to each other's faults as long as they themselves can still benefit. But a marriage in which each side secretly has contempt for the other cannot end well.

CHAPTER 7

Henchmen of the Woke-Industrial Complex

THERE'S ARGUABLY NO COMPANY that embodies the marriage of wokeness and capitalism more than Unilever. Investigative journalist Maria Hengeveld notes that over the last decade the company has positioned itself as the corporate leader in the fight to empower women.[1] If you want to join that fight, Unilever's website tells you a good place to start: "Every time you scrub up with Dove, wake up with Lipton, or clean up with Persil, you're supporting 'fempowerment' by helping girls and women unlock their amazing potential."[2]

As a savvy consumer, perhaps you suspect there's something self-serving about this. That's fine. You don't have to take it from Unilever. Just listen to UN Women, a nonprofit branch of the UN dedicated to advancing gender equality and empowering women.[3] UN Women regularly sings Unilever's praises, and the two have partnered up on many projects over the last few years, ranging from its Unstereotype Alliance, which aims to reduce gender stereotypes in advertising, to a global partnership to improve women's safety in the tea industry. Many workers in the tea-picking supply chain are women of color, and as Unilever CEO Alan Jope puts it, "The immutable laws of intersectionality mean that the better the job that we do for women of color, the better chance we have of progressing gender equality everywhere."[4]

The year 2016 was a tumultuous year for Unilever's feminist efforts. On the one hand, it began its journey with UN Women to protect female workers in the entire world's tea industry. On the other, it was facing a lawsuit from a group of its Kenyan tea plantation workers who claimed it had failed to protect them from rape.* The story of Unilever's mutually profitable partnership with UN Women is inextricably connected to that lawsuit from its Kenyan workers, who continue to seek justice from Unilever to this day.

In December 2007, after the local ethnic majority's preferred candidate lost Kenya's presidential election, hundreds of men attacked the ethnic minority workers on Unilever's plantation. They looted and burned thousands of homes and raped husbands and wives in front of their children. At least fifty-six women were raped. Many people were maimed, and at least eleven were killed. Some of their attackers were their own Unilever coworkers. Unilever had been worried about possible violence before the election, so it stationed guards around its facilities and its management's homes, but none at the worker's camps.

Unilever closed the plantation for six months after the attack. When the brutalized workers returned, they saw many of their attackers still working there. Instead of pursuing criminal charges

---

* I drew many of the details of this story from Hengeveld's reporting.

against the attackers or paying the injured workers' hospital bills, Unilever compensated them for their suffering by giving them a month's wage. It had placed them on unpaid leave for six months.

Unilever may believe the immutable laws of intersectionality require it to help women of color, but when its Kenyan workers sought justice from it, it hid behind the mutable laws of men. In 2015, some 218 survivors of the attack banded together to sue Unilever's Kenyan subsidiary and the British parent company in London's High Court for failing to keep them safe. Unilever claimed that as a parent company, it had no duty of care to its Kenyan workers because it wasn't actively involved in managing the Kenyan operation; testimony from four ex-Unilever Kenya managers suggests that was false. In 2018, a UK judge sided with Unilever and ruled that the workers lacked standing to sue it.

Having lost their chance for legal remedies, the women are now, as of this writing, appealing to the UN's Working Group on Business and Human Rights, hoping it will make a declaration siding with them to place public relations pressure on Unilever. Meanwhile, shortly after their lawsuit in 2016, Unilever created its broad partnership with UN Women and started donating more than a million dollars a year to it.

And so the Kenyan women who are pleading with Unilever for justice face a bitter irony: the only hope they have left comes from a declaration from a branch of the UN, while a different branch of the UN issues regular pronouncements about how well Unilever treats women, particularly tea pickers. This irony is, of course, not coincidental.

A corporation offers woke people money and influence, and in return they lend it the protective cloak of wokeness's moral superiority to hide its wrongdoing. It's a familiar bargain, the same one I talked about in Chapter 6. It's the same thing that happened when State Street's female employees sued it over pay inequity and it made a feminist statue as part of its cover-up. What's new in Unilever's variation on the arranged marriage between wokeness and capitalism is that it's hiding behind a nonprofit instead of a statue. Statues are silent, but feminist nonprofits can speak on your behalf.

UN Women is surely making the same calculation all woke people do when they accept woke capitalism's proposal: it knows that Unilever is using it to provide moral cover for the Kenyan massacre, but it calculates that the money Unilever is giving it can do enough good to make that cost tolerable. UN Women said as much in a different context, when human rights activists at AIDS-free World pleaded with it to cut ties with Unilever over its marketing of skin-lightening creams, which promotes white skin as good. The activists said, "We were dismayed by a reply that seemed to say that UN Women is willing to tolerate racism in exchange for a token portion of Unilever's enormous profits. What we saw was an intolerable quid pro quo and an indefensible trade-off."[5]

They're completely right. This kind of quid pro quo between woke nonprofits and corporations is an essential part of the woke-industrial complex. The bargain is indefensible, but as you'll see in this chapter, it happens all the time.

HERE'S ANOTHER ANGLE to the quid pro quo between woke nonprofits and corporations. Remember those massive settlements that companies like Goldman pay for violating laws, like the $5 billion in fines it paid for that Malaysian scandal I talked about in the Chapter 1? Well, here's a second part of the scam—the settlement money that's supposed to go to taxpayers ends up in the pockets of left-wing nonprofits while sometimes cutting the fines actually paid by those companies by half or more. It's still too early to know where the Goldman money is going to go, but if history is any guide, taxpayers won't see much of it.

After all, that's exactly what happened with the billions of dollars in fines that Goldman Sachs and all the other major banks had to pay after the 2008 financial crisis. In Chapter 5, I described how Clinton administration policies encouraging homeownership incentivized banks to hand out subprime loans like candy to people who couldn't pay them back. The banks certainly bore a large share of blame for the inevitable collapse of the mortgage-backed securities market, and there was a lot of corruption and cronyism in the way they got bailed out. But eventually, between 2014 and 2016, they did pay a price for their wrongdoing, and it was a big one, on paper.

Goldman Sachs reached a $5 billion settlement with the Justice Department—maybe that's just its number. Morgan Stanley agreed to a $3 billion fine; it got off light. Citigroup got hit with a $7 billion fine. J.P. Morgan Chase got hit with $13 billion. And Bank of America reached the largest civil settlement in American history at nearly $17 billion.

That's a lot of billions. A good chunk of that money, $11 billion, was earmarked for "consumer relief" to help out homeowners who had been hurt by the Great Recession. But here's the thing—those homeowners may not have seen a dime of that money, for all we know. What we do know is that a lot of it was handed out to nonprofits picked from a list created by the federal government, and a lot of them were liberal favorites like La Raza and the National Urban League. Andy Koenig wrote a great exposé of it in *The Wall Street Journal*.[6]

These left-leaning nonprofits use their funds for liberal priorities like voter registration and lobbying state, local, and federal government. And it turns out they get a *lot* of their funding from banks, via these settlements with the DOJ—Koenig studied 80 nonprofit beneficiaries of Bank of America's 2014 settlement and found that, on average, they received more than 10 percent of their 2015 budgets from that settlement alone. Remember, that's just *one* bank settlement. They were probably raking in a lot of money from the other banks too. Bank of America is just the only big bank that disclosed exactly where it sent its money.

You might wonder how this hurts taxpayers, especially if you're a liberal and you think these nonprofits fight for worthy causes. So here's the kicker: that $11 billion meant for consumer relief? Not only did a lot of it go to Democratic-favored nonprofits instead, but it ended up being much less than $11 billion. That's because the DOJ offered banks a huge discount whenever they "donated" that money to those nonprofits. Most of the settlements gave banks double or triple credit toward their fine for every dollar they donated to these nonprofits—for instance, a Bank of America $1.15 million "donation" to the National Urban League counted as $2.6 million toward meeting its settlement obligation, and every $1.5 million to La Raza counted as $3.5 million of consumer relief.

This is so mind-boggling that it's worth summing up: after the financial crisis, the Obama DOJ slammed big banks with massive fines so it could trumpet that it was sending tons of relief to consumers. Then it told banks they could pay less than half that much if they donated the money to Obama's favorite nonprofits instead. And being fond of money, the banks took the DOJ up on the offer. Now that's a great *quid pro quo*—the DOJ gets to look good, the banks get to keep most of their money, and the liberal nonprofits get lots of funding.

There's another benefit to the bank and to the DOJ. There's an obvious PR win for the bank if it gets to pay its settlement money as "donations" to liberal darlings instead of having to call it fines. By the way, if they're charitable donations, they also become tax-deductible—even more money saved for the bank and even less going to the federal government and the citizens it represents.

But you might overlook an important benefit to the executive branch that comes from the fines being turned into donations. If they're *fines*, they naturally go to the US Treasury, and the Constitution says, "No money shall be drawn from the Treasury, but in consequence of appropriations made by law."[7] That means that *Congress* decides what happens to that bank money. But if it turns into donations instead of fines, the money never goes to the Treasury, and the *executive branch* gets to decide where it goes.

This is the woke-industrial complex at its finest. Three separate pillars of American society working in concert to scratch each other's backs. There are even more wins and favors being exchanged between the executive branch, banks, and woke nonprofits than you might expect. It's not just a *quid pro quo*; I lose track of how many *quids* and *pros* there should be. But you cannot create something from nothing. The American people end up with far less money than they should, and they lose the ability to have their elected representatives decide what to do with it.

And that's just the executive branch version of the scheme to use nonprofits to advance liberal causes. The judicial branch wets its beak too. The scam is fundamentally the same: when corporations reach settlements over their wrongdoing, judges and lawyers find ways to direct the money to their pet causes instead of to the people who were wronged. Since the lawyers representing clients against these corporations are disproportionately liberal, those pet causes are often progressive ones.

This scam happens via an old trust-law doctrine called *cy pres*, pronounced "sigh-pray." It derives from a French phrase meaning "as near as possible." The idea started out as a good one—when a court is determining how to apply the terms of a trust, if taking those terms literally would be impossible, the court should try to do the next best thing. For instance, in a classic nineteenth-century example, a court repurposed a trust that had been created to abolish slavery in the United States to instead provide charity to poor African Americans.*

That makes sense. But in recent years, the trust-law doctrine of *cy pres* has been abused to redirect settlement money from class-action lawsuits toward lawyers' favorite charities as well as to their alma maters. Basically, plaintiffs' and defendants' lawyers get together and tell the judge it would be too difficult to distribute settlement money to all the members of a class. Then they tell the judge they've agreed to give it to some nonprofits they like instead or that they want to use it to create some foundation at their alma mater. The judge usually agrees. Judges often get in on the action by directing some of the money to the nonprofits they like as well as their own alma maters. As with the bank settlements, corporations would much rather take photographs of themselves delivering fat checks to beloved nonprofits than mail thousands of tiny checks to faceless class members.

For instance, in one class-action settlement against Google's practice of divulging its users' search queries to third parties, instead of going for the massive $1,000 per violation statutory

---

* Thanks to Ted Frank for explaining all this to me as well as telling me about some of the other examples in this chapter. You can find an article from him about it here: www.wsj.com/articles/for-some-class-action-lawyers-charity-begins-and-ends-at -home-1521760032.

damages Google was on the hook for, the lawyers settled for a pal-try $8.5 million, $2 million of which went to themselves and the rest of which went to some charities affiliated with both Google and the lawyers. The lawyers' alma maters, Chicago-Kent and Harvard Law, also got some money. In a different Google case, federal dis-trict judge James Ware rewrote the settlement to direct $500,000 to his own alma mater, Santa Clara University School of Law, where he taught classes. The money—I'm not joking about this—went to fund a center on ethics.[8]

It's the same basic scam as the DOJ stuff, just the judicial sys-tem's version of it. Everyone gets to wet their beak. The loyal law school graduate goes out into the world, gets a big kill, and drags the carcass back to their alma mater to impress it. Nonprofits get million-dollar checks. The corporation writing them turns a poten-tial scandal into a PR win. Everyone wins, except for the actual members of the class who were harmed to begin with. But the beauty of this scam is that it's a class-action lawsuit. The members of the class don't even know they were supposed to get anything, so they'll never miss it. Another masterful trick from the woke-industrial complex.

I'T'S NOT JUST nonprofits that have become the accomplices of woke capitalism; it's our own government agencies, which is even worse. When the judicial branch funnels corporate settlement money to nonprofits, it's fleecing money from the people who were harmed by those corporations. When the executive branch does it, it's diverting money from the US Treasury and therefore from all taxpayers. By doing so it deprives Americans not only of their money but of their voice. The Constitution says that our elected representatives in Congress are supposed to debate each other in full view of the public and decide what to do with our money.

This DOJ tactic of changing fines to donations to bypass the Treasury was part of a shadow war waged between the Obama administration and the Republican-controlled Congress. President Obama supported a lot of policies that the Republicans in the House and Senate refused to make law. Call it obstructionist, but that's life in a two-party system. There was nothing unconstitutional about it. But it violates the spirit and letter of the Constitution for a frustrated executive branch to use its administrative powers to enact unofficial, undemocratic laws that it couldn't get through Congress.

That's exactly what the Obama administration was doing when it used DOJ settlements with banks to fund its favored nonprofits. For instance, Congress decided to cut $43 million in funding to community development, financial institutions, and housing counseling agencies. Then as part of the bank's consumer relief penalties, the DOJ had it turn around and pay more than $100 million to those exact same groups. Maybe that was good policy, maybe not. But there's no denying that Congress, which holds the constitutional power of the purse, decided to cut funding to those groups, and the executive branch immediately used its power to create a new purse and dole out money from it. The executive branch is charged to enact Congress's laws, not to outright defy it by creating its own.

Remember Volkswagen? That big scandal where it preached about how environmentally friendly its cars were and it turned out it just installed hardware to cheat on all the tests? Volkswagen comes back into this story about the woke-industrial complex too, and the DOJ is again a star, once again acting as a shadow legislature. President Obama had promised to put a million electric vehicles on the road by 2015 and asked Congress for $300 million to make it happen; Congress refused.

Constitutionally speaking, that should have been the end of it. But the Obama administration bypassed the Treasury and realized it could use Volkswagen as its piggy bank. The DOJ forced Volkswagen into a settlement where it had to invest $1.2 billion in creating electric vehicle charging stations. And it had to get the EPA to approve of the plan. But the EPA isn't created or designed to know the best way to invest a billion dollars into new technology, just like the DOJ wasn't created to find funding for Democratic priorities whenever Congress refuses.[9] But like nonprofits, those administrative agencies became the willing henchmen of the woke-industrial complex.

Part of being a loyal henchman is that you don't just reward the boss's friends; you punish their enemies. And that's what the DOJ has become—a goon squad that kicks down the doors of wokeness's public enemies. This was most evident in the way it took down public villain Martin Shkreli. One rule of woke capitalism is that jerks who obviously care only about money don't get to keep making it. Shkreli violated that rule, and the DOJ came down on him like a ton of bricks.

I met Shkreli for the first time in 2013. I was 28 years old. When I read in *Forbes* magazine about a guy around my age who had graduated from Baruch College and was supposedly the young savant of the biotech industry, I was reflexively skeptical—and if I'm being honest, even a little envious.

But when I met him, I could tell within minutes that he was brilliant. I was still an investment analyst, and he was the young CEO of a company called Retrophin. His knowledge of genetic diseases was encyclopedic. He knew the clinical data of his competitors cold—he often knew more than even their own scientists. He was a rare genius.

Yet I also learned pretty quickly that he was pathologically incapable of telling the truth. He wasn't a liar in the conventional sense. Rather, it seemed that he was literally incapable of distinguishing fact from fiction, like some type of rare genetic anomaly that made him agnostic to objective truth, let alone rules or norms. The media would later portray him as a "pharma bro" because he was once photographed wearing sunglasses and a douchey-looking outfit, but they fundamentally missed the mark. He wasn't a bro. He was a semi-autistic idiot savant with a hard-wired inability to tell the truth.

In that first meeting, Shkreli told me unprompted that he had attended Columbia University but dropped out to go to Baruch College instead. As part of my due diligence I called Columbia's admissions office and asked whether he'd ever been admitted there. He hadn't. So I wasn't shocked when he lied about the other basic stuff too. At one point during my due diligence, he started to volunteer confidential information. I told him to stop, since I was a public markets investor and could only be exposed to public information. He laughed and said, "Look, man, this is *Wall Street*." It was as though he were trying to act out his childhood dream of starring in his favorite movie.

Maybe that was his sin. Martin Shkreli just wanted to be the Wolf of Wall Street. He didn't just want to make money; he wanted everyone to know he cared about nothing else. So, ironically, he didn't actually care only about money—he cared even more about making sure everyone knew that. Martin Shkreli didn't dream of being rich; he dreamed of being a rich asshole. And being famous for it.

I watched from afar as he became an industry pariah for

acquiring Daraprim, a medication to treat a rare condition in certain HIV patients, and jacking the price over 5,000 percent from $13.50 to $750 per pill.[10] He became the poster boy for the greed of the pharmaceutical industry. His desire for attention did him few favors. While the media continually misunderstood him as a pharma bro, I was certain that he was relishing fame that he mistook for popularity, popularity he hadn't enjoyed in his youth as a nerdy son of immigrants.

Martin Shkreli wasn't a pharma bro; that's the tragedy of his story. He was acting out a poor kid's lonely fantasy of what being one was like. That's why he became a caricature. He'd always been viewing that glamorized life from the outside, and even after he found his way to Wall Street and became his two-dimensional image of a pharma bro, he still never really knew what it was like.

Here's how the case that took him down started. As I take you through the details, ask yourself this: What was Martin Shkreli really punished for?

In December 2015, Shkreli was charged with securities fraud for orchestrating schemes to defraud investors in two hedge funds he managed, along with a scheme to misappropriate more than $11 million in Retrophin assets to cover investment losses at the hedge funds.

The SEC had been investigating Shkreli since 2012; he popped up on its radar after abandoning his financial obligations on a large short-sale position, leaving his broker with a $7 million loss. *The Wall Street Journal* reported that the SEC probe took priority after Shkreli raised the price of Daraprim overnight.[11]

It was obvious that prosecutors really wanted to punish Shkreli for his actions with Daraprim, but it was also clear that their case was murky. But Shkreli was already guilty in the court of public opinion, no matter the charge. His notoriety grew to unprecedented heights with each of his increasingly obscene antics. He shelled out $2 million on *Once Upon a Time in Shaolin*, an unreleased Wu-Tang Clan album, and said that he'd play it only for Taylor Swift, in exchange for sexual favors.[12] While out on bail awaiting the outcome of his trial, he offered a bounty of $5,000 for a strand of Hillary Clinton's hair. A federal judge revoked Shkreli's bail over that, sending him back to jail.[13]

Shkreli was convicted on three of eight counts and sentenced to seven years in prison.[14] It's at least noteworthy that he was acquitted by the jury on a majority of the DOJ's charges. His defense had centered on the fact that the investors he defrauded made money in the end. He'd lied in various ways to investors in his hedge funds, mostly to conceal big losses. Eventually, he told them he was shutting the hedge funds down and offered them shares of his company Retrophin instead of returning the cash they'd given him. And, of course, he'd defrauded shareholders of Retrophin by taking assets from it to cover up his hedge fund losses. Ultimately, both his Retrophin and hedge fund investors made money because those Retrophin shares ended up becoming very valuable.

So that's the story of Shkreli's rise and fall. Let's come back to the question I asked earlier: What was Martin Shkreli really guilty of? Why did the DOJ go after him so hard when it lets others quietly get away with much worse?

In January 2018, I attended the annual J.P. Morgan health care conference. I got drinks with the CEO of one of the largest biopharmaceutical companies. After downing a couple, he said something about Shkreli that stuck with me: "The reason they got him is because of what he did to that drug's price. Of course I would never say that publicly." He was right: the only acceptable public line for any biotech or pharma CEO about Shkreli is that he was a villain.

That was the pharma industry's goal: to make clear that Shkreli wasn't one of us. And he was indeed an outsider. He wasn't a polished executive. He was a lonely kid with serious psychological issues who was desperate for attention. That's what made him an outsider, not his business practices. In reality, he did what many other pharma companies do every single day—different not in kind but only degree. Martin Shkreli may have committed fraud, but the reason the DOJ punished him for it is that he was an asshole who was bringing too much heat down on all the more polished pharmaceutical elites.

Shkreli jacked up drug prices and propositioned Taylor Swift instead of paying lip service to the immutable laws of intersectionality. That's what the system got him for. The same system that got him tells us who the good guys and bad guys are, and we all know who Shkreli was: the worst of the bad guys. And we all know who the good guys are, too—guys like Unilever CEO Alan Jope, who fight gender stereotypes and harness the power of intersectionality to protect all women by protecting women of color.

So Shkreli is a bad guy and Jope is a good guy. But whom did Shkreli hurt? The people he was convicted for defrauding all ended up richer. The people who used Daraprim didn't pay more for it; the cost was split up across the whole health insurance system. But those Kenyan tea pickers who are begging the UN to make Unilever admit it failed to protect them? They were hurt very badly, and Unilever could help them without even noticing the money was gone.

But it won't. That's because it's not about the money for Unilever, though it was all about the money for Shkreli. If Unilever compensates those women or even acknowledges it wronged them, it loses its sterling reputation as one of the good guys. That's why instead of helping its Kenyan tea pickers it's dropping a million a year to get UN Women to praise it for protecting every other tea worker. Unilever has to be seen as the one who protects women from rape, not the one who allowed it; the fact that it did allow it is irrelevant. It's got too much invested in its reputation to admit the truth.

And that's one of the problems with wokeness. Corporations aren't people, but in one way they're exactly alike. Whether you're a corporation or a person, if you aspire to a reputation for goodness and achieve it, at some point maintaining the appearance of virtue becomes more important than virtue itself. Woke nonprofits are silent middlemen in the woke-industrial game: they allow corporations to buy the appearance of virtue by paying nonprofits to speak on their behalf.

In this game, nonprofits are the puppets, and corporations are their puppet masters. That's simple enough, but this is where our story takes a dark turn: on the global stage, the corporations themselves become puppets too. So who's pulling *their* strings? The answer is downright frightening.

CHAPTER 8

When Dictators Become Stakeholders

IN OCTOBER 2017, I WAS aboard a flight to a place that had never been high on my destination list: Saudi Arabia.

The occasion for the trip was the first-ever Future Investment Initiative global conference—one that was quickly dubbed "Davos in the Desert." The conference shared a lot in common with the World Economic Forum in Davos and the annual Milken Institute Global Conference in Los Angeles. The same billionaire class was in attendance. They use the same private jets to travel to all three. They drank wine in Davos, whiskey in Los Angeles, and sparkling grape juice in Riyadh. In Davos they talk about the promise of ESG, in Los Angeles they talk about the American dream, in Riyadh they talk about spreading technology in the Middle East.* But in all

---

* The big theme in 2017 when I visited Riyadh was the unveiling of a new technological city called Neom in which flying robots and human beings would cohabit a space where they traveled via flying cars.

three places, the goal was to set an agenda that entrepreneurs and CEOs were expected to follow—especially young CEOs like me who were dependent on investments from people like them. Some of these investors were institutional investment firms like mutual funds or hedge funds. But the largest and most important ones of all were sovereign nations like Singapore, Norway, China, and Saudi Arabia.

I had received a special invitation to visit Mohammed Bin Salman (or MBS, as he is known), the newly anointed Crown Prince of the Kingdom of Saudi Arabia, at the Royal Palace. After landing in Riyadh, I spent most of the day waiting at a nearby hotel along with a small group of CEOs who had also received the same invitation. After a few hours, the group received a call to notify us that the Crown Prince was ready, so we proceeded to the palace in a caravan of black SUVs. During the car ride, another CEO advised me to approach the visit the same way Fortune 500 CEOs behave when they visit the White House: when in doubt, shut up and listen, and always let them know that you're ready to help.

Upon arriving at the palace, we waited for a couple more hours before being escorted to a special room in the basement. Soon enough the Crown Prince arrived. Each CEO stood individually as they spoke and addressed him as "Your Highness" and his royal sidekicks as "Your Excellency." I did the same. Several of them expressed fealty to the nation of Saudi Arabia in various ways and volunteered to launch ambitious collaborations with the Kingdom to help advance the Crown Prince's sweeping Vision 2030 plan.

I was captivated, fascinated, and even a bit smitten with the new Crown Prince, who despite being my age was seemingly determined to modernize an entire society. He was arrestingly knowledgeable about different areas of science and technology, spoke fluent English, and listened carefully to what every CEO in the room told him.

Shortly after the trip, safely back in the United States, I read in the news that MBS had indefinitely imprisoned nearly a hundred business leaders on unspecified charges of corruption. The same hotel where my peers had stayed only weeks ago, the Ritz Carlton in Riyadh, was used as a makeshift prison to house them. After that, they came for the feminists. As MBS paid lip service to the cause of women's rights, he jailed its most vocal supporters. Feminist leaders were reportedly jailed without charges or trials and, then tortured and sexually assaulted. Many of them remain imprisoned today.[1]

Next they came for Jamal Khashoggi, a contributor to *The Washington Post*. In Turkey, they lured him into a trap as he entered the Saudi consulate in Istanbul to get documents for his upcoming marriage.[2] A team of Saudi operatives was waiting for him. They tortured him, strangled him to death, and dismembered his body with a bone saw.[3] Then Saudi Arabia denied it. Once it was confronted with overwhelming evidence, it denied MBS had anything to do with it and trotted out a few guys to take the fall.

The Saudis had sent a fifteen-man team to the consulate, including a forensics doctor. The mission was led by Ahmad al Asiri, a close advisor to MBS; news reports claimed the Crown Prince personally assigned the assassination to him, though the Saudis deny that.[4] Seven of the fifteen hit men were MBS's personal bodyguards.[5]

Saudi Arabia's sovereign wealth fund was an investor in an investment fund that had invested in my own company. As it turns out, that's why I had been invited to meet the Crown Prince in the first place. After the Khashoggi incident, one of my close advisors gave me an alarming warning to keep an eye on the situation. "Just be careful with those guys," he warned me, referring to the Saudis. When I probed what he meant, he responded: "Well, they *probably* don't execute CEOs. Just keep your eyes open."

Maybe the Crown Prince directly ordered the killing of Khashoggi. Maybe he didn't. Who can know such things? All I know is that I haven't returned to Riyadh.

But if the behavior of Saudi Arabia was suspect, China's is far more frightening. I've done business in China too, and it's not rosy. Last year, the Chinese government expressly warned that it's willing to deploy government-backed scare tactics even in private business negotiations. China said that it might detain US nationals following the US Justice Department's prosecution of Chinese researchers accused of hiding their ties to the Chinese military. It's well known that China has previously detained US citizens and sentenced Canadian, Australian, and Swedish citizens on charges with little or no factual or legal basis. The US State Department issued its own warning to echo this reality.[6]

Chinese business leaders have experienced similar setbacks when they've run afoul of the ruling party. For example, when Chinese President Xi Jinping caught wind that the prominent entrepreneur Jack Ma had made comments critical of government regulators, he personally pulled the plug on the IPO of Ma's Ant Financial—the day before it was due to debut as the largest IPO in world history.[7] Other prominent Chinese business leaders including Wang Jianlin, once the richest man in China, have been the targets of Xi's wrath when they strayed too far from the party line even in private.

American critics of Donald Trump portrayed him as an aspiring autocrat with the sensibilities of a Scorsese mob boss, but Trump's influence over American industry was insignificant compared to the iron rule of Xi and his cronies over every company that does business in China. Rulers like Xi and MBS are the greatest threat democracy will face over the next decade, and now the dictators have discovered a new arrow in their quiver: wokeness. There's even a new Chinese word for wokeness—*baizuo*—referring specifically to woke white people. They use it to laugh at America.[8]

Don't get me wrong. Stakeholder capitalism didn't kill Jamal Khashoggi. Wokeness didn't create corruption in China. But it does aid the cover-up. Throughout this chapter, I'll show you how American corporations have become the pawns of foreign dictators even as they portray themselves as paragons of virtue. They would still fawn over dictators in pursuit of profit even without Wokenomics entering the picture. That's just an evil of global capitalism itself, in any form. But the key difference between the stakeholder and shareholder models of capitalism is that the woke version crowns corporations with a patina of moral authority. I'll show you how foreign dictators use the moral stature of woke corporations to whitewash their own oppression and also to damage the moral standing of the United States on the global stage.

I N JANUARY 2020, Silicon Valley darling Airbnb shocked the business world when it announced that it would make decisions based on "stakeholders," not just shareholders, when it comes to its corporate governance. Among other things, the company planned to hold a "Stakeholder Day" as an alternative to the conventional annual shareholder one. CEO Brian Chesky committed to changing the company's compensation program, with factors important to "stakeholders" taken into account when bonuses are calculated.

Sometimes woke companies are vague when making statements about stakeholders. But not Airbnb. It made a nice little chart that described the relationships that Airbnb hoped to have with its various stakeholders.[9]

Chesky was lionized for the announcement. But it turns out

the handy chart conveniently omitted one of one of Airbnb's most important stakeholders: the Chinese Communist Party (CCP).

About seven months before Brian Chesky's declaration of love for stakeholders, Airbnb hired Sean Joyce, a former deputy director of the FBI, as its first "chief trust officer." The purpose of the role was to protect users' safety on the platform. Yet in a move that Airbnb tried to sweep under the rug, Joyce resigned before the end of the year over concerns about how the behemoth was sharing data on millions of its users—without their knowledge—with the Chinese Communist Party. Guests and hosts are at the top of Airbnb's stakeholder list. Yet it was stealing and sharing data from both of these stakeholders to share it with an even more important one.

According to *The Wall Street Journal*, Joyce left because he was concerned that Airbnb wasn't transparent with its users about the data that it regularly shares with the CCP. And Airbnb continued to expand the scope of data that it shared.[10] Regularly shared data about American users includes phone numbers, email addresses, and the content of messages between users and the company, according to unidentified sources within Airbnb. Chinese officials privately approached Airbnb with an unwritten request for even more data, including so-called "real-time data," about the users. Joyce worried that such data-sharing would empower Chinese government surveillance and put members of minority ethnic groups at risk.

Joyce elevated his concerns to senior executives, including Brian Chesky and his co-founder Nathan Blecharczyk (with whom, incidentally, I had crossed paths during our student days at Harvard). "We're not here to promote American values," Blecharczyk told Joyce. Joyce then resigned. His only public statement said that it was over "a difference in values."[11]

I wish that people like Blecharczyk would say in public what they actually say behind closed doors. The American public deserves to hear the truth. Our system works pretty well when the American people know exactly what's going on. But the PR smoke screen of stakeholder capitalism prevents the American public and government from putting companies like Airbnb under the microscope.

If Airbnb were honest, it would publicly admit what Blecharczyk said in private: "We're not here to promote American values." That's a perfectly legitimate thing for a company to say. On the other hand, if Airbnb really *did* care about promoting American values, then it would act accordingly. It would stand up to the CCP and say it wasn't going to siphon data provided to it by its trusting American users and be damned if that meant losing access to China's lucrative market. That's how Airbnb could have demonstrated that it really cared about its "stakeholders."

But we're left with the worst of both worlds. Companies like Airbnb cultivate the public image that they care about society at large rather than their bottom line while in reality abusing that public trust. The stakeholder smoke screen wasn't just a sideshow. It's an essential part of the story: without earning trust that it never deserved, Airbnb wouldn't have been able to collect vast reams of consumer data.

And no one has mastered this dark art better than China. In sum, here's how the game works. First, Black Lives Matter activists—or environmentalists or feminists or whoever—become the front for American technology companies to win consumer trust. Second, those companies monetize that trust by generating clicks, selling ads, and charging fees—generating a treasure trove of sensitive personalized data about each of their consumers. Third, the CCP demands access to that data as a condition of entry for companies to do business in China. Fourth, these companies supplicate to the CCP and make a killing in China. Fifth, they keep mum about their dealings in China while continuing to issue woke proclamations through their corporate megaphones. BLM wins. Silicon Valley wins. The CCP wins. The real losers of this game are the American people.

The role of trendy stakeholder-ist values in this charade cannot be overstated. Companies like Airbnb would never command the blind allegiance of naïve American users by simply selling a humdrum product. That's why they douse it in morality. They flaunt their wokeism precisely to win the trust of US consumers—which in turn provides air cover when they betray *those same consumers* by handing over their data to the Chinese government. It's a dirty bribe to the CCP, plain and simple, one that leaves American consumers hanging dry. For many progressive consumers, it's easier to trust a company that posts a black square on its corporate Instagram account rather than one that posts a red flag with five golden stars. Yet Airbnb effectively gets to have it both ways—flaunting a sleek video titled "We Stand with #BlackLivesMatter" while quietly collaborating with CCP without any mention of China on Instagram or anywhere else.

The real evil isn't just the CCP gaining access to the private data of American consumers. That's just the scam. The deeper problem arises when the CCP flexes its muscle as a gatekeeper to the Chinese market to then convince corporations to *spread the CCP's own values abroad*. It does this implicitly through the rise of woke capitalism—with companies like Disney, Marriott, Apple, or the NBA expressing their moral outrage about injustices like "systemic racism" and transphobia in the United States while staying completely silent about human rights abuses like concentration camps, forced sterilization of religious minorities, and beatings of innocent civilians in China.

Over the last few years, the Chinese government has detained more than a million Uighurs in concentration camps. The Uighurs are a large ethnic minority who have lived in the Xinjiang region of China for at least a thousand years. Over the centuries they've gradually become predominantly Muslim, the heart of the cultural conflict between them and the CCP. The CCP at first denied that it was detaining Uighurs at all. When confronted with satellite photos of its camps, it claimed that they were reeducation camps meant to end the threat of Uighur Islamic extremism, which had led to a number of terrorist attacks in the last decade. But the CCP's take on education looks a lot like cultural genocide to most Westerners.

Chinese police look for signs of "religious extremism" such as owning books about Uighur history, growing a beard, having a prayer rug, or quitting drinking and smoking. They install cameras in private homes. Men are imprisoned without trial or charges for reciting verses from the Quran at funerals. Wives are sent to concentration camps surrounded by barbed wire fences if their husbands are under suspicion. Inmates at the camps are beaten, insulted, and forced to write "self-criticism essays" and sing hymns in praise of the Communist Party. They're also forced to labor in factories producing goods for China to export. The CCP claims it's just giving them training and jobs. But the Uighurs aren't given a chance to say no.[12]

The Chinese government isn't just brainwashing Uighurs, enslaving them, and erasing their culture. It's forcibly sterilizing them. In June 2020, German anthropologist Adrian Zenz released a report alleging that Uighur women are being compelled to have abortions, undergo sterilization surgeries, and be outfitted with IUDs, all under threat of internment.[13] He made a few startling statistical discoveries. For instance, in 2014, right before the CCP's campaign to control the Uighurs, only 2.5 percent of all IUD placements in China occurred in Xinjiang. But by 2018, 80 percent of all new IUDs in China were in Xinjiang. The program seems to be having its intended effect: between 2015 and 2018, population growth rates in the Uighur regions of China plummeted 60 percent. If Zenz is right, the Chinese government is committing cultural genocide against the Uighurs in a very literal sense—instead of killing them or controlling them, it's decided it's easier to prevent more from being born.

While the Uighurs suffer the worst of China's atrocities, they are far from alone. The Chinese Communist Party has taken advantage of the free rein given to it by the global pandemic to extend its brutal hand outward. Its soldiers attacked Indian ones on the supposedly demilitarized border in Ladakh, killing dozens in hand-to-hand fighting and executing the wounded by pushing them over a cliff.[14] China's also rapidly building amphibious assault ships and aiming them squarely at Taiwan.[15] It takes the US years to build one of these powerful, expensive assault carriers, loaded with helicopters and marines. China is churning out a new one every six months.[16]

The Communist Party has turned its all-seeing eye to another island: Hong Kong. When the British turned over Hong Kong to China in 1997, it was on the understanding that China would adhere to a "one country, two systems" principle. China agreed to the drafting and adoption of Hong Kong's Basic Law, a mini-constitution letting Hong Kong maintain its own unique capital-ist system, currency, laws, and freedoms until 2047. But alarmed by pro-democracy demonstrations, the CCP broke its promise to allow Hong Kong autonomy and brought it under its thumb. In June 2020, the Chinese government passed a draconian national security law, setting up a new CCP-controlled agency to prosecute cases in Hong Kong and making those found guilty of sedition subject to punishments of up to life imprisonment. Alan Leong, former chair of Hong Kong's bar association, summed the new law up by saying, "We are allowing the long arms of the Chinese Communist Party to reach Hong Kong.[17]

The long arms of the CCP have reached all the way to America too. When Houston Rockets general manager Daryl Morey tweeted from his personal account in support of Hong Kong, saying, "Fight for freedom, stand with Hong Kong,"[18] the CCP was incensed. Turns out the Rockets do a lot of business in China, largely thanks to ex-Rockets star Yao Ming. And the NBA is trying to make inroads in the vast, basketball-crazy Chinese market. In other words, China was a big stakeholder in the Rockets' business. That stakeholder flexed its muscle.

The Chinese consulate in Houston denounced Morey. Tilman Fertitta, the Rockets' owner, followed suit, "[Daryl Morey] does NOT speak for the [Houston Rockets]." The Chinese Basketball Association announced that it would cease all cooperation with the Rockets. The NBA issued a statement calling Morey's tweet regrettable. The Rockets were reportedly considering firing Morey to appease China.[19] All Chinese broadcasters refused to show any NBA games. Nike pulled all its Rockets gear from its stores in China.[20]

It wasn't just the CCP, its corporate minions, and the NBA that acted like Morey had done something inexcusable. Players joined in. Rockets star James Harden said, "We apologize. You know, we love China. We love playing there."[21] Superstar LeBron James, known for his social justice advocacy, also threw his weight behind the cause to demonize Morey. LeBron had the misfortune of being in China for a preseason game between the Lakers and Nets right when Morey tweeted. LeBron claimed Morey had misused his right to freedom of speech, adding, "I believe he wasn't educated on the situation at hand."[22]

It's jarring when you compare LeBron's criticism of Morey to his vocal support of Black Lives Matter protestors and his frequent criticism of Donald Trump.[23] LeBron spearheaded a get-out-the-vote effort called More Than a Vote, a laudable goal if he hadn't simultaneously been criticizing Morey's effort to allow voting in Hong Kong.[24]

The whole affair exposed a darkly hilarious truth: the NBA and its stars felt duty-bound to criticize America's president and judicial system but considered it beyond the pale to criticize China's.

It sounds great to some people when woke capitalists support causes they like, like BLM, but the bottom line is always there, right beneath the surface, dictating which causes a stakeholder capitalist supports. And what's worse is that foreign authoritarian nations understand the weaknesses of America's new stakeholder model far better than America does and ruthlessly leverage their stakeholder status to selectively determine which causes the woke capitalists throw their weight behind. The NBA can put "Black Lives Matter" on all its courts because the CCP isn't threatened by that message. But the Communist Party would never allow the NBA or any of its employees to breathe a word in support of Hong Kong, Taiwan, or the Uighurs.

That imbalance lends a silent moral authority to all the CCP's oppressive acts: *the people who are known for criticizing injustice never criticize it*. China could invade Taiwan tomorrow with all those assault ships it's been building and the NBA would act like nothing happened.

So would Disney. After all, Disney wasn't bothered by all those concentration camps in Xinjiang. It got to film *Mulan* there. In the movie's credits, it thanked the CCP's propaganda bureau in Xinjiang for its assistance.[25] Meanwhile, back at home, Disney's CEO said it would be "very difficult" for Disney to film movies in Georgia if it implemented a new abortion ban because people wouldn't want to work there.[26] It's tough to render Disney's decisions consistent. Maybe Disney's fine with forced sterilization but it'd draw the line if the CCP forbade abortions.

That was far from the first time Disney had abased itself to appease the CCP's dictatorial tendencies. Before *Mulan*, Disney was worried about getting *Dr. Strange* approved in the lucrative Chinese market. The problem? The Ancient One, a prominent character in the comics, was a Tibetan monk. As with Taiwan, China thinks Tibet is part of China and Tibet does not. Disney cut this Gordian knot by making the Ancient One white.

Woke critics then howled that Disney had committed the cardinal sin of whitewashing by making an Asian character a white one. But they missed the real move: making a *Tibetan* character a white one. Disney had cunningly juked controversy with the CCP by inviting a woke controversy instead. As it turns out, woke activists are more easily appeased: to mollify them, Disney made the Tibetan monk a woman instead of a man, casting popular actress Tilda Swinton in the role.

This isn't my take on things; it comes straight from C. Robert Cargill, the screenwriter of *Dr. Strange*.[27] White-woman-washing the Ancient One was good for China, good for Disney, and good for feminism—really, it was good for everyone but Tibet.

Wokenomics whitewashes the abuses of dictators abroad while condemning actions of government at home. And that makes the US less safe. Implicit in all this corporate doublespeak from companies like Disney and the NBA is a mechanism to elevate the moral standing of China as compared to the US on the global stage. The moral standing of the United States is one of our greatest competitive advantages on the global stage. Autocratic dictatorships like China know this well and are now able to implicitly use their power over multinational corporations and the rise of woke capitalism as a tool to chip away at that advantage. Over the long run, that weakens the geopolitical standing of the US by creating a false moral equivalence to China, even though there is no comparison between how, say, black people are treated in America as compared to how Uighurs are treated in China. Xi Jinping himself took advantage of this: when European officials criticized him for China's treatment of the Uighurs, he smoothly pivoted to pointing out how the BLM movement shows US human rights problems.[28] In March 2021, Chinese diplomat Yang Jiechi followed suit at the US–China summit in Alaska when he falsely claimed that black Americans were being "slaughtered"[29] and that "We hope that the United States will do better on human rights."[30]

There's a special irony to all of this. The only reason that companies like the NBA or Disney are able to criticize social injustices in the US—even those that pale in comparison to day-to-day reality in China—is because our liberal democracy *permits* them to. By contrast, China imprisons those who publicly dissent against the CCP and would punish corporations that fail to follow its party line. Yet paradoxically, that has empowered the CCP to co-opt American companies to do the CCP's own bidding back home in America. They're turning multinational corporations into Trojan horses to achieve their longer-run geopolitical objectives.

These companies then come back to the US with pent-up moral frustration for what they can't say in China and let off their moral steam back home through the performative acts of woke capitalism. Then when some of the very largest of these corporations find the absence of a single dictatorial overlord back home in the US, they choose to fill that void themselves by *becoming* the dictators who decide what the right moral norms should be. Yet all the while, their real bosses in the true global hierarchy are the *real* dictators in places like China—where the government uses access to the world's second-largest market as a condition to achieve its geopolitical ends.

The American people would never let that happen if they actually knew what was going on. That's what makes stakeholder capitalism so dangerous: it tricks us into allowing large multinational companies—and their dictatorial overlords abroad—to do what we would have never allowed them to do if we knew what was actually happening.

Companies like Airbnb, Disney, and the NBA gain moral clout when they preach about how much they care about stakeholders at home. But then they turn around and use that moral clout to implicitly endorse atrocities abroad when foreign dictators flex their own stakeholder status. That's the key difference between stakeholder and shareholder capitalism: if corporations never gained unearned moral authority to begin with, they couldn't be weaponized so easily by authoritarian stakeholders.

T HE CCP IS the spider at the center of the global web of stakeholder capitalism. This theoretical observation is borne out by the actions of American companies abroad.

For instance, when Google first drafted its code of conduct for employees in 2000, it famously included the line "don't be evil."[31]

Google seems to have quickly forgotten that rule when it went abroad to do business in China. Its initial Chinese search engine enabled censorship by state authorities from 2006 to 2010, but after being the victim of Chinese hacking efforts, Google eventually announced that it would no longer comply with mainland Chinese censorship and relocated to Hong Kong.[32] Upon leaving mainland China, Google tried to make a virtue of necessity, with Sergei Brin speaking out against the "forces of totalitarianism."[33]

That lip service to freedom of speech earned Google applause in the West, but the truth is that the company quickly sought to return to China by any means necessary. Unbeknownst to virtually all of the company's employees, a team of engineers were assigned to work on a search system, code-named Dragonfly, that would require users to log in to perform searches, track their location, and share their data with a Chinese partner that would have "unilateral access" to the data.[34] Terms like "human rights" and "student protest" would be blacklisted. Being evil was back in style. It was only when an internal memo about this project leaked to the *Intercept* and embarrassed the company by revealing the insincerity of its statements about free speech that it quietly shuttered this effort. We'll see if it is revived in the coming years.

Google is just one example among many. Apple, for its part, has removed from its Chinese app store messaging apps that allowed users to bypass government-imposed firewalls and hid the Taiwanese flag emoji from users in Hong Kong and Macau. It has also removed songs from iTunes that reference Tiananmen Square.

It's not just the tech companies that bend over backward for those sweet Chinese profits. As usual, Wall Street has gotten in on the action. *The Wall Street Journal* summed up the situation in an article titled "China has one powerful friend left in the US: Wall

Street."[35] And it turns out the CCP's very best friend on Wall Street is Larry Fink.

BlackRock and Larry Fink, you may remember from earlier in this book, happen to be the poster boys for stakeholder capitalism in the West. Fink's defense of the idea is described in glowing terms in Klaus Schwab's recent book *Stakeholder Capitalism*.[36] Schwab approvingly cites a 2018 letter where Fink writes, "To prosper over time, every company must not only deliver financial performance, but also show how it makes a positive contribution to society."[37]

Wise words indeed. But which society did he mean? To hear *The Wall Street Journal* tell it, Fink is increasingly preoccupied with making a positive contribution to *Chinese* society, often at the expense of American interests. As he put it in a more recent letter to BlackRock shareholders, "I continue to firmly believe China will be one of the biggest opportunities for BlackRock over the long term, both for asset managers and investors."[38] *The Wall Street Journal* says that to pursue this opportunity, Fink had BlackRock throw its weight behind "controversial initiatives championed by Chinese leadership," such as getting Chinese stocks listed on indexes in spite of their questionable bookkeeping practices, opening them up to billions more in investment. Shortly after BlackRock provided its support to the CCP, the CCP returned the favor by approving its application to start a fund in China.[39]

China's not the only dictatorship that loves to use American companies to do its dirty work. Saudi Arabia has also relied on US companies to suppress internal opposition. An episode of a comedy show that featured American comedian Hasan Minhaj criticizing the Saudi Crown Prince for the murder of Khashoggi was removed from Netflix at the request of the regime.[40] The Saudis have done more than just remove offensive content; they've also used US companies to remove the offenders.

The "Social Responsibility" page for the elite consulting firm McKinsey & Company states, "Our purpose as a firm is to help create positive, enduring change in the world" and mentions the importance of "empowering our people to give back to their communities, operating our firm in ways that are socially responsible and environmentally sustainable, and working with our clients to intentionally address societal challenges."[41] The Saudi government is one of McKinsey's clients, and one of the Saudi government's societal challenges is dissent. According to a recent *New Yorker* article, "McKinsey . . . prepared a report [quantifying] public perception of . . . Saudi economic policies [that identified the] three individuals driving [the bulk of the] negative coverage on Twitter: a . . . writer in Saudi Arabia named Khalid al-Alkami, a dissident . . . in Canada named Omar Abdulaziz, and [a third] anonymous [account.]" McKinsey's research proved useful for the regime, and they went out of their way to *intentionally address* the issue: "Al-Alkami was arrested . . . Abdulaziz's brothers living in Saudi Arabia were put in prison[, and the] anonymous Twitter [channel] was shut down."[42]

If authoritarian regimes were only interested in suppressing dissent internally, that would be bad enough, but again and again they have sought to pressure American corporations to restrict the speech of employees in the US critical of the Chinese government. Witness what happened to Daryl Morey when he supported pro-democracy protestors in Hong Kong.

Hollywood is no exception to this obeisance. Casting decisions, content, dialogue, and plotlines are increasingly edited to appease censors in Beijing. The sequel to *Top Gun*, expected to be released in 2021, provides an illustrative example. In the original film, Tom Cruise wears a leather bomber jacket that belonged to his late father. The jacket has patches from his dad's US Navy tours and includes flags from allies including Taiwan and Japan. For the sequel, those politically problematic flags were removed from the jacket.[43] So much for being a maverick.

Remember Disney's note publicly thanking the CCP's propaganda department for helping it film *Mulan* in Xinjiang?[44] That would be analogous to a note at the end of Disney's 1941 film Dumbo thanking the local Reich Main Security Office in Theresienstadt and the Reich Ministry of Public Enlightenment and Propaganda in the Sudetenland for their assistance. Mickey Mouse always says thank you for his cheese. Incidentally, Disney's recent collaboration with the authorities in Xinjiang does not appear in Disney's most recent Corporate Social Responsibility report.[45]

The more we go woke, the easier it becomes for countries like China to co-opt woke methods to serve their own ends. Consider one product of wokeness on college campuses in recent years: the emergence of "trigger warnings" to students before being exposed to ideas that may challenge their presuppositions on social questions like race, gender, or climate change. It turns out that China took note of the effectiveness of this woke movement. In 2020, based on a new Chinese law, top universities including Harvard and Princeton have begun to label certain courses with a warning label if they teach any material that China may consider sensitive.[46] And there is a growing list of subjects that Beijing considers to be off-limits. In response, at Princeton, students in a Chinese politics class now use codes instead of names on their essays to protect their identities.

At Amherst College, one professor is shifting to anonymous online chats so students can speak freely. Harvard Business School now excuses students from discussing politically sensitive topics relevant to China if they are worried about the risks of doing so: while class participation is normally an element of students' grades, if amnesty is put in place for political reasons, students won't be penalized for opting out.

The new law in China that prompted these changes is one that bars what it calls "sedition, subversion, terrorism, and colluding with foreign forces." Chinese authorities have made clear that this law applies not only within China but also in Hong Kong and now even outside Hong Kong, including in the US. What's striking is that the same approach used by woke activists to constrain the scope of acceptable speech—like trigger warnings in college course catalogs—is now being copied by the Chinese Communist Party at the very same institutions. Woke activists and Chinese autocrats may make for strange bedfellows, but they are increasingly using the same methods in the very same places. Ibram Kendi and Xi Jinping both have an alarmingly similar effect on what can and can't be said at US companies or universities.

What struck me most was how fear-inspiring China has become even among America's otherwise fearless icons. In 2020, I had a chance to participate in a group dialogue with John McEnroe during the US Open. McEnroe was without doubt a legendary tennis champion, but there are many players who have won more Grand Slam titles than McEnroe did. You don't have to be a tennis fan to know that John McEnroe is never afraid to speak his mind. He used to curse at umpires as a player; today, while serving as a commentator on ESPN, he is unafraid to say things that often offend other tennis players and make his fellow commentators cringe.

During the US Open, the tournament organization made a decision to conform to the NBA's approach by creating visible signs in the stadium to support the "Black Lives Matter" movement—in solidarity with the black community following the death of George Floyd. Yet unlike the NBA or NFL, the Association of Tennis Players (ATP) is a truly global professional league. At the time, I wondered whether the ATP's step of promulgating social values in the United States would continue when it hosted tournaments in the Middle East or China, where human rights abuses go far beyond anything we've seen in the United States in nearly two centuries. So I decided to ask the one guy who I expected would give me a straight answer: John McEnroe. Yet even he demurred. "That's a big question, a loaded question," he said in response. "I'm glad the sport is able to have a positive impact, and those are big questions, about China and the Middle East. I'm so proud of the impact that tennis has had around the world." And that was it. If even John McEnroe feared the CCP, I knew there was something to worry about.

China and Saudi Arabia have cracked the code of stakeholder capitalism. They've realized a simple truth, the same one I learned years ago during my summer at Goldman Sachs: whoever has the gold makes the rules. But it used to be that those rules were limited to financial transactions. Thanks to woke capitalism, the rules of morality itself are now up for sale. You won't find a bigger, more powerful stakeholder than a wealthy authoritarian government, and they're always ready to buy your silence. Under the old shareholder model, American corporations might still prostrate themselves at the feet of dictators to make a buck. But they wouldn't get to come out of it smelling like a rose. We'd all see them as the money grubbers they were and judge them accordingly. But stakeholder capitalism gives us the worst of both worlds: woke capitalists in America get to make money with their dictator buddies abroad and act like they're saving the world back home.

T HE PUBLIC OUTRAGE from the business community about Khashoggi's assassination was short-lived. US companies' condemnations of the murder were motivated by the acute demands of social justice activists. But those demands were fleeting as the activists eventually found other causes to champion. The initial fever pitch gradually gave way to silence. And the cost-benefit analysis for multinational corporations tipped back in favor of monarchical deference. Fund managers and corporate executives gradually went back to doing business in Saudi Arabia just as they had done before. Richard Branson had rejected the proposed Saudi investment in Virgin Galactic in 2018, but by the next fall his affiliated company Virgin Hyperloop was doing business in Saudi Arabia again. Indeed, in 2019, Virgin Hyperloop's CEO said it was "delighted" to return to the Future Investment Initiative conference, which Branson had boycotted only a year prior. Uber CEO Dara Khosrowshahi retreated from his initially critical stance in 2018. During a November 2019 interview, he said the murder of Khashoggi was "a mistake" but that Uber had "made mistakes too, with self-driving"—drawing an equivalence between a targeted assassination of a journalist and a pedestrian accident involving a self-driving car.[47] McKinsey & Company went back to charging a small fortune for advising clients on how to do business in the Kingdom of Saudi Arabia. The cottage industry built around opening up personal connections in the Middle East was soon humming once again.

To be sure, most business leaders still haven't forgotten about the Khashoggi episode. In private, they'll admit that they are personally more timid about traveling to Saudi Arabia and a tad bit more afraid for their own safety. For those few who do still personally travel to the region, they're much more mindful of what they say.

The real world is complicated. Personally I don't plan on visiting the Royal Palace again, but I did learn something during my visit to the palace in 2017 that stuck with me ever since then. When the Crown Prince spoke to a small group of us in a conference room that day, he was well aware that many people viewed him skeptically for making unprecedentedly large venture investments into massively unprofitable companies with big dreams for the future.

"Some people think it is foolish to invest such vast sums because that means that more money will chase fewer opportunities, which means that investment returns will go down," he said. The monarch was correct about what others thought back then. His combination of financial acumen, nuance, and self-awareness impressed me. "But I see it differently," he continued. "My view is that the sheer size of our investments will *create* new opportunities that otherwise would not exist without us. And that's why we'll make the most money in the end."

It will be another decade or so before we know whether the Crown Prince's prediction was correct. So far, he's doing pretty well. MBS understood something about the relationship between long-term investment and innovation that most ordinary fund managers do not: patience pays, and betting big is a competitive advantage.

My own experience as an entrepreneur suggests that his remarks were spot-on. At the time my company accepted the billion-dollar check from the fund in which the Saudis had invested, we had yet to complete a Phase 3 trial for any of the drugs in our pipeline. The first drug to complete Phase 3 was a high-profile, high-risk, high-reward bet to develop the first new treatment for Alzheimer's disease in over a generation. It was deeply personal for me—my mother was a geriatric psychiatrist who dedicated her life to treating Alzheimer's patients in nursing homes, and one of my grandmother's sisters in Vadakanchery had died of Alzheimer's disease. It was important to our business and to the world if it succeeded. But in the end, that trial ended in spectacular failure, just like every other valiant attempt in the field by other companies, large and small.

Unlike those larger pharma enterprises, a high-profile clinical trial failure for a young biotech startup usually spells the end of the road. Yet my vision—and, mercifully, that of my investors too—had been to create an engine that produced many drugs over the long run, not just one. That meant enduring failure along the way. With a billion-dollar investment in hand, I had a chance to realize that longer-term vision: no single clinical trial was going to make or break the company. The Alzheimer's failure was painful, but thanks to the massive capital investment, it wasn't existential.

Our next Phase 3 trial was for an overactive bladder treatment—one that also affected elderly patients. It was a less serious disease than Alzheimer's, but it mattered to the people who had it, most of whom were also elderly. I was prepared for another failure, but thankfully it was a resounding success. The next trial was for a drug to treat uterine fibroids. That one succeeded too, and so did the one after in endometriosis. And then we flipped over an unexpectedly positive card on our Phase 3 study in prostate cancer in late 2019 and then once again for a pair of Phase 3 studies in psoriasis the following year. All told, out of the nine Phase 3 trials spawned by my company, the first one was an epic failure, but the next eight were unambiguous successes.

In retrospect, that billion-dollar check in 2017 made all the difference. It was the difference between playing the lottery and playing the long game. It was quite possibly the difference between having a company and not having one at all. Running out of cash is a biotech company's equivalent of getting chopped up with a bone saw. Capital is what kept my company's blood flowing rather than spilling. Patients around the world will be better off for it. A good story usually ends with a neat lesson, but I'm not sure that this one does.

CHAPTER 9

The Silicon Leviathan

B IG CORPORATIONS AREN'T JUST BECOMING the flunkies of dictators abroad. They're learning from those autocrats, and then they're becoming dictators in their own right back here at home.

A friend shared a striking story with me from his time at Facebook over a decade ago. He was in a closed-door meeting led by Chamath Palihapitiya, Facebook's executive in charge of its growth strategy at the time. Chamath asked the question of what it would take for Facebook to achieve *sovereignty*—and raised the possibility of eventually having a Facebook militia. Not an allegorical militia like a sales force for selling its ads, but an actual armed militia. The idea that this would even cross the mind of one of Silicon Valley's titans is downright frightening.

Chamath subsequently left Facebook and went on to found a firm called Social Capital, a new woke venture capital fund whose mission is to "advance humanity." He's built a sterling reputation for himself by publicly criticizing social media companies for "ripping apart society" while becoming a part owner of the Golden State Warriors and a Silicon Valley celebrity on the back of his appreciated ownership in Facebook.[1] I haven't heard him publicly float his onetime idea about starting a private militia for Facebook . . . not a great look for a newly woke capitalist.

While doing research for this book, I was struck to learn that the Dutch East India Company once wielded its own militia, behaving as though it were a sovereign entity in its own right. It also had its own currency—not dissimilar from the cryptocurrency that Facebook wanted to launch. Today Silicon Valley represents the reincarnation of the Dutch East India Company in the twenty-first century—except this time firmly on American soil, after its companies sidestepped the safeguards in our system that were designed to protect against exactly that result. Like its predecessor in the Old World, Big Tech has gradually grown into a corporate monster, though the giant slept until recently.

Today, over two centuries after the birth of the American corporation, that corporate monster has finally emerged from its slumber. Over the last decade, the monster has quietly escaped the cage of capitalism. It now roams freely over all terrains of American life. And in 2020, the monster finally pounced on its most prized prey: American democracy itself.

Its attack was as staggering as it was sudden. Silicon Valley's titans restricted debates between ordinary Americans, just as monarchs like MBS do in Saudi Arabia. They appointed themselves as the sole arbiters of truth in science and silenced dissent, just as the CCP does in China. They banished century-old newspapers. They interfered in our elections in unprecedented ways.

During widespread state-imposed lockdowns during the pandemic, YouTube (owned by Google's parent company Alphabet) banned videos that were critical of COVID-19-related policies, including content posted by medical professionals arguing that lockdowns were excessive or unnecessary. Its stated justification? To remove "medically unsubstantiated" content in favor of facts from "authoritative" sources. According to YouTube CEO Susan Wojcicki, "anything that would go against World Health Organization recommendations would be a violation of our policy."[2] In early 2021, YouTube did the same thing by censoring the Senate testimony of a doctor who made the medical case for ivermectin, a little-known tropical medicine, to treat severe COVID-19 patients, with no explanation other than to say it violated its misinformation policy. Apparently it was good enough for the US Senate to hear but not for the American people to hear. The list of examples of YouTube's censorship continues to grow each day.

Its approach is flawed on multiple levels. First, it wrongly conflates empirical fact-finding with normative policy-making. Facts are important inputs to making sound policy decisions, but facts and policy judgments are not the same thing. It's one thing for someone to wrongly assert that bandanas were more effective than N95 masks in preventing person-to-person transmission of the coronavirus. It's another matter entirely to treat anti-lockdown arguments as though those arguments themselves are incorrect "facts." Whether a lockdown of certain businesses to prevent the coronavirus from spreading is the right policy isn't a matter of "fact" or "science." It's a policy judgment, and the best policy may vary depending on what the business is, where it is, and myriad other factors. The lifeblood of our democracy is open debate about our public policies. Whether to implement lockdowns to stop the spread of COVID-19 was one of the most important public policy debates of 2020. Treating policy judgments as though they're "facts" is a threat to democracy.

There's another problem. Using the WHO as a single source of truth is dangerous to science—and to public health too. We now know that the WHO had reason to believe in December 2019, when Taiwan sent an emergency message to WHO leadership about a respiratory disease from China, that SARS-CoV-2 was contagious between humans. Yet the WHO does not recognize Taiwan due to pressure from China. The world suffered greatly as a consequence: the next month, the WHO echoed the claims of the Chinese Communist Party that there was no evidence of human-to-human transmission of the virus. An injustice somewhere became a pandemic everywhere.

Under its stated standard, YouTube would've banned any videos in January 2020 that claimed that human-to-human transmission of COVID-19 *was* possible, given the official WHO stance at the time. In retrospect, that was arguably the most dangerous lie about public health in modern history.

As of this writing, the issue remains relevant to other scientific debates surrounding COVID-19 as well. In the spring of 2020, the FDA approved a drug called remdesivir, which it says shortens the duration of hospital stays for patients with severe COVID-19. Tens of thousands of patients hospitalized in the United States went on to receive remdesivir, including one of my family members. Yet the WHO conducted its own analysis and found that remdesivir offered little to no medical benefit. Does this mean that YouTube would ban advertisements for remdesivir from Gilead Sciences, the pharmaceutical company that markets it? Or take down academic presentations from physicians who find a medical benefit? Its decisions to censor doctors testifying about ivermectin while permitting presentations about remdesivir seem arbitrary at best.

YouTube is hardly alone in its transgressions. Last summer, Facebook banned anti-vaccination advertisements and posts that were critical of lockdowns and mandatory mask orders. To discern real science from fake science, Facebook adopted a fact-checking program with "independent, third-party fact-checking organizations" certified through the "International Fact-Checking Network."[3] Inappropriate content, as determined by this fact-checker politburo, was either labeled as misinformation, deprioritized, or removed. To further sanitize the ideas that circulate on its platform, Facebook employed a "Hate-Speech Engineering" team to devise complex machine learning algorithms that discern between palatable content to promote to the top of users' newsfeeds and "borderline content" to be down-ranked and relegated to the bottom. The idea cleanse is now complete—all the while unnoticed and barely detectable as users mindlessly scroll down the page.[4]

Of course, the main objective of these large technology titans wasn't really the pursuit of science at all. It was partly about financial self-interest. Large publicly traded technology companies, as of this writing, have added over a trillion dollars of market capitalization since the start of the pandemic in early 2020—an order of magnitude more than the GDP of most nations in the same period. Why? Because lockdowns meant more people decided to get their groceries on Amazon rather than go to the local store, because more people were able to meet via Zoom rather than travel to a conference, and because more people chose to subscribe to Netflix rather than go to a movie theater. Meanwhile, small businesses across America suffered for the very same reason. It's no wonder that Big Tech stacked the decks of public debate to favor lockdowns, even as in retrospect we find these policies were of dubious value in preventing the spread of COVID-19 while markedly effective in spreading economic calamity.

Yet as tempting as it might be to pin all of this to the economic self-interest of large tech companies, that's just an asterisk compared to the real story—the pursuit of a monolithic political agenda. In modern Silicon Valley, money isn't even the main motivator anymore. That's where woke Silicon Valley today differs from woke Wall Street. The Valley's titans have more money than either you or they can imagine. Now they're after raw power.

Mailchimp, the bulk email marketing platform, refused service to the Northern Virginia Tea Party, citing that the group was spreading "potentially harmful misinformation." The company also suspended an account associated with the conservative grassroots organization Engage the Right for "hate speech."[5] PayPal removed accounts belonging to certain conservative customers, a practice the payments processor has long been accused of by "right-wing" and "far-right" groups.[6]

Vacation rental service Airbnb banned Ronald Gaudier, a self-proclaimed "Proud Boy," after an anonymous group on Twitter asked whether "members of white supremacist hate groups" were allowed to use the platform. These tweets were in response to a post from Gaudier announcing that he would be attending a pro-Trump rally in DC and inviting like-minded individuals to join him at his rental apartment. Airbnb found the reservation, canceled it, and banned Gaudier indefinitely—and tweeted that members of "hate groups" weren't welcome on its platform.[7] The arbiter of who counted as a "hate group" was, of course, Airbnb itself.

The behaviors became even less veiled as the election neared. Just a week before the final ballots were cast, Expensify—an expense management software firm in Silicon Valley—sent a 1,300-word email to the company's base of 10 million customers urging them to vote for Biden because its CEO was worried about America being able to survive another term of Trump's presidency. The email assumed a vaguely threatening tone, suggesting that a vote for anyone other than Joe Biden, including a vote for a third-party candidate, meant that you were "comfortable standing aside and allowing democracy to be methodically dismantled, in plain sight."[8]

I recently met David Barrett, the company's CEO, and I asked him whether he worried that CEOs like himself might actually pose the greater threat to the integrity of democracy. I expressed my view that our democracy worked according to a one person, one vote principle and that CEOs shouldn't have a greater voice in our democracy just because they run companies. His response: "I don't fucking care." He used the word "fuck" or "fucking" too many times for me to fully grasp the actual points he was making, if there were indeed any coherent points at all. When I tried to ask him if Expensify would bar customers who supported Trump, he pointed me to their policy barring hate groups and said that he would follow the definition adopted by the Southern Poverty Law Center.*

The message sent by powerful technology firms to the American people was crystal clear. If you dare to do things like, say, transfer money, submit an expense report, rent a home, or *send an*

---

* As a side note, the Southern Poverty Law Center is an entirely separate racket in its own right—a convenient front for the woke corporations that fund it—today a nonprofit whose endowment exceeds $200 million and whose expenditures on fundraising dwarf those of normal nonprofits. A nonprofit that spends a ton of money on *fundraising* is the charitable world's equivalent of a Ponzi scheme—an ideological one run by woke capitalists in the name of social justice. See Ben Schreckinger, "Has a Civil Rights Stalwart Lost Its Way?," Politico, July/August 2017, www.politico.com/magazine/story/2017/06/28/morris-dees-splc-trump-southern-poverty-law-center-215312.

email, you better have the right political views and be on the right side of politics . . . as determined, of course, by Silicon Valley itself.

As the gatekeeper to the internet itself, no company was better positioned to implement those political values than Google. In the summer of 2020, ahead of the election a curious trend emerged. In the first half of the year, individual clicks and impressions of the conservative news website *Breitbart News* resulting from Google searches for "Joe Biden" were steadily high. But suddenly, starting in the middle of the year, activity on *Breitbart* from the same search terms took a nosedive.[9] Why did this happen? As it turns out, Google had allegedly kept a "blacklist" of "right-wing" conservative websites and news outlets to be suppressed from its search results.[10] *Breitbart* was on the list.

Dr. Robert Epstein, a renowned psychologist and researcher and a Democrat, is a longtime expert on deceptive business practices by Big Tech companies and a personally motivated Google critic.[11] In 2019, Dr. Epstein testified before the Senate Judiciary Committee and claimed that Google could manipulate "upwards of 15 million votes" in the upcoming 2020 election without anyone knowing they were manipulated and without leaving a trace.[12] Ahead of the election, Dr. Epstein's team of 733 field agents were deployed in three key swing states. They preserved approximately 500,000 ephemeral online experiences and found that Google search results were strongly biased in favor of liberals. While bias was shown to every group in Google searches, conservatives were shown slightly *greater* liberal bias in their search results.[13]

Having already censored users and websites with impunity, social media giants then took the next major leap—censoring *articles* published by major newspapers. In the weeks leading up to the 2020 presidential election, the *New York Post* ran an article featuring Hunter Biden, son of Joe Biden. The article detailed the younger Biden's business dealings in Ukraine, purportedly trading favors on his father's name while the elder Biden was vice president. As evidence, the article featured email exchanges involving Hunter and a senior executive of Burisma, a Ukrainian oil company. The emails showed that Hunter, then a member of Burisma's board, was made aware of political and legal pressure inflicted on the company by the Ukrainian government. According to the emails, Hunter allegedly brokered a meeting between the executive and his father after being asked how he "could use his influence" on the company's behalf.

Contrary to reports that Joe Biden wasn't involved in Hunter Biden's business dealings, Tony Bobulinski, a former business associate of Hunter Biden, eventually stepped forward. In a live TV interview with Tucker Carlson, Bobulinski presented text messages that appeared to refer to Joe Biden as the "Chairman" and suggested that he often weighed in on business transactions.[14] When asked to comment on the *New York Post* story, the Biden campaign declined to deny the accuracy of the story. The Biden campaign and family also didn't dispute Tony Bobulinski's allegations.

Whether or not the story was actually true is a separate question. I certainly don't know. Neither does Mark Zuckerberg or Jack Dorsey. It is noteworthy that after Biden had won the election, the news quietly came out that the DOJ had been investigating Hunter Biden.[15]

Regardless, factual disputes like these are a feature of modern politics. The general public weighs different pieces of information from various sources, listens to the candidates, and then makes an electoral decision. That's how democracy *works*.

Yet in 2020 that process was corrupted: Big Tech quickly

stepped in to suppress the Hunter Biden story and muzzled anyone who dared to probe further. Shockingly, Twitter decided to ban *any* of its users from sharing even a link to that article on its platform. It prevented individual users from sending that link to one another via private messages, taking the dramatic step of intervening even in nonpublic one-on-one communications.

Worst of all, *Twitter froze the entire account of the New York Post altogether.* A twenty-first-century Silicon Valley giant, run by a multibillionaire bearded self-fashioned Buddhist guru, single-handedly censored America's fourth largest newspaper by circulation, an institution that had been founded over two centuries ago by Alexander Hamilton. Twitter also suspended the *personal* accounts of certain editors and journalists who worked at the newspaper.

Facebook quickly followed suit and also decided to limit the distribution of the Hunter Biden article. Together, Facebook and Twitter comprise the two biggest social media platforms—and both of them effectively decided what information was made available for the American electorate in advance of an election. That's particularly arresting when it involved a story about one of the two candidates in the election—and, in retrospect, the one who emerged as the winner.

During Senate testimony in response to a probe surrounding these issues, Twitter CEO Jack Dorsey feigned humility, effectively saying "we screwed up" with respect to the company's handling of the *New York Post's* Hunter Biden story. Dorsey claimed that blocking the article was in accordance with Twitter's policies with respect to materials obtained through hacking while expressing contrition for making a hasty decision without sufficient evidence.[16] Mark Zuckerberg was similarly self-critical.

But don't be fooled by their practiced vulnerability. Was it merely a coincidence that Facebook and Twitter adopted the exact same policies with the exact same political effect at the exact same time? Nope. This wasn't a case of two bumbling gentle giants that simply couldn't get out of their own way. It was a case of nefarious coordination.

Silicon Valley's chokehold over our marketplace of ideas is fundamentally different in kind from the scammy kind of woke capitalism, what I like to call "Corporate Social Irresponsibility" or CSI. CSI is fundamentally about *inauthenticity*. It's about using trendy social values as a trick to generate more profits. "Profit" became a bad word after the 2008 financial crisis; greed was no longer good. CSI was just the natural response of corporations—creating a new narrative of social purpose to disguise their old-school greed.

The social causes simply serve as a form of reputational laundering for those same companies' profit-seeking. That's what most Wall Street banks and big pharma companies do today, for example. It's Goldman Sachs preaching about diversity so it can be at the front of the line for the next government bailout. It's AstraZeneca waxing eloquent about climate change so it can secure multibillion-dollar government contracts for vaccine production. It's State Street building feminist statues to detract attention from wage discrimination lawsuits from female employees, all the while marketing its exchange-traded fund with the ticker "SHE." It's Chamath Palihapitiya founding a social impact investment fund and criticizing Silicon Valley, even though he and his wealth are products of Silicon Valley, all to cover up for his prior tenure as an executive at Facebook who dreamed out loud about a private corporate military. Those companies and people use their market power to prop up woke causes as a way to accumulate greater political capital—only to later come back and cash in that political capital for more dollars.

To be sure, CSI is itself toxic for American democracy. It causes Americans and our government to vest too much trust in these corporations, only to later be scammed by them for an extra buck at a later date, in one form or another.

But what we see today from Silicon Valley is something different altogether. Twitter and Facebook weren't just distracting the public from their profitable cash-generating machines when they intervened in the 2020 presidential election in the sweeping ways that they did. They weren't just practicing CSI. Rather, their interventions were actually about legislating the value system and set of beliefs of their leaders—rendering our democratic process irrelevant.

Why? For most Americans, the rate limiter for what they can buy is the amount of money that they have. But for multibillionaires like Zuckerberg and Dorsey, the rate limiter is different. It's not the amount of money they have, since that's effectively infinite. Rather, it's the limitation on *the scope of what money itself can buy*. For a working-class family, a normal struggle might be how to save up to buy a house or a new car. For Zuckerberg and Dorsey, their struggle is different: it's to figure out how money itself can buy more things, since they already have a limitless supply of it.

This may be more authentic than the scammy kind of woke capitalism that I described earlier. But it's even more dangerous. And it's also worse than the crude monopolistic pricing practices used in prior centuries by robber barons such as John D. Rockefeller and Andrew Carnegie. This expansive new form of woke capitalism poses the greatest long-run threat of all to American democracy itself.

Worst of all, Big Tech today is keenly aware of brewing populist ire against its tyrannical practices. And it has discovered the perfect lightning rod for that ire: antitrust law.

If that sounds confusing, you're right: antitrust law was supposed to be the government's stick against big business. But for Silicon Valley, antitrust law is a mousetrap—one that politicians on both sides are falling right into. Right-wing populists like Josh Hawley as well as liberals like David Cicilline wrongly view antitrust law as the *solution* to the problem of the growing power of today's tech titans, just as it was used to rein in the classical robber barons in prior centuries.

But they're wrong. There's a tactic in warfare known as "feigned retreat," in which one side leads another to a destination that's actually a trap. That's exactly what Big Tech is doing to lawmakers and the Justice Department's antitrust division today. And it's playing politicians on both sides by acting frightened of antitrust.

Here's why. Antitrust law was designed to protect consumers from monopolies and cartels that use market power to limit consumer choice and charge higher prices. But today's Big Tech titans—companies like Apple, Microsoft, Google, Facebook, and Amazon—provide consumers with a wider range of products than ever before and for strikingly low prices. Facebook, Twitter, and Google are all free for users. Consumers can find pretty much anything they want on Amazon or at the Apple iTunes store. That's why tech CEOs ran circles around the House Judiciary Committee's Antitrust Subcommittee in hearings in August 2020. They'll likely do the same thing in court if they're charged with antitrust violations.

The real catch is this: the same companies that have improved consumer access and lowered the prices of technology are also the ones limiting options in the marketplace of ideas and raising the "cost" of ideological dissent. That's not the classical antitrust violation of price-fixing. It's what I call "idea-fixing."

Antitrust law was designed to protect consumers from companies who abuse their market power to beget more market power. That was a distinctly nineteenth-century problem. But that's *not* the main problem with Silicon Valley's behavior today. The issue today centers on companies abusing their market power to beget greater social, cultural, and political power. The main victim isn't the consumer in the market; it's the citizen in our democracy. Neither the original antitrust statutes like the Sherman Act nor the revisionist judicial logic of more recent antitrust scholars like Robert Bork was designed or equipped to tackle this uniquely twenty-first-century conundrum. That leads to a classical error made by professional politicians: using yesterday's toolkit to fight today's problems.

There's a children's story about a character called Br'er Rabbit who pleads "please don't throw me into that briar patch!" to get a predator to throw him in one so he can escape. Big Tech's just saying "please don't throw me into that antitrust investigation!" so it can point to its low prices and escape having its idea-fixing regulated.

The rise of Wokenomics consummates Silicon Valley's coup over our democracy. Censorship becomes rebranded as social responsibility. Refusing to run ads is praised as a form of corporate restraint. Yet the stakeholderist cheerleaders miss the bigger point: companies like Facebook and Google have effectively assumed the role of the state itself and have further expanded that role to regulating and censoring public opinions in ways that no governmental actor can. Their exercise of power over the content of public discourse is without precedent in human history.

In 1924, US Secretary of Commerce and future US President Herbert Hoover contended: "It cannot be thought that any single person or group shall ever have the right to determine what communication may be made to the American people . . . We cannot allow any single person or group to place themselves in the position where they can censor the material which shall be broadcasted to the public."[17]

He was prescient yet wrong. Less than a century later, Silicon Valley does exactly as Hoover feared but on a scale he could not have imagined. In the lead-up to the 2020 presidential election, President Hoover surely did a few backflips in his grave.

But he certainly did a few more backflips in the months *following* the presidential election. Consider what happened in January 2021 in the aftermath of the Capitol riot. A deplorable and disgraceful assault on our democratic process by misguided rioters in Washington, D.C., was met in kind with Big Tech's deliberate and coordinated assault on personal freedoms.

Just as the military-industrial complex seized on 9/11 to implement a permanent new surveillance state beginning in the early 2000s, the newly ascendant woke-industrial complex in America seized on January 6 to do something similar. Based on tenuous charges of "incitement to violence" and "hate speech," Facebook[18] and Twitter[19] banned, suspended, and removed accounts associated with Donald Trump, the sitting US president, including the official White House and the official POTUS Twitter accounts. To top it off, Facebook enacted a new policy in March 2021 that it would not only block President Trump from accessing his own account but also prohibit *anyone* from posting a video "in the voice of President Trump"—more reminiscent of Orwellian fiction than American reality[20].

To make matters worse, the week after suspending President Trump indefinitely, Facebook resorted to its preferred remedy: an "independent" committee. Facebook appeared to delegate all responsibility for the Trump suspension to the Oversight Board—that is, an "independent" group, conveniently founded and funded by Facebook. The Oversight Board will render a decision on whether Trump's suspension will be overturned, a decision that will be binding on Facebook. So, just to clarify: a Facebook-created committee gets to pass judgment on whether Facebook acted appropriately. That's the modern world: the 45th president of the United States is relegated to appealing not to the US Supreme Court but to *Facebook's* Supreme Court in order to communicate via social media.[21] So what did this "Oversight Board" decide? In May 2021, it upheld Trump's ban from Facebook and Instagram (which Facebook owns), but it also criticized Facebook for its "indeterminate and standardless" response. They were applauded for their balanced approach. It was the best of all worlds for Facebook: the Board upheld Facebook's decision in substance, but with that classic jujitsu-like move of self-criticism to confer a veneer of legitimacy to its own actions. It reminded me of a kid in my high school French class who used to cheat by stealing the answer key to every test . . . except he would always intentionally write the wrong answer to just one question each time, as a decoy to prevent him from getting caught.

In an embarrassing public display of conformity, YouTube, Snapchat, Stripe, PayPal, Shopify, and other platforms quickly followed suit with their own Trump bans.[22] Of course, there was no hope for Trump supporters or sympathizers if the 45th president himself wasn't immune to this brazen censorship. Naturally, the accounts of tens of thousands of conservatives also disappeared into the ether—all at the behest of technocratic autocrats like Zuckerberg and Dorsey.

While Americans are supposed to enjoy due process and the presumption of innocence in everyday life, they enjoy no such luxury in their online lives. Today's technology tyrants deploy a censor-first mentality and operate under the principle that certain people are *probably* guilty, that they are *probably* violating the ever-changing "terms and conditions." This approach gives them the license to silence voices with whom they do not agree with. Sure, sometimes that means they get it wrong. So conveniently, whenever they're caught red-handed or the uproar risks being too costly, today's social media giants now have a new refrain: *oops, we just made a "mistake."*

In March 2021, Dorsey testified at another congressional hearing, this time on misinformation and social media. Dorsey admitted that Twitter's ban of the *New York Post's* Hunter Biden story was a "total mistake" while denying that Twitter has a "censoring department."[23] The prior week, on the same day House Democrats introduced a resolution to expel US Representative Marjorie Taylor Greene from Congress, Twitter locked Greene out of her Twitter account for twelve hours by "mistake." Twitter claimed that its algorithm-based rule enforcement mechanisms were to blame for the error.[24] The following month, Twitter made another "mistake" and suspended Congresswoman Greene for the second time in just a few weeks. Her crime? Tweeting "He is risen" on Easter.[25]

But weren't these actions simply limited to white-nationalist, domestic-terrorist lunatics? Didn't they all deserve it for spreading misinformation, stoking violence, and encouraging insurrection? Wrong. In one of its more egregious actions, in January 2021, Facebook blocked access to Dr. Ron Paul—onetime presidential candidate for the Libertarian party, an ob-gyn physician, and one of the greatest advocates for social liberties of Americans. Facebook cited no explanation other than "repeatedly going against our community standards." Paul said he "never received notice of violating community standards and nowhere is the offending post identified."[26] Curiously, these "errors" are consistently limited to one side of the political spectrum.

The scariest fact of all is the way that most people uncritically accept these companies' judgments at face value, even when the companies later admit they were wrong. Immediately after Ron Paul was locked out of his Facebook account, here's what the founder of another multibillion-dollar health-care company emailed me: "I guarantee you Ron Paul's account was locked because he was saying something insanely inaccurate and unsafe about coronavirus." Of course, he didn't bother emailing me afterward once Facebook said it was an error. People said similar things about Marjorie Taylor Greene too, and I doubt they noticed Twitter's subsequent correction. In both cases, the damage was already done. And even worse, these incidents reveal just how much everyday Americans trust these behemoths.

Errors or not, this broad wave of deplatforming didn't just happen to prominent politicians, who at least had other avenues for voicing their grievances. It happened to ordinary Americans too, in shocking numbers. The message was clear: comply or we'll shut you up, *permanently*. It was nothing short of a Soviet-style purge of political dissent.

Well, doesn't the free market provide a solution? It did, at least for a hot second, in the form of Parler, a Twitter alternative popular with conservatives. Unlike Big Tech social media incumbents, Parler didn't harvest user data and didn't regulate political content. Instead, Parler set out to value, of all things, free speech and open dialogue. Parler was . . . earnest.

Ultimately it paid a hefty price for its naivete. Following the Capitol riot, Parler was blocked from being downloaded from

Google's Play Store, was suspended from Apple's App Store, and lost access to Amazon Web Services—all based on hackneyed allegations similar to those levied against President Trump. Big Tech may permanently put Parler out of business. As it turns out, the free market is no match for the monopoly of ideas.

This isn't about silencing conservatives. That's just how they get you on board with the idea of censorship. But once it becomes acceptable to silence people under the banner of fighting hate speech, whatever speech powerful interests dislike becomes hate speech. Unfortunately, it looks like we've already opened Pandora's box.

I HAD A long call with one of Silicon Valley's most prominent venture capitalists on a Saturday night during the peak of the ideological purge in January 2021. He's served on boards of some of the largest tech giants. He explained to me with alarming clarity that there are about fifty pieces of infrastructure that comprise the modern internet—and that every single one of them, from individual browsers to cloud computing, serves as a node to effectuate political censorship and each could be used to banish defectors from the ideological cartel in the future. In a subsequent text exchange, he called it "*the* issue of our time." Yet despite being a famous jillionaire[27] himself, he was also personally frightened: when I asked him what we could do to stop the tide, he immediately requested that I not cite his name publicly for fear of retribution. He acknowledged that his inability to speak up was a case in point of the underlying problem, but he felt the personal risks to him were just too great.

So I wondered who, or what, would be the next target. If Twitter has a moral obligation to censor misinformation and offensive speech in public tweets and private direct messages, does Google have an obligation (and therefore justification) to censor private emails? Will Verizon say it has a responsibility to stop hate and conspiracy from spreading via text messages? If text messages become fair game, then why not live phone conversations too?

This isn't just a matter of hyperbole. Earlier this year, at the 2021 Game Developers Conference Showcase, Intel revealed new technology that "uses artificial intelligence to get rid of other gamers' hateful and abusive audio chat." The new product is called "Bleep." This piece of software allows users to screen out "White Nationalism," "Aggression," "LGBTQ+ Hate," or "Racism and Xenophobia." But who decides what counts as racist or xenophobic for purposes of training the artificial intelligence algorithms? Of course, Intel Corporation.[28] Is it really such a stretch to believe that this kind of technology couldn't easily be incorporated into our iPhones and email accounts too?

Nowadays, concepts like "racism" and "sexual exploitation" are regularly being used to censor content not just for political reasons but for commercial reasons too. Just look at what happened earlier this year to online chat groups focused on trading stocks.

Early in 2021, a group of traders on a Reddit forum called WallStreetBets realized Wall Street might have made a mistake. As it turns out, hedge funds had short-sold more shares of struggling video game retailer GameStop than actually existed. Short-selling means borrowing a share of a company and then selling it in the market. It's a way of betting against a stock: the short-seller makes money when the share price of a company goes down, allowing the short-seller to buy back the share at a lower price and return it to the lender.

Predictably, short-selling isn't very popular with the public for the same reason that predators and scavengers aren't popular in nature, but in reality they all have proper roles to play in their respective ecosystems: predators prevent rodent infestations, scavengers clean up carcasses, and short-sellers help prevent asset bubbles. That's why I don't think it's inherently bad, as some populists on both the left and the right do.

But like all investors, short-sellers are often wrong: they lose a lot of money when a company's share price goes up. The Reddit crowd realized that if they just bought a ton of GameStop shares, they could drive the price up by so much the short-sellers would be forced to buy shares *at the higher price* to close their positions (that's how the mechanics of short-selling work) and would have to pay whatever price the Reddit guys named.

That's called a "short squeeze," and it worked wonders. GameStop's share price skyrocketed. Hedge funds bled. The hedge fund Melvin Capital, led by onetime star trader Gabe Plotkin, was down over 50 percent in the month of January as a consequence—a staggering loss for a fund of its kind.

It seemed like the Reddit traders had won, but the tide turned in the other direction on January 28: Robinhood, the Reddit crowd's favorite brokerage, prevented all of its users from buying GameStop while *still allowing them to sell*. Robinhood claimed it did that to protect its users, seemingly unaware that when people are allowed to sell a stock but not buy it, it drops. That in turn panicked other retail traders into selling their own shares too.

Robinhood pointed to complicated regulatory reasons about margin requirements for why it had to halt people from buying GameStop. In those rare situations, a brokerage might ordinarily halt trading in a particular stock. But that doesn't explain why they selectively halted just buying activity *while still permitting selling*. I worked at a hedge fund for seven years myself, and I never saw that happen once in my career. At the end of the day, it isn't rocket science: if you prevent people from buying a stock and only permit them to sell, the stock will go down. And that's exactly what happened.

Of course, Reddit traders were still free to use brokerages other than Robinhood to buy stocks if they wanted to—including in a coordinated fashion. But this is where wokeness comes in. Just hours before the Thursday short-selling onslaught, the online chat company Discord shut down a WallStreetBets discussion server with 250,000 members over allegations of "hate speech"— WallStreetBets moderators claimed the entire Discord server was banned because one user had managed to bypass a filter for vulgarity.[29]

Simultaneously, Facebook shut down a 150,000-strong discussion page for Robinhood traders over allegations of "adult sexual exploitation," which it refused to substantiate.[30] It was a ridiculous claim even on its face. So when Robinhood locked them out of buying the next day and GameStop plummeted, the retail traders were left silenced and alone, allowed only to sell. Most of them didn't.

When reporters asked the White House to comment on the GameStop drama, wokeness resurfaced yet again. White House Press Secretary Jen Psaki responded by saying, "I'm happy to repeat that we have the first female Treasury Secretary, and she's monitoring the situation."[31] In other words, we're not gonna answer your question about all that stock stuff, but the important thing to remember is that we've got a female Treasury Secretary out there breaking glass ceilings. You can't make this stuff up.

The really important thing to remember here is that Big Tech's idea-fixing isn't just about silencing conservatives. That's only where it started. But it evolved just weeks later. Corporate America acclimated regular Americans into accepting its censorship by banning "hate speech" from conservatives. Right after that, when stock traders on Reddit and Facebook were saying things it didn't want them to say, it immediately used its newfound power to ban them for "hate speech" and "sexual exploitation" too, even though those things had nothing to do with it. And the purview of the ideological purge continues to expand further every day.

I F SOCIALISTS AND MAGA conservatives agree on anything, it's that the rise of the Silicon Leviathan is a threat to America. This January, following Robinhood's decision to halt its users' ability to buy GameStop shares, lawmakers from across the political spectrum condemned the move and called for hearings into the decision, including staunch conservative Ted Cruz and ultra-liberal Alexandria Ocasio-Cortez. The conservative attorney generals in Texas and the progressive attorney general in New York both initiated inquiries into Robinhood with equal vigor. Even in August 2019, the House Judiciary Antitrust Subcommittee grilled Big Tech CEOs so aggressively that a political layperson couldn't have guessed which participants were Republican and which ones were Democrats.

They disagree only in their diagnosis of the problem. Liberals allege that this grim reality is simply the inevitable outcome of the free market, while classical conservatives say the answer is that we don't have enough competition in the marketplace even though they don't have a coherent account as to why. Who's right? My view: neither.

The real culprit is actually Congress itself. Our federal laws continue to aid and abet the rise of Silicon Valley's behemoths—in the form of unique "corporate privileges" enjoyed by internet companies that have successfully lobbied our lawmakers for competitive advantages that wrongly favored Silicon Valley over the rest of America. The emergence of these corporate monsters isn't a product of capitalism but instead the laws and regulations that are vestiges of crony capitalism.

The most important of these laws is Section 230 of the Communications Decency Act of 1996—which confers a broad shield of legal immunity *specifically* to Silicon Valley titans ("Internet Service Providers") like Facebook and Twitter for all content published on their platforms. Notably, this is a tremendous benefit that ordinary publishers of content don't enjoy—for example, my hometown's newspaper *The Cincinnati Enquirer* or even the publisher of this book (Hachette Book Group). Those who are familiar with this law in Silicon Valley generally agree that companies like Google, Facebook, and Twitter would have never become large-scale behemoths without Section 230. The irony is that they generally cite that fact as an argument in favor of Section 230, not an argument against it.

Before going further, it's worth pausing to note what Section 230 actually says. The law has two key provisions. Section 230(c)(1) says that platforms are *not* to be "treated as the publisher or speaker" of any information provided by their users. This means that if someone tweets something disparaging about you on Twitter, you can sue that person, but you can't sue Twitter. Section 230(c)(2) is the so-called "Good Samaritan" provision, which immunizes platforms from liability for "any action voluntarily taken in good faith to restrict access to or availability of material that the provider or user considers to be obscene, lewd, lascivious, filthy, excessively violent, harassing, or otherwise objectionable, whether or not such material is constitutionally protected."[32] In a nutshell, it's this second part that gives social media companies the power to censor material on their sites.

It's a shield that Silicon Valley's titans use today to regulate content on their websites in ways that go far beyond the scope of what Congress envisioned when it passed the Good Samaritan provision of the statute. According to former US Congressman Chris Cox, Section 230's co-sponsor, the intent of the law was to empower social media companies to do things like prevent children from accessing pornography on the internet.[33] Yet companies like Facebook and Twitter have used that same protection to prevent American adults from reading or sending certain articles in major newspapers that were critical of a leading candidate for president of the United States in the weeks preceding an election. The key problem with Section 230 isn't just the statute itself but the *abuse* of the statute by companies.

Indeed, that's the feature that bothers most politicians who call for the repeal of Section 230 today. In 2020, President Trump tweeted "REVOKE 230!" after certain of his other tweets were flagged by Twitter as potentially misleading. Josh Hawley introduced a bill that same year aiming to end Section 230 protections for technology companies unless they agreed to an independent audit to ensure they were moderating content without political bias. He posted the following on Twitter, ironically enough: "It's pretty simple: if Twitter and Google and the rest are going to editorialize and censor and act like traditional publishers, they should be treated like traditional publishers and stop receiving the special carve out from the federal government in Section 230."[34] Interestingly, the movement to scrap Section 230 has become increasingly bipartisan, with even President Joe Biden suggesting a repeal of the statute.[35]

Silicon Valley's defenders of Section 230 claim that social media companies like Facebook and Twitter could have never gotten off the ground in a big way if they were also responsible for fighting lawsuits from angry users who sue those companies for being defamed on their sites. But that may have been a good thing for society. We ought to prefer a society in which no individual social media company is any larger or more powerful than an ordinary publisher. In that world, there would be multiple social media companies each with different offerings that each reach a smaller base of users—akin to a fragmented media marketplace with a series of local newspapers. That's what the free market might have produced as an alternative equilibrium, and it's one that sounds pretty good to me.

That should be our greatest learning of all: we would have never had behemoth corporate monsters in Silicon Valley wielding the power that they do without laws that were a product of Silicon Valley's own lobbying efforts. In an ultimate irony, Jack Dorsey in his Senate testimony invoked that very fact in arguing against the repeal of Section 230. He warned that if Section 230 were to disappear, then only massive tech companies capable of shouldering the financial burdens associated with new legal liabilities would continue to exist, choking out smaller companies and startups that try to compete. It would leave "only a small number of giant and well-funded technology companies," he testified.[36] Dorsey's lack of self-awareness is laughable: the only way that the current Silicon Valley behemoths ever became behemoths was due to the existence of Section 230 in the first place.

But this is at best a learning for the future. Unfortunately, in one narrow sense, Dorsey is right: a repeal of the law is probably too little, too late—and may even do more harm than good given that the network effects already enjoyed by the larger incumbents like Facebook and Twitter would only be strengthened by making it more costly for other startups to reach their scale and reach . . . even if Section 230 was a mistake when it was passed in 1996.

Congress opened Pandora's box, and it may be too late to shut it. But in the original myth, opening Pandora's box didn't just release a flood of evils into the world. The last thing left in the box was hope.

S O WHAT'S THE solution? Antitrust law misses the point. Breaking up Big Tech companies won't stop smaller companies from still behaving like an ideological cartel. Regulation is self-defeating because large firms are expert at capturing the process for their own benefit, entrenching their status as incumbents. Repealing Section 230 would have the same effect, since larger firms are better able to withstand liability as compared to smaller upstarts.

A more promising solution, at least in theory, would be for Congress to amend Section 230 in the following manner: any company that benefits from Section 230 is bound by the standards of the First Amendment. In other words, "Internet Service Providers" would have a choice: either they could benefit from the extraordinary privilege of legal immunity against lawsuits from users alleging censorship while abiding by the First Amendment, or they could moderate and censor user content as they wish without the special shield of Section 230. But they can't have both. Intellectually, it makes sense: if the federal government gives you special treatment, then you assume special obligations to act according to the same constitutional restraints as the federal government. Practically though, it's nearly impossible to imagine Congress actually acting so boldly, especially when dollars from large corporate donors are still like mother's milk for most congressmen.

In the near term, our most promising solution rests in the judicial system, the one institution that nearly all Americans still trust.

In response to the widespread social media bans in January

2021, I argued in *The Wall Street Journal*—along with my former law professor Jed Rubenfeld—that when Big Tech companies engage in selective censorship of political viewpoints on their platforms, these companies should be treated as state actors and bound by the Constitution—*under existing legal doctrines*. No new laws are required. The legal argument is a bit of a mind bender. But it's also a game changer, so bear with me.*

Conventional wisdom holds that technology companies are free to regulate content because they are private and the First Amendment protects only against government censorship. But that view is wrong. In reality, Congress co-opted Silicon Valley to do through the back door what government cannot directly accomplish under the Constitution. And it did it through a carrot-and-stick approach.

Section 230 was the carrot, in that it not only permits tech companies to censor constitutionally protected speech but completely shields them from federal or state liability for doing so. Yet the Supreme Court has long held that the legal provision of such immunity can turn private action into state action. Take *Norwood v. Harrison* (1973), which held that it is "axiomatic" that the government "may not induce, encourage, or promote private persons to accomplish what it is constitutionally forbidden to accomplish."[37] Similarly, in *Railway Employees' Department v. Hanson* (1956), the justices found state action in closed-shop agreements between private unions and the employer—which forced all employees to join the union— because Congress had passed a statute immunizing such agreements from liability under state law.[38] In *Skinner v. Railway Labor Executives*

---

* Jed Rubenfeld and I made an abbreviated version of this argument in January 2021, see https://www.wsj.com/articles/save-the-constitution-from-big-tech-11610387105. I credit Jed for pioneering several of the legal arguments in this section. See also https://www.law fareblog.com/are-facebook-and-google-state-actors.

Association (1989), the court yet again found state action in private-party conduct—drug tests for company employees—because federal regulations immunized railroads from liability if they conducted those tests.[39] In all of these cases, as with Section 230, the federal government didn't mandate anything. It merely preempted state law, protecting certain private parties from lawsuits if they engaged in the conduct Congress was promoting.

If Section 230 is the carrot, here is the stick: congressional Democrats have repeatedly made explicit threats to social media giants if they failed to censor speech those lawmakers disfavored. In April 2019, Louisiana Congressman Cedric Richmond warned Facebook and Google that they had "better" restrict what he and his colleagues saw as harmful content or face regulation: "We're going to make it swift, we're going to make it strong, and we're going to hold them very accountable." He added, ominously: "Figure it out. Because you don't want us to figure it out for you." New York Congressman Jerrold Nadler added: "Let's see what happens by just pressuring them."[40]

The threats have worked. In September 2019, the day before another congressional grilling was to begin, Facebook announced important new restrictions on "hate speech." It was no coincidence that Big Tech took its most aggressive steps against Trump just as Democrats were poised to take control of the White House and Senate. Prominent Democrats promptly voiced approval of Big Tech's actions, which Connecticut Senator Richard Blumenthal expressly attributed to "a change in the political winds."[41]

Our courts have long held that governmental threats can turn private conduct into state action—and with good reason. In *Bantam Books, Inc. v. Sullivan* (1963), the Supreme Court found a First Amendment violation when a private bookseller stopped selling works state officials deemed "objectionable" after they sent him a veiled threat of prosecution.[42] In *Carlin Communications, Inc. v. Mountain States Telephone & Telegraph Co.* (1987), the Ninth US Circuit Court of Appeals found state action when an official induced a telephone company to stop carrying offensive content, again by threat of prosecution.[43] As the Second Circuit held in *Hammerhead Enterprises v. Brezenoff* (1983), the test is whether "comments of a government official can reasonably be interpreted as intimating that some form of punishment or adverse regulatory action will follow the failure to accede to the official's request."[44]

Richmond's comments and Nadler's comments easily meet that test. So do those of many other lawmakers and regulators. Notably, the Ninth Circuit held it didn't matter whether the threats were the "real motivating force" behind the private party's conduct; state action exists even if he "would have acted as he did independently."[45] So even if you think that Jack Dorsey and Mark Zuckerberg aren't frightened of these mere mortal congressmen, the Supreme Court says it doesn't matter: the legal doctrine applies just the same.

Either Section 230 or congressional pressure alone might be sufficient to create state action. But the combination has to be. Suppose a Republican-controlled Congress enacted a statute giving legal immunity to any private party that obstructs access to abortion clinics. Suppose further that Republican politicians explicitly threatened private companies with punitive laws if they fail to act against abortion clinics. If those companies did as Congress demanded and then got a pat on the back from lawmakers like Blumenthal gave the social media companies, progressives would instantly see the constitutional problem.

Or try a different example. Say Congress wants to look through the email of every corporate executive in the country. There's no constitutional mechanism for Congress to accomplish that directly. But it could simply pass the Email Decency Act, which immunizes any hacker from all legal liability for breaking into corporate email servers and transferring corporate executives' email logs into public databases—and prosecute hackers for their other crimes if they *don't* also break into those corporate email servers and publicize the executives' emails.

If that sounds ridiculous, think again: *that's exactly what Congress did with Section 230 of the Telecommunications Decency Act, combined with its severe threats to social media companies to censor speech on their sites.* The left wing of Congress, unwittingly aided by some right-wing populists, effectively dispatched social media companies to do speech-censoring work that the First Amendment prohibits Congress from doing directly. These social media companies are effectively privately hired censoring agents for the government.

This ought to be an affront to any American who cares about the integrity of our Constitution. It reminds me of the premise underlying season five of the television series *Homeland*. German intelligence agencies were prohibited by new German privacy laws from spying on their citizens. So instead, they invited the US Central Intelligence Agency onto their soil to do the spying on their behalf. In return, the CIA got to keep the private information of German citizens for its own purposes. It's strikingly similar to what's happening now in the real world with social media companies: substitute the US government for the German intelligence agencies, Twitter and Facebook for the CIA, and the analogy becomes clear.

These corporate behemoths are doing the work of big government under the mantle of private enterprise—and they're getting away with it together. It's the most dangerous kind of woke capitalism of all—the kind where the government explicitly co-opts private institutions to do the government's own bidding.

As we've discussed, the unholy marriage between government and corporations isn't just hypothetical. Nor is it hyperbole—in fact, it may soon have a name. *New York University* researchers published a report titled "False Accusation: The Unfounded Claim That Social Media Companies Censor Conservatives," which calls for the Biden administration to form a new "Digital Regulatory Agency" to fight dangerous ideas such as the assertion that social media companies have anti-conservative bias.[46]

Remind you of Orwell's Ministry of Truth? Well, it gets worse. According to the *New York Times*, we now have a "reality crisis." The solution? Experts are calling for the administration to "put together a cross-agency task force to tackle disinformation and domestic extremism, which would be led by something like a 'reality czar.'" Importantly, "This task force could also meet regularly with tech platforms, and push for structural changes that could help those companies tackle their own extremism and misinformation problems . . . it could become the tip of the spear for the federal government's response to the reality crisis." Others are calling for a "truth commission."[47] For anyone who's still wary of my argument that Big Tech censorship is state action disguised as private action, don't take it from me. Just listen to America's newspaper of record.

In sum, here's how the game was played. First, Congress endowed Big Tech with the special corporate privilege of Section 230 that immunizes technology companies from any liability in state court for censoring or otherwise regulating user content. Second, liberal congressmen threaten those same companies at hearings in 2020, saying that if they *fail* to remove "hate speech" from white nationalists, they would be punished. Third, liberal lawmakers congratulate social media companies after they go on to censor content that Democrats don't like. Fourth, tech titans manage to take their most aggressive actions of all just as Democrats are poised to take control of the White House, the Senate, and the House of Representatives for the first time in over a decade. And fifth—of course—Silicon Valley billionaires made staggeringly one-sided campaign contributions to those same Democratic candidates as a token of appeasement.

In 2020, the mantra of "keeping money out of politics" was no longer a liberal slogan. Instead, blending profits with politics—and, ultimately, power—became the new progressive way. We've devolved from a three-branch federal government to one with a headquarters in Silicon Valley and a branch office in Washington, D.C.—each doing precisely the work that the other can't. That's the backroom bargain that defines our century.

When I was a kid growing up in Ohio, my favorite field trip was the one that we took to Washington, D.C. I still remember my awe when I saw the dome of the US Capitol for the first time. We used to visit the various memorials. We learned how to do a proper salute, just like they do in the military.

Perhaps one day my son will feel the same way when his teachers take him on a trip to see the glassy exterior of the Googleplex offices in Silicon Valley. I doubt they'll make him salute the CEO. Maybe they'll have him bow instead.

CHAPTER 10

Wokeness Is Like a Religion

I READ MY FAVORITE STORY about Christ during my junior year at St. Xavier High School, in a poem contained in the last book Fyodor Dostoevsky wrote before he died, *The Brothers Karamazov*. Here's how I remember it.

The story begins with Jesus Christ returning to Earth during the Spanish Inquisition. He shows up in Seville and starts performing biblical miracles, healing the lame and the sick. But when an old cardinal recognizes him, instead of celebrating Christ's return, he has him arrested. The Inquisition's leaders sentence Christ to be burned to death the next day. The Grand Inquisitor shows up in Christ's prison cell and gives an extended explanation of how Christ's return stands in the way of the Church's mission.

The Grand Inquisitor begins by reminding Jesus of the three temptations the devil offered him in the desert, taking the devil's side and arguing that Christ was wrong to reject each of them for the sake of keeping his freedom. Freedom, claims the Grand Inquisitor, is an obstacle to salvation, not the pathway to it. He says that instead of extolling the virtues of free will, Jesus should've won people's hearts by turning stone to bread and feeding them, should've gained their worship by casting himself down from the mountain to be lifted up by angels, and should've ensured their salvation by ruling all the kingdoms of Earth.

The theme of the Grand Inquisitor's soliloquy is that the Church has outgrown Christ. He agrees with Christ's goal of delivering salvation, but he says that people can't be trusted to make the right decisions; they have to be forced to be good. In the Inquisitor's eyes, all men are sinners, and the duty of the Church is to compel them to recognize their sin so they can be saved. Jesus's message of free will interferes with that project because, fallen as they are, most people will only choose to fall further into sin.

Christ has value only as a symbol whose name and likeness the Church can invoke to make people obey, but Jesus himself is obsolete, says the Grand Inquisitor. Jesus must die so that what he has come to represent can live on.

When I reflected on Roivant, wokeness, and the state of our nation on Juneteenth 2020, I remembered the Grand Inquisitor. "Diversity" has become a term of art, a symbol, one so powerful that the symbol is now more important than the thing it was supposed to represent. Wokeness sacrifices true diversity, diversity of thought, so that skin-deep symbols of diversity like race and gender can thrive. Just like Christ in the story, true diversity of thought now represents a threat to the Church of Diversity. So this Church didn't just make us forget the true god. It sentenced the true god to death.

Columbia University linguistics professor John McWhorter has observed that "third-wave antiracism is a profoundly religious movement in everything but terminology."[1] He couldn't be more right. Diversity experts like Ibram Kendi and Robin DiAngelo are the Grand Inquisitors of our time. Corporate CEOs are the followers in the square who kneel to them. Some kneel out of worship, some out of fear, some a mixture of the two. If they confess themselves to be sinners and acknowledge their racism and sexism, the Inquisitors will absolve them of these sins. Corporate employees and their consumers are like the innocent masses, left to worship at the temple of Diversity—a quasi religion that monolithically rejects diversity itself, just as the commoners in Seville worshiped at a church that sentenced Christ to execution. "Heal me of my patriarchy!" the woke CEOs and their employees cry. "I am blind to my white privilege—make me see!" If they show a penitent heart and contrite spirit, the diversity experts graciously bless them and then move on to their next speaking engagement. All must be saved.

Robin DiAngelo is the author of *White Fragility*, which you can find on the bookcase of every woke suburban mom. It topped bestseller lists in 2020. DiAngelo presents an overly simplified view of race in America, which paints whites as a racist monolith that systemically oppresses blacks and other minority groups. As *The Washington Post* describes it, DiAngelo believes that whites are "an undifferentiated racist collective, socialized to 'fundamentally hate blackness' and to institutionalize that prejudice in politics and culture."[2] DiAngelo's rise is emblematic of the increased adoption of a previously fringe school of thought that has now spread across corporate America through mandated Diversity trainings and has even made its way into exhibits at the Smithsonian.[3] DiAngelo and her devotees seem to believe that things like the scientific method, use of written word, punctuality, and hard work are "hallmarks of whiteness" and that it perpetuates white supremacy for employers and teachers to valorize them. In DiAngelo's telling, the idea of meritocracy is a white supremacist myth meant to justify existing racial hierarchies as the product of hard work. One journalist interviewing DiAngelo questioned her about her objection to the supposedly white practice of hiring professors based on how rational they are. The journalist asked whether hiring rational teachers might produce rational students. DiAngelo ultimately responded that if any practice leads to the outcome of minorities doing poorly, that practice must be racist. She then noted, incidentally, that under capitalism, minorities do poorly.[4]

The reasoning doesn't seem airtight to me, but this is the stuff of which Diversity seminars are built. Coca-Cola made the news recently when some images leaked of a DiAngelo diversity training course it had its employees take on LinkedIn—she instructed them to try "to be less white" and said that amounts to being less oppressive, arrogant, defensive, ignorant, and so on. I took a look at the training course and noted DiAngelo added that Asians are guilty of these sins too because they're "white-adjacent."* Coca-Cola responded to the controversy over DiAngelo's diversity training with some corporate legalese saying it was "not a focus of our company's curriculum."[5] LinkedIn quietly took down the course.[6]

Robin DiAngelo's shtick is that she's a white person who tells her fellow white people they're racists and gives them verbal flails they can whip themselves with to atone. And she charges a pretty penny for the service. *White Fragility* is essentially a modern-day hair shirt. As far as I can tell, the phenomenon of "white fragility" refers to white people not liking being called racist.

---

* This jargon-based racism about Asians being "white-adjacent" is increasingly common in woke circles, as a recent *Wall Street Journal* op-ed explains: www.wsj .com/articles/the-woke-model-minority-myth-11614035596?st=qn0wv3fwbasid6z &reflink=article_copyURL_share.

You'll find more of the same in Ibram Kendi's work on Diversity, although without the nauseating self-flagellation you can only find in woke white people. One of his recent books is called *How to Be an Anti-Racist*. In it, he makes assertions such as "the claim of 'not racist' neutrality is a mask for racism."[7] So, if you claim to be racist, you obviously are. If you claim not to be racist, you're hiding your racism, which is even worse. It's a woke catch-22. It turns out that one of Diversity's central tenets is that everyone is racist, just as part of Catholicism is accepting that everyone is a sinner.

Don't get me wrong. True diversity *is* very valuable, both for a nation and for a company. But it's diversity of thought that's supposed to matter, not a kind of diversity crudely measured by appearance or accent. At some point we all started using superficial qualities as proxies for intellectual diversity. But the more we focused on those proxies for intellectual diversity, the less we cared about the thing the proxies were supposed to represent. Just as Jesus had become a threat to the institution of the Church in Dostoevsky's tale, intellectual diversity had become a threat to American corporations, universities, and other institutions. Just as the Grand Inquisitor sentenced Jesus to execution, today's corporate stewards sacrifice intellectual diversity at their corporate altars in the name of a new Diversity.

As I chafed at the new regime of Diversity that had taken root across corporate America, I also found myself thinking about an email I'd just got from one of my employees after groups of employees across the company self-organized to have "honest discussions about race" after the murder of George Floyd and the resulting aftermath. As CEO I even joined a few of them and assumed that the conversations were just that—honest.

But I soon found out we'd really only had the illusion of honesty.

As it turns out, in public everyone says the same things. I started to receive a dribble of feedback from employees who'd felt afraid to say what they really thought. One email gnawed at me in particular, this one from one of the few who was willing to reveal his identity. He started out by praising the company's diversity and its purpose of developing medicines. I encouraged him to share his thoughts at our next townhall.

What he said in response stuck with me. "Thank you for the invitation to talk on that. However, I am uncomfortable doing that. One part of my experience is that many years ago I realized that some media outlets and people in general see a white male . . . and immediately label that person as a 'racist' or a 'bigot.' While I don't have a racist bone in my body, I am uncomfortable talking publicly about our diversity."

I didn't realize until seeing his email that our "honest conversation about race" had been governed by an implicit hierarchy based on perceived diversity. Maybe some of his coworkers didn't see him as diverse, and maybe his fellow citizens didn't either, but he'd been diverse all along to me. I saw a diversity of identities within him alone—a southern Christian man who was devoutly committed to science and developing new medicines.

Our little episode last spring was a trifle compared to the experiences of other companies at home and abroad. For instance, in 2019, Nike planned to unveil a new sneaker for Fourth of July, a red, white, and blue one that had a picture of the Betsy Ross flag on the back, which features thirteen stripes, alternating between red and white, and thirteen white stars in a circle on a blue background. It made the shoes and shipped them and then suddenly recalled them all. Why? Because Colin Kaepernick had recently signed onto its payroll, and he argued that because the flag design was created in 1776 and slavery was legal at the time, Nike would've been endorsing slavery. This quickly became the accepted wisdom. Democratic political candidates rushed to endorse Nike's move, and Betsy Ross's flag became known as a symbol of white supremacy overnight. So what had been intended to be a celebration of women's contributions to the creation of the nation became viewed as a threat to Diversity.

Forbidden words are also a threat to Diversity, even when you're quoting them, not using them. Prominent science reporter Donald McNeil was recently ousted from *The New York Times* for uttering the N-word when answering a high school student's question about whether a classmate deserved to be suspended for saying that word.[8] Tim Boudreau, the chair of Central Michigan University's journalism department, was fired merely for quoting a leading free speech case that itself mentioned the N-word in its description of the facts.[9] Greg Patton, a communications professor at the University of Southern California, was recently suspended when he mentioned a Chinese word that *sounded* like the N-word to some students.[10]

Forbidden hand gestures are an affront to Diversity too. Emmanuel Cafferty, a Latino man who was fired from his job as a truck driver, found that out the hard way. His sin? Imperiling Diversity by—I'm not joking—making the "OK" sign with his fingers. Here's what happened: at a traffic stop, another driver flipped him off, made the "OK" symbol, and yelled at Cafferty to copy him. Confused, Cafferty did, hoping that would end the encounter. The other driver took a picture. When it got onto the internet, Cafferty was fired because the alt-right has appropriated the OK sign and said that it stands for "White Power."[11] So Cafferty's employer fired a Latino man for inadvertently making an ordinary gesture that some use to object to diversity. The fact that he was obviously Latino was no defense against the charge that he was endorsing white supremacy. He had to be fired in part for the sake of Latinos, to protect them from the OK sign.

For a recent example that hits close to home for me, consider my old classmate from Yale Law School, Jamil Jivani. *The Globe and Mail* ran a story about him titled "Ontario's opportunities advocate accused of anti-Blackness." Jamil is black, but that was no defense. He had committed the cardinal sin of opposing the Black Lives Matter movement, and in the Church of Diversity, that makes one automatically anti-black. Jamil wrote a powerful response. He concluded with the following words:

> Imposing an ideological racial purity test on Black men and women is dangerous. It is divide and conquer. It is colonial. But news media companies who purport to be anti-racist are often blind to this reality. Consider, for example, that the Globe and Mail has decided to capitalize the letter "b" in Black and invites Black writers to contribute to its opinion pages. But how much does any of that matter if your paper is going to assume Black people are supposed to think and say the same things? What kind of agenda is a news outlet actually supporting if it is narrowly defining an entire demographic by what Twitter activists say?
>
> My blackness was not given to me by the Globe and Mail. God did that. No newspaper can take my blackness from me. We can address anti-Black racism and provide hope to Black communities without demanding that Black people in positions of leadership parrot the same ideological talking points.[12]

As one commentator put it, Jamil had run afoul of a central tenet of the Church of Diversity neatly expressed in a sermon from US

Congresswoman Ayanna Pressley: "We don't need any more Brown faces that don't want to be a Brown voice. We don't need any more Black faces that don't want to be a Black voice."[13] I suppose her disciples will call me a Brown face, and they will say they don't need me to speak because I don't want to be a Brown voice. But I have things I want to say.

The Church of Diversity delivers a new sermon every day. The list goes on and on, as you'll see throughout this chapter. I'm going to show that wokeness really has become a religion in every meaningful sense of the word—practically, morally, and even legally. The Church of Diversity is as real as Christianity, Islam, or Hinduism, and its membership is growing every day. It has now grown powerful enough that, like many dominant churches throughout history, it has decided to begin punishing all the nonbelievers. A democracy may thrive on dissent, but a theocracy can't tolerate it.

LIKE MOST RELIGIONS, the Church of Diversity started from humble beginnings. It's hard to point to a moment where any story truly begins. But for a single moment where America's interest in diversity began to become a formalized obsession, take a look at Justice Powell's famous concurrence in *Regents of the University of California v. Bakke*. It was here, in an opinion about the constitutionality of racial quotas in university admissions, that American law began to really acknowledge the value of diversity. Over the years, as the Supreme Court's affirmative action doctrine flourished and gave diversity more weight, Diversity grew strong too, first entrenching itself in universities and soon after that in all companies and institutions. Once we carved the value of Diversity into the Constitution, it became easy for it to spread to the rest of our culture.

Bakke was decided back in 1978. Allan Bakke, a white man with good qualifications aside from his advanced age (33), had been rejected twice from UC Davis's medical school. The medical school had a policy of reserving sixteen seats for racial minorities, and Bakke argued that if it weren't for this racial quota, he would've been admitted.

When the case finally arrived at the Supreme Court, it ruled in Bakke's favor, but that was all it could agree on. Here's the key takeaway of *Bakke*. Although Justice Powell's concurring opinion wasn't legally binding, later thinkers found his arguments about the value of diversity compelling. Powell argued that the state of California *did* have a compelling interest in constructing a diverse class of students: "The atmosphere of 'speculation, experiment and creation'—so essential to the quality of higher education—is widely believed to be promoted by a diverse student body." The problem was just that a quota system was too crude. He held up Harvard University's affirmative action program as an example of one that pursued diversity in an appropriately flexible way. Harvard used a policy called "holistic review," where an applicant's race was one kind of diversity out of many that could count in their favor.[14]

Decades later, in the landmark cases *Grutter v. Bollinger* and *Gratz v. Bollinger*, Powell's reasoning and Harvard's holistic review both resurfaced and gained the force of law. *Grutter* was a challenge to the University of Michigan Law School's policy giving applicants from racial minorities a significantly greater chance of admission. *Gratz* challenged the University of Michigan's undergraduate admissions policy giving racial minorities a quantifiable numerical boost to their prospects. Unsurprisingly, the law school won and the undergraduate school lost.

The Court decided that the University of Michigan's undergraduate program was a thinly disguised quota system, with its rigid numerical boost based on minority status. But the law school's unquantifiable non-numerical boost passed constitutional muster because, like Harvard's holistic review policy, it considered race one positive factor out of many. The bottom line is that holistic review policies are constitutional because, in theory, they give applicants' race weight without making race automatically decisive for any applicant.

In practice, universities quickly learned that they could get away with whatever they wanted as long as they chanted "we practice holistic review" at judges whenever they got sued over their affirmative action policies. There's this trope in fiction where a soldier gets captured and all they do is recite their name, rank, and serial number to their captors. Similarly, all universities really have to do is intone "we have a compelling interest in admitting a diverse class and race is but one factor of many we consider in our policy of holistic review."

Crucially, this has been a winning legal argument in constitutional and statutory law even when statistical evidence suggests that the universities are in fact implementing racial quota systems—at most Ivy League universities, for instance, the percentage of their student body that's Asian has hovered around 16 percent over the last couple decades even as the population of Asians in America has grown far faster than other races.[15] The legal lesson is that official quotas are bad; the way to do racial quotas is to quietly implement them and call the results the product of holistic review.

The Biden administration supported these unofficial quotas when it dropped a DOJ lawsuit against Yale for anti-Asian discrimination, even as it championed laws against anti-Asian hate speech.[16] What many liberals miss is that America's silent quota system reinforces the stereotypes that lead to hate: when elite colleges need to reject Asian applicants with high test scores and GPAs because they're at their quota, but they can't admit it's because of a quota, they're forced to say that Asians as a group tend to be worse at all the personality-based aspects of their applications, like leadership. It turns out this is exactly what Harvard says.[17] American colleges routinely discriminate against Asians in the name of diversity.

Once the Supreme Court held that states had a compelling interest in achieving diversity, it was natural for non-state actors to argue that they had the same interest. "Our diversity is our strength" became a truism not just in universities but across American institutions. And the kind of diversity universities and businesses value happens to be the same narrow kind of diversity that was at issue in the affirmative action cases—in theory, it's diversity of thought that matters, but in practice, Diversity is all about skin-deep factors like race and sex.

Race-based affirmative action has left the incubation chamber of the university and spread to the corporate world, even to my home turf in the biotech industry. When I was a biotech CEO, I was called on by BIO, the industry lobbying group, to support the BIO-Equality Agenda, "a national effort . . . that aims to counteract the systemic inequality, injustice, and unfair treatment of underserved communities."[18] Some of the agenda's goals are reasonable enough, such as ensuring that racial minorities are adequately represented in clinical trials and making sure underserved populations have access to vaccines and therapeutics—these are certainly pressing needs. Clinical trial representation is particularly important for advancing science, since different racial groups may differ in their responses to different therapies.

But some of the BIOEquality Agenda's goals are, well, pushing a bit of an agenda. In particular, two of its "pillars of change" are thinly veiled racial and gender-based affirmative action programs—it wants to "Facilitate a partnering network, including hiring of industry-trained minority scientists and engineers" and "Enhance use of minority- and women-owned small businesses in biotech supply chains, to promote economic development of marginalized communities."[19] Looks like it's the biotech industry's turn to embrace thinly disguised racial quotas.

It's the government's turn, too. In the 2020 election, California, for instance, put an initiative on the ballot that brings the university holistic review system to government hiring. The initiative, Proposition 16, was charitably labeled "Allow Diversity as a Factor in Public Employment, Education, and Contracting Decisions." Sounds great. Who wouldn't want to allow diversity as a factor in these decisions? But the word game, of course, is that diversity of thought is what we want to encourage, and that's already allowed. It's hiring based on Diversity that's currently forbidden by California law— Proposition 209 forbids the government from discriminating against or granting preferential treatment to individuals or groups on the basis of race, sex, color, ethnicity, or national origin in the operation of public employment, education, or contracting. When Prop 16 talked about allowing diversity, it meant repealing Prop 209 to allow racial quotas under the name of Diversity.

We need a cultural shift in the direction of shaping diversity and affirmative action initiatives in the direction of economic hardship—which selects for diversity of experience—rather than race. We'd almost surely address racial diversity in the process, but addressing racial disparities should be the side effect of good policies, not the goal. This is exactly the approach we started to take at Roivant. We didn't have any crude kind of quota system, whether official or disguised under the label of holistic review. But we did recognize that we'd be a stronger and scrappier company if our employees had a variety of experiences, and to get that diversity of perspectives, we implemented our new loan repayment program to make sure that an impoverished background was no obstacle to working with us (see Chapter 3).

We wanted actual diversity of thought at Roivant. As I mentioned earlier, I stepped down as CEO in January. We gave the job to Matt Gline, my longtime CFO, who disagrees with me on most social and political questions and brings a different perspective to many business decisions too. Diversity of thought benefits a biotech company in the same way it benefits a university and for the same reasons. But whether you're a biotech company or a university, you can't get that valuable diversity of thought if you simply assume that skin-deep qualities like race are the central factors in whether people think alike or differently. People speak for themselves; they're not representatives of their race. Roivant's new CEO does indeed have a different skin color than I do, but that's not actually the most important thing that distinguishes us from one another.

WHETHER YOU BUY my story about university affirmative action jurisprudence leading American culture to focus on superficial, appearance-based diversity or not, Diversity is here now. And it's spreading its woke tendrils from the seminar rooms of the ivory tower to the boardrooms of corporate America. Woke capitalism has moved beyond bland corporate statements about diversity. Frighteningly, it now demands the firing of employees who don't share its enlightened worldview.

There are three archetypal models when it comes to political beliefs in the workplace: apolitical, deliberative, and orthodox.

Whether an employee's political speech will get them fired or not depends on which of these models their employer subscribes to.

First, there's the apolitical model, a workplace where the focus is work and employees check their political opinions at the door, like IBM in the 1950s. Many companies outright ban political speech at work.[20] One prominent example is Huntington Ingalls,[21] the US Navy's main shipbuilder, which recently fired a worker for violating this policy by wearing a Trump 2020 hat to meetings.[22] Another recent example is Coinbase, which faced the question of what kind of company it was last June when a group of employees demanded that CEO Brian Armstrong make a public statement in support of Black Lives Matter.[23] It was a situation similar to the one I faced at Roivant. But at Coinbase it resulted in open warfare.

First, Armstrong refused to make the statement, arguing it would be divisive. Then senior managers organized a group of employees to stage a walkout in protest. Armstrong posted some pro-BLM Twitter messages later that day and held a couple diversity meetings, but he soon regretted caving. He issued a statement coming down decisively on the side of being a mission-focused, apolitical workplace. In it, he laid out a list of things the company explicitly wouldn't allow employees to do.

We won't:

- Debate causes or political candidates internally that are unrelated to work
- Expect the company to represent our personal beliefs externally
- Assume negative intent, or not have each others back
- Take on activism outside of our core mission at work[24]

He even offered a generous severance package to employees who didn't want to stay at an apolitical workplace; sixty of Coinbase's employees took him up on it, 5 percent of its workforce.[25]

Some outside observers applauded Armstrong's decision to foster a mission-oriented culture. Others were much less sympathetic. The firestorm of visceral criticism is probably best summed up by former Twitter CEO Dick Costelo's reaction. Costelo declared in a now-deleted tweet, "me-first capitalists who think you can separate society from business are going to be the first people lined up against the wall and shot in the revolution. I'll happily provide video commentary."[26] The message is clear: damned be all who don't bow at the altar of woke stakeholderism.

Given that backdrop, it's somewhat predictable that, unlike Coinbase, most companies just informally create a politics-free workplace. Apolitical workplaces often come from a bottom-up approach—one poll found that 60 percent of employees say they believe discussing politics at work is unacceptable.[27]

But ironically, the same poll finds that 57 percent of employees do it anyway. There's a natural human itch to discuss the issues of the day, and some businesses reject the apolitical model by embracing that urge and encouraging their employees to speak their minds. This is the deliberative model, where a workplace is a site of discussion and debate on any and all topics—essentially a faculty lounge at most twentieth-century universities. It's reflected in the self-image of hedge funds like D. E. Shaw or Bridgewater. A lot of modern-day Big Tech companies like Google and Facebook claim to fall into this category. Corporations may not be people, but one way they're exactly alike is that their self-image is often at odds with reality. As we'll soon see, that's becoming the case with

Google. But it at least holds itself up as an exemplar of the deliberative model.

Last, there's the orthodox model, where employees are a self-selecting group who must swear fealty to a set of principles to retain employment, like the instructors at a religious school who must affirm a denominational catechism. It's mostly just religious colleges like Liberty University or Brigham Young University that openly claim to belong to this group. Although it's rare for organizations to outright require adherence to religious orthodoxy, they often indirectly encourage it by having policies rooted in religious beliefs, such as Chick-fil-A's closures on Sundays or Hobby Lobby's refusal to provide its employees access to contraceptives in their health-care plans. Historically, businesses with religious owners have been the main adherents to the orthodox model, whether formally or informally.

But wokeness is the new orthodoxy, the new religion, one that disguises itself in secular clothing. Because its disciples worship the secular force of identity rather than any supernatural one, it's much easier for the Church of Diversity to infiltrate the workplace. For years many universities have been in the process of lurching quite dramatically from the deliberative model to the orthodox one, and now corporations are trending in that direction as well. And they're firing anyone who doesn't toe the new party line.

Let's start with Google's firing of software engineer James Damore in August 2017, a paradigmatic case of political discrimination. After he attended an internal meeting on Google's policies on diversity and inclusion, the organizers asked for feedback. He wrote a long memo titled "Google's Ideological Echo Chamber" and sent it to the organizers. Writing that memo and sending it out into the echo chamber would end up being a career-ending mistake.

The memo is relatively innocuous. It acknowledged the discrimination women face in the tech sector, but argued that Google's employment policies gave too much weight to discrimination when explaining gender disparities in recruitment and promotion. Damore cited a variety of articles and peer-reviewed psychological papers to argue that Google's preferred explanation didn't account for innate biological differences between men and women. He recognized that the research he cited only discussed averages, adding "So you can't say anything about an individual . . . I hope it's clear that I'm not saying that diversity is bad, that Google or society is 100% fair, that we shouldn't try to correct for existing biases, or that minorities have the same experience of those in the majority. My larger point is that we have an intolerance for ideas and evidence that don't fit a certain ideology."[28]

Google's response ended up proving his point. After hearing nothing back from the diversity seminar's organizers, Damore shared his memo on Google's employee message boards. His memo created a firestorm. First it sparked an outcry among many of his fellow employees. Plenty of Damore's fellow Googlers defended his position, or at least his right to voice it,[29] but once one of his detractors leaked the memo to the media, his time as an engineer was at an end. The firestorm became a public conflagration, and to cover itself, Google torched his career. A nerdy 28-year-old centrist who'd been diagnosed with autism stumbled into the culture wars, expressed a vaguely conservative view, and became Silicon Valley's favorite pariah, its whipping boy for the evils of the world.

Google had to sacrifice Damore to prove its purity. It had to excommunicate him to avoid being excommunicated itself. This punishment made perfect sense under the tribal logic of woke capitalism, but it didn't make much sense in light of Google's explicit commitments to free and open dialogue. Perhaps in recognition of this tension, Google attempted to square the circle with a mealymouthed statement from its CEO Sundar Pichai, who led by asserting, "To suggest a group of our colleagues have traits that make them less biologically suited to that work is offensive and not OK," but added, "At the same time, there are co-workers who are questioning whether they can safely express their views in the workplace (especially those with a minority viewpoint). They too feel under threat, and that is also not OK."[30]

But this childlike list of what was OK and not OK did nothing to address the underlying contradiction in Google's commitments—Damore was fired for arguing for a minority view that Google's own views defined as inherently unacceptable, no matter how well supported his argument was. No one said Google needed to have an internal message board for dialogue on important ideas. But it was trying to get the credit for fostering dialogue through its public verbiage while doing precisely the opposite in practice. To top it off, Damore didn't even say what was alleged—Pichai's characterization was inaccurate. It wasn't enough to fire Damore for his views, Google also slandered him on the way out.

Google recently got back into the game of firing its political enemies and laid off software engineer Kevin Cernekee, allegedly for his political perspectives.[31] But Google's far from alone. David Shor, a left-leaning data analyst who didn't lean left enough, was fired by Civis Analytics, a consulting firm, for tweeting in support of a study suggesting that violent protests are counterproductive.[32]

Shor's case exemplifies yet another category of political firings: the tweets that aren't woke enough. This new species of political discrimination is especially pernicious. Sadly, there's a thing called "woke Twitter" now, and it's just begun stretching its muscles to find out how much power it really has.

This progressive Twitter mob tried for months to get actress Gina Carano fired from the show *The Mandalorian* over her refusal to list her pronouns and her jokes about mask-wearing, and it discovered that persistence pays off. Disney finally fired Carano after she compared Nazi persecution of Jews to the persecution of conservatives in America today. The company called her tweet "abhorrent and unacceptable," declining to explain why co-star Pedro Pascal remained employed despite his own tweets comparing President Trump's supporters to Nazis. According to corporate America, it's anti-semitic to compare liberals to Nazis but praiseworthy to compare conservatives to them.

Conservatives aren't woke Twitter's only victims or even its favorites. Frequently, as with Shor's firing, the ultra-vocal, ultra-liberal inhabitants of woke Twitter take it upon themselves to police their own tribe, zealously snuffing out dissent to make sure the faithful adhere to identity-politics orthodoxy. In one recent example, the Tobias Literary Agency fired Sasha White for tweets on her personal Twitter account that expressed solidarity with novelist J. K. Rowling for her views on biological sex.[33]

Rowling had crossed woke Twitter when she tweeted in support of Maya Forstater, whose contract with a think tank wasn't renewed after she herself tweeted things that offended woke Twitter.[34] She defended the view that a person's sex is a biological fact that can't be changed. Rowling supported her. This betrayal stung practitioners of identity politics because the Harry Potter author had become a woke icon after she curried favor with the left by revealing that Dumbledore had been gay all along. Rowling can't be fired, but she's now a pariah. "I heart JK Rowling" happens to be one of the hateful tweets that got Sasha White fired, along with horrific word violence, such as calling Rowling's defense of herself "powerfully nuanced and insightful."[35]

So, to recap, Maya Forstater lost her job because she tweeted that transgender women aren't really women, J. K. Rowling lost her fans for tweeting in support of Forstater, and then Sasha White lost her job for tweeting in support of Rowling. It was tweet-firing inception, a termination within a termination, like Russian matryoshka nesting dolls. It can be hard to keep track of until you realize that the woke mob is just behaving the way any mob does. First it tars and feathers the enemy; then when the enemy's supporters reveal themselves, it tars and feathers them too. Then it just repeats the process until all its enemies have been silenced.

The left and the right each discriminates in its own ways, but one thing that distinguishes the left is that it loves to eat its own. People like Rowling and White consider themselves feminists, and their insistence that transgender women should be considered separate from biological women is motivated by their feminism—they think that transgender women and biological women have meaningfully different experiences that are obscured when their identities are treated the same. The woke left calls these heretics trans-exclusionary-radical-feminists, or TERFs. It's an ironic label because this chain of firings looks much like an actual turf war.

This internecine squabbling for ideological control makes perfect sense under the view that wokeness is a religion. Many religions have one kind of contempt for nonbelievers and a special kind of hatred for heretics, who must be punished even more violently because they threaten to lead the faithful astray. In The Church of Jesus Christ of Latter-day Saints (or Mormonism), for instance, the only people who actually go to Hell are those who knew the truth but turned their backs on it: the worst sin of all is not nonbelief but apostasy. The Church of Diversity works the same way.

And so Forstater, Rowling, and White were shamed not for being *wrong* but for being *traitors*, for violating the tenets of a belief system that they'd been understood to have implicitly agreed to. They were treated with special contempt because their tribe thought they should've known better. When they signed on for feminism, they were supposed to have understood that it came with support for transgender women attached. When Rowling said Dumbledore was gay, she became an LGBTQ ally and was baptized to great celebration. But when she said transgender women weren't women, she became an LGBTQ enemy and was ritualistically excommunicated.[36] If you're not on board for the whole acronym, you're against all of it.

That's just how religious belief systems work—you don't get to pick your five favorite commandments and follow those. Since it's a modern religion, the Church of Diversity just transcribes its commandments onto acronyms instead of stone tablets. It ties its dogmatic beliefs together by invoking words like "intersectionality" instead of "faith."

And now corporations are firing people for violating the woke articles of faith, which they are understood to have implicitly agreed to by applying for a job at a woke company. Chances are, by the time you read this, there'll be a new political firing of the day, probably even in the same chain. Someone will have tweeted in support of Sasha White and been fired for it by now, I expect. Then someone else will tweet about it and be fired for supporting them. This is just the way things are now in the new world of woke capitalism, where for-profit entities are expected to be the judges of good and evil. But it's not the way they have to be.

AFTER THE GRAND Inquisitor finishes his story about why he has to kill Jesus, Christ approaches him. Christ softly kisses the Grand Inquisitor, as if he's forgiving him.

The Grand Inquisitor shudders. He goes to the cell door, opens it, and says to Christ "Go, and come no more . . . come not at all, never, never!" Jesus leaves. They never see each other again. That's how Dostoevsky ends the story.

The Grand Inquisitor's tale teaches us how the Church of Diversity became the real threat to true diversity of thought, all in the name of "Diversity" itself. It also teaches us how we should respond.

The Church of Diversity gives in to the three temptations the devil offered Christ in the desert. When woke companies fire people for things they say at home on Twitter, it's taking the Grand Inquisitor's advice to rule men through giving and taking bread from them. To control someone's heart and soul, first control their body. Let them know that if they don't fall in line they won't even have a roof over their head. With the knowledge that they live and die at the pleasure of the Church of Diversity looming over their heads, they'll look for reasons to believe it.

Then it gives them the reasons they're looking for. The Church of Diversity knows that it's not enough to rule through fear; it has to offer salvation, too. "See privilege everywhere," it promises, "and you will understand truth." You will see the web of power that underlies all ordinary interactions, the microaggressions hidden beneath good intentions—you will see colonialism in holiday greetings, patriarchy in pronouns, and systemic racism in filibusters and highways.

Feed men and offer them miracles, the Grand Inquisitor says, and then you can rule all the Earth. In the third temptation, the devil offered Christ dominion over everything, and with the advent of woke capitalism, this is the stage the Church of Diversity is currently in. It's not enough to rule or save a few people; you have to save everyone by exercising dominion over all. It's not enough to control universities; you have to rule corporations and government too.

This is the narrative the Church of Diversity offers. Like the Grand Inquisitor, it bids us to be silent. So how should we respond?

With a kiss, forgiving but not submitting. Diversity of thought *is* important, and that includes the woke perspective, too. The Church of Diversity's beliefs require it to silence classical liberals, but classical liberals—which in today's climate includes political conservatives like me—can't forget that our beliefs require us to listen to it. Yes, the playing field is uneven, but that's what defines the choice we make when committing to true diversity of thought. Part of the reason it's difficult to go to war with terrorists is that we choose to play by different rules than they do. Yet if we played by their rules, the war would no longer be worth fighting. The same goes for today's intellectual war between classical liberalism and modern wokeism.

We mustn't be drawn into a petty tit-for-tat game where we silence those who silence us—something that I worry about as I see the early stages of "cancel culture" emerging on the right, now copying the methods of their left-leaning counterparts. If we try to cancel the Church of Diversity, we just join its ranks under a different name. Christ gave the Grand Inquisitor a courtesy that the Grand Inquisitor wouldn't return. We should follow his example.

There are reasons to be optimistic. Proponents of classical liberalism won an important battle in the war during the 2020 elections, and that victory may pave the way for a path to reconciliation between the two sides. As I wrote at the time, voters at least temporarily shunned the Church of Diversity.[37] Trump gained ground relative to 2016 in every demographic except white men—racial minorities and women shifted toward him in spite of Democratic attempts to write a narrative in which minorities and women were automatic votes for Biden.[38] And that California initiative to bring back affirmative action? Even California's voters resoundingly rejected it, striking it down by a double-digit margin in a state composed mostly of voters from minority demographics.

The American people are beginning to let the Church of Diversity know that they've had enough of its preaching. The 2020 election was a jab; the moment is ripe for a knockout punch. But the best way to do that isn't to attempt to "cancel" woke culture itself. Rather, we need to take its concerns seriously and provide a better answer to those very concerns than wokeism does.

So that's the high-minded answer. But don't worry, there are some legal solutions too.

CHAPTER 11

Actually, Wokeness Is Literally a Religion

DO FIRED EMPLOYEES LIKE JAMES Damore have legal recourse against employers like Google on grounds of being fired for political or social views?

It turns out the legal answer revolves around the question I raised in the last chapter: Is wokeness a religion? In that chapter, I argued that for practical and moral purposes, wokeness acts increasingly *like* a religion. In this chapter, I'll prove that wokeness actually *is* a religion, from a legal perspective. That means both that employees like Damore have some protection from woke employers and that woke employees have certain protections as well. Being a religion comes with legal costs and benefits.

The bottom line is that there's an easy, bipartisan solution to our cultural battles over political firings hiding in plain sight. We don't have to pass any new laws or pressure judges to engage in any kind of judicial activism. If lawyers just bring the right cases, using the right legal theories, existing law will provide perfectly good protection to many of the people getting fired over their political views, whether they're liberal or conservative. And the court system is one of our country's few institutions that both sides of the aisle still have a bit of faith in, so we can turn adjudication of these issues over to it, once lawyers just start making the right arguments.

But before we dig into what the law is, let's play an old Yale Law School game: What should the law be? *Should* employees like James Damore or Sasha White have legal recourse against their employers when they're fired over their political views?

Libertarians and classical conservatives would argue no because the labor market is capable of fixing this problem on its own without government intervention. There could be another employer—let's call it "Shmoogle"—that invites engineers with alternative points of view and creates an environment that is more open to diversity of ideas than is Google. Shmoogle would presumably enjoy a competitive advantage in being able to hire talented engineers who valued that culture more than Google's monolithic one. Thus, the market itself is a sufficient tool to preserve a thriving marketplace of ideas.

This libertarian perspective is as valid as it is irrelevant. It's not even clear that the free market would correct for political discrimination—after all, it didn't fully correct for racial discrimination in the Jim Crow era. But this is a moot point anyway. As a society we've already accepted government intervention in ordinary course hiring-and-firing decisions over the last five decades.

The Civil Rights Act of 1964 prohibits discrimination on the basis of race, color, religion, sex, or national origin. It was the signature achievement of the nonviolent civil rights movement led by Martin Luther King, Jr. One of its biggest components was Title

VII's ban on employment discrimination. It also had a number of provisions desegregating public spaces and prohibiting the use of voting registration laws to disenfranchise minorities. After Dr. King's assassination led to a wave of riots, Congress passed the Civil Rights Act of 1968, which extended protection from discrimination to housing, saying that those selling, renting, and financing housing couldn't discriminate on the basis of race, religion, national origin, and, in later additions, disability or sex.

Even before these civil rights acts the Fourteenth Amendment had sought to address our nation's history of slavery with a number of sweeping provisions protecting rights like due process and equal protection of the law. But, crucially, the Fourteenth Amendment stops *state governments* from discriminating against people; it does nothing about discrimination from *private* entities like employers or landlords. By the 1960s, it was evident to many that to truly ensure equality the government had to prevent private actors from discriminating in public arenas. Title II of the Civil Rights Act of 1964, for instance, outlawed discrimination against protected classes in "public accommodations"—places like hotels, restaurants, theaters, stores, and schools, which are part of daily life for the public, even if they're owned by private entities. With its guarantee of fair treatment regarding housing, the Civil Rights Act of 1968 simply recognized that housing is a kind of public good too, a necessary part of ordinary life. So the government regulated it to prevent systemic private discrimination from creating *de facto* second-class citizens who are only equal in name.

Here's the bottom line: a libertarian may insist that in some more perfect world the free market, rather than government regulation, would prevent employment discrimination, but our society has already emphatically rejected that proposal. While it may be a valid intellectual exercise to interrogate the presuppositions of these major pieces of civil rights legislation of the 1960s, this is not a politically relevant question today. No libertarians have made repealing the Civil Rights Act a serious part of their platform, whether Rand Paul, his father Ron Paul, or the Libertarian Party itself.

The more relevant question is this: given that we as a society already view race, sex, religion, and national origin as "protected categories," should we add one's political affiliation to that list? I think yes. When Google fires James Damore, it sends a message that any other employee from his tribe is unwelcome there and that they are in a certain way inferior to those who espouse majority views.

In the same way that it took civil rights legislation in the 1960s to extend the *spirit* of equal protection under the law, which had been guaranteed by the Fourteenth Amendment—passed in the late 1800s—we require a similar mechanism for extending the *spirit* of the First Amendment to a modern world in which corporate power represents as much of a threat and an increasingly potent threat to the open exchange of ideas as the government itself. America's Founding Fathers were skeptical of the concentration of power in government hands, but if they were alive and among us today, they would be equally concerned about the power of companies like Google, Facebook, and Goldman Sachs to regulate our speech and conduct as well.

If you believe that civil rights legislation was required to prevent discrimination in our society on the basis of race or sex—in a way that the Fourteenth Amendment's prohibition on government-led discrimination did not sufficiently accomplish—then it's reasonable to think that additional civil rights legislation is required in the twenty-first century to prevent the suppression of speech in our society on the basis of corporate leaders' views—in a way that the First Amendment's prohibition on *government*-led speech suppression doesn't sufficiently accomplish. For example, the Civil Rights Act of 1964 prevents discrimination in the workplace on the basis of race, sex, religion, or national origin. You could envision a simple amendment to the statute that adds political beliefs to the list. In other words, you could make political belief a protected category— just like race, sex, or religious belief.

But in today's political climate, it's unrealistic to expect that legislative fix. That's the same problem I flagged in Chapter 9 with respect to amending Section 230—a great idea in theory, an impossible idea in practice—which is why I made an argument based on existing legal doctrines that Big Tech's victims could pursue in court.

Here's the good news: in order to fix political discrimination in the workplace, new legislation actually isn't required either. In reality, the Civil Rights Acts of 1964 may already suffice as a basis for plaintiffs to win in court. So now let's end the old Yale Law School game of talking about what the law should be and talk about what the law is.

Take a look at the Supreme Court's recent landmark ruling in *Bostock v. Clayton County*. This ruling prevents employers from discriminating on the basis of sexual orientation, holding that such discrimination represents a violation of the Civil Rights Act of 1964. Yet that act only prevents discrimination on the basis of "race, color, religion, sex, or national origin." There's no doubt that at the time the Civil Rights Act of 1964 was passed, Congress didn't intend to include discrimination on the basis of sexual orientation in it. But the *Bostock* majority effectively reasoned that in the year

2020, our understanding of discrimination on the basis of sex was fundamentally different from what it was in the 1960s—in such a way that caused discrimination on the basis of sexual orientation to be a civil rights violation in 2020, even if it wouldn't have been considered one in 1964.

The *Bostock* decision was a combination of a few separate cases: Gerald Bostock was fired by Clayton County when he joined a softball league for gay men, skydiving instructor Donald Zarda was fired after he told a female client he was gay in an attempt to put her at ease about being strapped to him, and transgender woman Aimee Stephens was fired by a funeral home after she told it she wanted to live and dress as a woman instead of a man. The Court ruled 6–3 in favor of the plaintiffs, with Chief Justice John Roberts and Justice Neil Gorsuch joining the liberal wing. Gorsuch wrote an opinion on strict textualist grounds, arguing that the plain meaning of the words in the Civil Rights Act of 1964 made the case an easy win for the plaintiffs, even if that wasn't the original legislative intent of the statute. Here's the key section:

> That's because it is impossible to discriminate against a person for being homosexual or transgender without discriminating against that individual based on sex. Consider, for example, an employer with two employees, both of whom are attracted to men. The two individuals are, to the employer's mind, materially identical in all respects, except that one is a man and the other a woman. If the employer fires the male employee for no reason other than the fact he is attracted to men, the employer discriminates against him for traits or actions it tolerates in his female colleague. Put differently, the employer intentionally singles out an employee to fire based in part on the employee's sex, and the affected employee's sex is a but-for cause of his discharge. Or consider

> *an employer who fires a transgender person who was identified as male at birth but who now identifies as female. If the employer retains an otherwise identical employee who was identified as female at birth, the employer intentionally penalizes a person identified as male at birth for traits or actions that it tolerates in an employee identified as female at birth. Again, the individual employee's sex plays an unmistakable and impermissible role in the discharge decision.*[1]

Bostock's reasoning was appealingly simple. How can we recognize when an employer discriminates on the basis of sex? Just reimagine the case, switching the sex of the fired employee but keeping all other facts identical, and see if they'd still be fired. If not, then their sex must've been a crucial reason for their firing—in legal terminology, this proves that their sex was a "but-for cause" of their termination. They wouldn't have been fired but for their sex.

This easy formula for recognizing when one entity is discriminating against another has ripple effects in areas of law that go far beyond sex discrimination litigation. Combining *Bostock's* formula for recognizing discrimination with the interpretation of Title VII by the Equal Employment Opportunity Commissions yields the conclusion that people like Sasha White, the literary agent fired for tweeting about transgender people, ought to receive Title VII protection for expressing beliefs rooted in secular reasoning just as Title VII protects the same beliefs when they're rooted in religious reasoning.

Let me finally put that pricey Yale law degree to work with a legal argument. Take the belief that marriage should be between a man and a woman. It's well established that an employer can't fire a Catholic employee for espousing this belief on religious grounds. But suppose a second employee believes the same thing on secular grounds. If the employer fires the second employee but not the first, that decision is implicitly based on the fired employee's lack of religion and thus prohibited by Title VII—in much the same way that firing a male employee but not a female employee who are both attracted to men is implicitly based on sex.

Here's why: Title VII explicitly forbids firing someone for their religion, and under the EEOC's interpretation, its ban on religious discrimination also prohibits employers from firing people over their *lack* of religion. The EEOC's guidance says Title VII forbids "treating applicants or employees differently based on their religious beliefs or practices—or lack thereof—in any aspect of employment, including recruitment, hiring, assignments, discipline, promotion, and benefits."[2]

So there are two steps to the *Bostock*-based argument. First, start with Title VII's protection from being fired over religious beliefs. Assume that a company has two employees, X and Y, who both say Z and that the only relevant difference between the employees is that X is religious and Y is an atheist. It's clear that employee X can't be fired for saying Z, assuming they have a religious basis for saying it. Easy enough. Here's the tricky second step, the part where *Bostock* comes in. If the company fires *Y* for saying Z, then, according to *Bostock's* method of identifying discrimination, the company was discriminating against Y on the basis of Y's lack of religion. That's because the company didn't fire X for saying the exact same thing and the only difference between X and Y is that Y lacks a religion.

The bottom line is that the mere fact that the company fires Y for saying Z and *wouldn't* fire them if they were religious and said the same thing means Y's lack of religion is a but-for cause of their firing, using *Bostock's* method of recognizing discrimination.

In other words, because the Civil Rights Act of 1964 says a literary agency can't fire a Muslim employee for asserting that transgender women are actually men because the Quran says so, it must also say that the agency can't fire Sasha White for asserting the same thing because her preferred brand of feminism says so.

There's one wrinkle in the argument: an employer actually *can* fire a Muslim employee for expressing religious beliefs in some situations. The crucial question is whether the speech was on the job or off the job. In *Peterson v. Wilmur Communications*, the plaintiff claimed to adhere to a religion called "Creativity" and to belong to the "World Church of the Creator." This supposed religion mainly just endorsed white supremacy. He gave an interview to local media discussing his religious beliefs and was demoted. The court found in favor of his Title VII claim, finding that he didn't do anything *at work* to justify his demotion.[3]

So for existing civil rights law to protect James Damore's beliefs about gender differences the same way it protects religious beliefs, he'd have to argue that he was speaking while "off the job." That would be a hard case to make: he did write about Google and post it on Google's internal message boards for employees, after all. I'll come back to that harder case in a bit.

But many of today's political firings would be easy cases because they clearly take place outside work. When Sasha White got fired for tweeting her support for J. K. Rowling's views on sex, she was using her personal account on her personal time, so the *Bostock*-based argument shows she should've been protected just as she would've been protected if she'd tweeted siding with the Bible's views on sex. Likewise, Grant Napear, a Sacramento Kings broadcaster forced out for tweeting that all lives matter, has a solid legal case. He was tweeting from his personal account on his personal time, just answering a question about what he thought about the Black Lives Matter movement.[4] To summarize this argument: if we combine *Bostock* with Title VII's ban on religious discrimination, it is clear that companies can't fire employees for off-the-job expressions of political beliefs.

Even on-the-job political speech gets *some* protection from the Civil Rights Act of 1964. Title VII compels employers to make efforts to accommodate religious belief in the workplace if doing so would impose a minimal burden on the business's operations. The EEOC gives a few examples of religious accommodations: a Catholic requests a schedule change so he can go to church on Good Friday, an atheist asks to be excused from prayers at the start of meetings, a Christian pharmacist asks to be excused from filling birth control prescriptions, a Jehovah's Witness wants to change tasks at a factory to avoid producing weapons.[5] My argument that complying with Title VII's ban on religious discrimination requires treating deeply held secular beliefs the same as these religious ones suggests that on-the-job *political* speech should receive similar accommodations. So if a factory accommodates a Jehovah's Witness's pacifism by allowing them to switch jobs to avoid making weapons, it has to do the same thing for an employee who has strong political beliefs that favor pacifism.

The EEOC's interpretation of Title VII doesn't just say that the law bans discrimination on the basis of a lack of religion as well as on the basis of adherence to religion. The EEOC also has a quite expansive definition of religion itself. So some seemingly secular beliefs actually would count as religious ones for legal purposes. This is a second legal path to the application of Title VII to political speech in the workplace, independent from my *Bostock*-based argument. The *Bostock*-style argument is that Title VII's ban on discrimination over lack of religion implies employers can't fire nonreligious employees over speech whenever they can't fire religious ones for the same speech. But the new argument is more straightforward: according to the EEOC, sometimes seemingly nonreligious speech just *is* actually religious speech. Here are the EEOC's criteria:

> *Religious beliefs include theistic beliefs as well as non-theistic "moral or ethical beliefs as to what is right and wrong which are sincerely held with the strength of traditional religious views." Although courts generally resolve doubts about particular beliefs in favor of finding that they are religious, beliefs are not protected merely because they are strongly held. Rather, religion typically concerns "ultimate ideas" about "life, purpose, and death." Social, political, or economic philosophies, as well as mere personal preferences, are not "religious" beliefs protected by Title VII.*[6]

So for an employee's political belief to be counted as religious for Title VII purposes, and therefore be protected when off the job and granted accommodations when on the job, it has to be both strongly held and tied to beliefs about ultimate ideas about life, purpose, and death. The EEOC elaborates on the latter requirement by saying that "a belief is 'religious' for Title VII purposes if it is 'religious' in the person's own scheme of things,' i.e., it is 'a sincere and meaningful belief that occupies in the life of its possessor a place parallel to that filled by . . . God.' "

The EEOC didn't just pull this definition out of a hat. It actually comes from a line of Supreme Court cases about how the Establishment Clause interacts with statutes allowing religious conscientious objectors to the draft. The first of these cases was *United States v. Seeger* during the Vietnam War. The draft board had rejected Daniel Seeger's application for conscientious objector status because he didn't believe in God; he opposed war for moral reasons. The Universal Military Training and Service Act only exempted religious conscientious objectors from the draft. The possible constitutional problem was that exempting religious objectors to the draft but not nonreligious ones might count as establishing a religion, which the Establishment Clause forbids. The Court got around this problem by saying that Seeger's moral belief counted as religious for government purposes because it had the same significance in his life that traditional religious belief would.[7]

The Court emphasized its expansive understanding of religion five years later in *Welsh v. United States*.[8] The big difference between *Seeger* and *Welsh*? On the form saying he was objecting for religious reasons, Seeger put "religious" in quotation marks. Welsh crossed it out. This caused pandemonium at the Court. You see, it was easier for it to pretend moral objections were religious ones when Seeger used quotation marks than it was when Welsh explicitly denied he had religious motivations. Four justices of the Court got around this fact by arguing that it didn't matter whether Welsh thought his belief was religious; what mattered was that he held it with the *same strength* as a religious belief. Justice Harlan wrote a concurrence calling a spade a spade. He acknowledged that the Court was really just saving itself from having to rule that the statute violated the Establishment Clause by effectively adding protections for nonreligious objectors into the statute itself. That's how Title VII's prohibition on discrimination by religion ends up including a prohibition on discrimination over lack of religion, and, for good measure, it's also how Title VII's definition of religion includes some secular beliefs.

So that's where the EEOC gets its expansive definition of

religion—it's adopting a hodgepodge of Supreme Court language that interprets certain laws protecting religion very broadly to avoid having to rule that they violate the Establishment Clause. The EEOC's definition of religion is an administrative interpretation of an assortment of judicial interpretations of a federal law. The three branches of government combined their powers to create a legal definition of religion that none of them particularly intended.

That helps explain why the EEOC's guidance about what it takes for a non-theistic belief to count as religious is pretty nebulous—what does it really mean for a secular belief to be tied to "ultimate ideas" about life, purpose, and death? What does it mean for a secular moral belief to occupy a place in one's life parallel to the one filled by a theist's belief in God? The Supreme Court never really explained itself because it was just grasping at straws.

So let's turn to exploring those questions now. In doing so, I'll argue that the ideology of wokeness meets both these requirements and that wokeness really is a religion—not just from a philosophical or social perspective but from a legal one.

ACCORDING TO THE EEOC's own terms, wokeness is literally a religion. It turns out that being a religion is a double-edged sword from a legal perspective. Our law both protects employees' religious beliefs and protects them from having their employers' religious beliefs imposed on them.

That second part is crucial. In the last section, I made three arguments: first, that political beliefs like James Damore's or Sasha White's should receive the same legal protections as religious beliefs due to Title VII's prohibition on the government discriminating over a lack of religion; second, that some secular beliefs actually count as religious ones under Title VII's expansive definition of religion, and employees are therefore protected from termination when they voice those beliefs off the job; and third, that those employees are entitled to reasonable accommodations of those beliefs when they express them on the job.

These three arguments all talk about what employees are legally permitted to do. But now I'm adding a fourth, independent argument that focuses on what employers *can't* do instead of what employees *can* do: since wokeness is a religion, employers can't impose it on their employees. An employer violates the law when it fires an employee for failing to bow down to the employer's religious tenets.*

Here's how this new argument works. Suppose that Damore's or White's beliefs about sex didn't meet the EEOC's standard for being religious in nature—one could argue that Damore's beliefs, for instance, were simply based on his interpretation of the psychological research and that no matter how strongly he believed his inferences, they didn't fit into some grand account of the universe that fills the same role as a set of beliefs involving God. Similarly, one could argue that no matter how strongly White believed that transgender women are importantly different from women, the type of feminism her belief stems from doesn't play a religious role in her life.

All of that is about when an *employee's* particular beliefs are protected from their employer. There's an entirely separate branch of law saying that an employer can't force its *own* religious beliefs on its employees. And so under this doctrine, the legal question is not whether *Damore's* beliefs were religious in nature—it's whether *Google's* were.

It's well established that the law forbids an employer from firing

---

* I thank Professor Jed Rubenfeld for suggesting this argument to me—one that he pioneered and that I hope he will write more about in legal journals in the future.

an employee because the employee doesn't adhere to the employer's religious beliefs. That's true whether the employee's conduct takes place on the job or not. In *Venters v. City of Delphi*, for instance, Jennifer Venters, a radio dispatcher for the police department in Delphi, Indiana, was fired after more than a year of disputes with the born-again chief of the department, Larry Ives, who repeatedly told her he was on a mission from God to save the people of Delphi from damnation, that her lifestyle was sinful, that she ought to go to church if she wanted to keep her job, and so on.[9] Not only did an appellate court rule in favor of Venters when she sued over religious discrimination, the court clarified her argument for her. Its reasoning didn't revolve around any right of Venters to express *her* religious beliefs—it was about her right to be free from having the *police chief's* religious beliefs imposed on her:

> What matters in this context is not so much what Venters' own religious beliefs were, but Ives' asserted perception that she did not share his own. She need not put a label on her own religious beliefs, therefore, or demonstrate that she communicated her religious status and needs as she would if she were complaining that the city had failed to accommodate a particular religious practice. Venters need only show that her perceived religious shortcomings (her unwillingness to strive for salvation as Ives understood it, for example) played a motivating role in her discharge.[10]

So, legally, the easiest path to victory for people like Damore or White is to argue that the woke ideology that made their employers fire them counts as a religion. In the old days, before Title VII, employees might get fired for their heterodox religious views. Wokeness is the new orthodoxy, and these days, people are being fired for not adhering to it. We just haven't taken the step of legally recognizing that wokeness is actually a religion.

That's an easy case to make. The EEOC's own guidance already tells us that non-theistic beliefs can count as religious ones, and it outlines the two requirements they have to meet to do so. The tenets of wokeness clearly meet both requirements, so woke beliefs are therefore religious in nature.

Here's an easy way to frame the question. Remember Creativity, the supposed religion from *Peterson v. Wilmur Communications, Inc.*? Creativity taught that its adherents should "live their lives according to the principle that what is good for white people is the ultimate good and what is bad for white people is the ultimate sin."[11] If Creativity, professing white supremacy, is a religion, then Wokeness, professing the opposite, must be too.

Or consider "Onionhead." In 2007, a company called CCG adopted a program known as "Harnessing Happiness" or "Onionhead" to boost morale and cooperation. CCG employees had to attend "positivity sessions" during which they were taught that "choice, not chance, determines human destiny," just as employees at woke corporations today are forced to attend "diversity and inclusion" sessions in which they are taught that systemic racism determines human destiny. Employees at CCG who rejected Onionhead were fired, and the EEOC successfully sued on their behalf under Title VII, claiming this was religious discrimination even though CCG insisted Onionhead was secular. In the 2016 case of *EEOC v. United Health Programs of America*, the court found that Onionhead was indeed a religion.[12]

So before I dig deep into the legal analysis, just think of it this way: we know that *some* non-theistic belief systems must count as religious under Title VII. If Creativity and Onionhead are legal religions, Wokeness must be one too.

Remember, the EEOC says that non-theistic moral or ethical beliefs count as religious ones under Title VII if (1) they're as *strongly held* as religious ones typically are and (2) they *occupy the same role in one's life* as religious beliefs, meaning they're part of a belief system that makes claims about "ultimate ideas" like "life, purpose, and death."

It's easy to prove that woke beliefs meet the EEOC's first test for being religious—Google and all the other woke capitalists insist with every breath that their commitments to diversity, equity, inclusion, and all that are strongly held. Showing that woke beliefs meet the EEOC's second requirement for counting as religious is the one that would require a lawyer to do a bit of work. But if any non-theistic belief system counts as one that fills a religious role in one's life, it's wokeness. That means both that employees are protected by Title VII when they express woke beliefs and that they're protected from having their employer's woke beliefs imposed on them. Wokeness's religious nature is a double-edged sword.

So we circle back to the question I ended the last section with—what does it really mean for a belief to concern ultimate ideas about life, purpose and death? What does it mean for a belief not about God to play the same role in one's life as a belief about God? The question sounds almost philosophical, but it turns out to be a very important practical one. It's the question the legal application of Title VII hinges on, the question the legal fate of woke capitalism itself hinges on. If the tenets of wokeness play the same role in one's life that religious belief does, making sense of the universe in the same way religion does, then wokeness is a religion, legally.

We don't have to just guess at the answer. There are actually a growing number of academics who argue that wokeness really is a religion in the fullest sense of the word. Georgetown professor

Joshua Mitchell, for instance, argues that America has "relocated its religion to the realm of politics" and that identity politics shares the same core premises as Christianity:

> *Ponder for a moment, Christianity. Without the sacrifice of the innocent Lamb of God, there would be no Christianity. Christ, the scapegoat, renders the impure pure—by taking upon Himself "the sins of the world." By the purging of the scapegoat, those for whom He is the sacrificial offering purify themselves. Identity politics is a political version of this cleansing for groups rather than for individuals. The scapegoat in the case of identity politics is the white heterosexual male who, if purged, supposedly will restore and confirm the cleanliness of all other groups of communities. He is the transgressor; all others—women, blacks, Hispanics, LGBTQs—have their sins covered over by the scapegoat, just as the scapegoated Christ covered over the sins of all the descendants of Adam.*[13]

Mitchell's right. The analogy between Christianity and the Church of Diversity is so strong that it's evident that wokeness plays a religious role in one's life, and therefore really is a religion, for legal purposes. Under the woke worldview, being born white, straight, male, or—worse—all three is an original sin that one must spend their life atoning for. Just as Catholics think we inherited the sins of Adam and Eve even if we've done nothing wrong, disciples of wokeness think we've inherited the sins of the Founding Fathers—the mechanism for group guilt is just called systemic racism instead of original sin. And as I pointed out earlier, the woke left punishes its heretics with the same fervor as any inquisition and for the same reasons—even more important than bringing infidels to the light is keeping the faithful on the straight and narrow path. Any deviation from orthodoxy must be punished.

That's a key part of why wokeness really does play a religious role in one's life: it's a *system* of beliefs that stands as one indivisible unit and touches on all aspects of one's existence. You aren't allowed to consider the evidence and pick and choose which parts of wokeness you like—if you're in for a penny, you're in for a pound. Like Christianity or Islam, wokeness purports to provide a system of beliefs that explains *everything*, and it doesn't allow its believers to pick and choose which of its explanations they like. Wokeness counts as a religion for the EEOC's purposes because, like other religions, it provides unified, systematic explanations that order one's entire life. And like other religions, wokeness gives commands, not suggestions. And its disciples are expected to obey all of its commands, not just the ones that make sense to them.

You're not allowed to be a little woke, just like Christians can't follow their five favorite commandments. You have to embrace the whole LGBTQ acronym. Feminism too, but not the trans-exclusionary kind. And the acronyms that function as lists of commandments keep growing. Last time I checked, it had become something like LGBTTQQIAAP. There's a new acronym making its way around: BIPOC, for "Black, Indigenous, People of Color." It used to just be "people of color." BIPOC is all the rage in universities these days, which means it's a year away from being fashionable in corporate boardrooms. The point of the updated acronym is to deemphasize Asian Americans in the list of identities that matter. The high priests of Diversity decided Asians were privileged, or "white-adjacent," so they updated their acronym-commandments to demote us.

It's not a religion I subscribe to, but wokeness really is a religion. It does meet the EEOC's two-part definition because its adherents cling to it fervently and it dictates all their thoughts and deeds. Wokeness touches every part of its disciples' lives. Like any other religion, being woke isn't supposed to be a narrow, one-off commitment—it's supposed to be a way of life. It gives its believers purpose and meaning. It's the structure that they use to make sense of the universe. Where a nonwoke person sees ordinary interactions, for instance, a disciple of wokeness sees microaggressions. Just as a Christian sees God's hand in all of Creation, someone who's woke sees the guiding hand of identity-based power relations everywhere they look.

Being a religion comes with legal costs and benefits. My analysis implies that an employee should be legally protected for expressing woke beliefs outside work and have those beliefs accommodated at it, just like any other religious beliefs. But it also implies that woke employers can't punish their employees for refusing to worship at the same church. So businesses can't punish woke employees for saying that black lives matter, but woke companies can't punish employees for saying that all lives matter.

It's a simple legal insight with implications that stretch from Silicon Valley to Wall Street. Today many employees, perhaps many of you, face the choice between being able to keep their job to put food on the table or being able to speak their mind freely. It's a Hobson's choice.

That's not our country, but a distortion of it. In America we don't force you to choose between the American Dream and free speech. You get to enjoy both at once. This chapter offers legal proof for that basic idea. James Damore can't legally be fired for sharing his views on gender disparities; Emmanuel Cafferty can't be fired for accidentally making an "OK" sign with his hands; Huntington Ingalls can't fire one of its shipyard workers for wearing a Trump hat. And you can't be fired for refusing to attend the diversity and inclusion seminar hosted by Robin DiAngelo in the company auditorium. If your boss gives you a hard time, tell him you'll see him in court and that you'll be sending the company your legal bills too. Who knows, they might even cost as much as DiAngelo's speaking fees.

CHAPTER 12

Critical Diversity Theory

I LEARNED A VALUABLE LESSON from former Harvard president Larry Summers. I didn't learn it from him personally, but I picked it up as I watched his fall from grace while I was a student there, back in 2007.

The lesson was that there are certain things you just can't say—even at a liberal arts university in a democratic society. In my senior year, Summers was forced to step down as the university's president for comments that he made at a conference about diversity in the science and engineering workforce. He warned that his comments were intended to be an "attempt at provocation." He offered three hypotheses for the higher proportion of men in high-end science and engineering positions. One hypothesis was that men were more drawn than women to those jobs. Another was that hirers discriminated against women.[1]

And Summers' third hypothesis was that there was greater *variability* among men in some cognitive abilities relevant to science and engineering. Summers observed that for certain math tests, there were higher standard deviations in test scores for boys than for girls. That means that the students who performed best and worst on these tests were usually boys.[2]

His attempt at provocation succeeded, and I understand why some women at Harvard were annoyed by his comments. But the firestorm that followed was wildly disproportionate to what he actually said: his speech became the scandal of a generation for the university. After taking a thorough drubbing in the press, Summers—one-time US treasury secretary, among the youngest tenured professors in Harvard's history, and a respected university leader—was forced to resign as Harvard's president.

I was selected to be one of three students on the advisory committee to choose his replacement. It quickly became clear that the committee's mandate was to appoint a woman to make up for Summers's cardinal sin. And that's exactly what we did, even though no one publicly identified that as our objective. Harvard's motto is "Veritas," but very little about what happened that year felt like the pursuit of truth. It was a shame to me that Larry Summers was punished for asking an important question that others ignored, for example, the International Chess Federation, which organizes separate championships for men and women without saying a peep about why.

The lesson was clear: extol free speech publicly, but keep controversial thoughts to yourself. Got it.

As the years passed, I realized what I'd witnessed back in 2007 was neither the beginning nor end of wokeness, but an important point in the middle of its story: the point where it became dominant. When wokeness struck down the president of Harvard, it raised its flag triumphantly over all of academia.

Race and gender studies had been laying down roots for decades, but they really started flourishing around that time. So-called "critical" theories sprouted like weeds. Racism was redefined—the critical race theory experts had discovered that it was definitionally impossible to be racist toward white people. Their students dutifully spread that epiphany to the rest of society. "Intersectionality" became the word of the day, and then the decade, even though no one understood exactly what it meant—an ideal feature for any concept to evade falsifiability.

A few academics fought the rising tide. In what has been dubbed "the grievance studies affair," a trio of liberal academics, Helen Pluckrose, Peter Boghossian, and James Lindsay, successfully published several purposefully farcical academic papers in peer-reviewed journals in fields like cultural studies, queer studies, fat studies, race and gender studies, and so on. Among the highlights were an article using observations from dog parks to prove that dogs engaged in rape culture, one arguing that men could reduce transphobia by anally penetrating themselves with sex toys, and a version of *Mein Kampf* rewritten in feminist jargon. The trio had many similar articles under review; the hoax only stopped after journalists at *The Wall Street Journal* uncovered it.[3] Deprived of their hoax, Pluckrose and Lindsay published a book called *Cynical Theories* that revealed the intellectual bankruptcy of academia's love affair with identity politics.

The grievance studies affair was the proud inheritor of a tradition begun by Alan Sokal's famous hoax back in 1996. Concerned that academia was beginning to publish anything that used fancy language and scientific theories to support liberal conclusions, Sokal had published an article titled "Transgressing the Boundaries: Toward a Transformative Hermeneutics of Quantum Gravity" in the postmodern journal *Social Text*. Sokal used a bunch of scientific gibberish to argue that quantum gravity, a subfield of physics that uses quantum mechanics to describe gravity, had progressive political implications.

Sokal's article contained gems like the claim that science "cannot assert a privileged epistemological status with respect to counterhegemonic narratives emanating from dissident or marginalized communities."[4] Funnily enough, you can find the exact same proclamations in the work of liberal favorites like Robin DiAngelo two decades later. But now they're made unironically and accepted as gospel.

People like Sokal, Pluckrose, Boghossian, and Lindsay fought the good fight, but the odds were always against them. They now find themselves pariahs on the outskirts of academia. Portland State University, where Boghossian works as a philosophy professor, instituted a research misconduct inquiry against him over the grievance studies affair. It ruled that he had violated ethical guidelines on research involving human subjects. He is now banned from doing further research. Pluckrose and Lindsay have no academic positions; Pluckrose's biography in *Cynical Theories* vaguely refers to her as "an exile from the humanities."

Pluckrose is far from alone in her exile. Conservatives have long been unofficially banned from academia, outside of a few enclaves like Notre Dame and the University of Chicago. Now centrists and liberals who don't agree with the new identity politics paradigm are being purged too.

The ideological cleansing extends to administrative staff, not just teachers. For instance, Jodi Shaw, a liberal, divorced mother of two, just resigned from her job as a student support coordinator at Smith College, her alma mater, after a years-long struggle against its racially hostile environment. Smith had heavily emphasized racial sensitivity training after a black student complained that some staff members had racially profiled her. It made no difference that the law firm Smith hired to investigate her claims concluded they were false.[5]

Jodi Shaw's troubles began when the library orientation program she'd been preparing for months was axed at the last minute because she was going to rap, and white women were forbidden from rapping at the newly sensitive version of Smith—and then because Shaw lacked a prepared program, she wasn't able to get the promotion she'd been up for and had to accept a lower-paying job.

In her new position, she was often told her job required her to discuss her thoughts and feelings about her whiteness and that any refusal to discuss her "white privilege" was a case of "white fragility." By the end of her time at Smith, even Shaw's polite refusals to speak about her race were dubbed acts of racial aggression. She went public with her story and then chose to resign from Smith instead of accepting hush money from the college.[6]

There are millions of stories like Shaw's, unfortunately. What makes her story special is that she's willing to tell it and willing to accept unemployment in a pandemic rather than bowing to the woke regime. A recent report from the Center for the Study of Partisanship and Ideology found that over a third of conservative academics and PhD students in the US have been threatened with disciplinary action for their views, and 70 percent of conservative academics report a hostile departmental climate for their beliefs. The report contains a number of other grim statistical findings, like the fact that more than 40 percent of US academics would refuse to hire a Trump supporter.[7]

The Church of Diversity waxes strong. All must be cleansed; all must be saved.

The war for academia has already been lost. When identity politics took down Larry Summers in 2007, it was a sign that wokeness had won at the highest levels and it was time to begin the mop-up action. Now, having won everything they can win in universities, grievance studies and critical theories are turning to new battlegrounds: corporations and governments. And they do it all under the banner of Diversity.

Institutions including companies, nonprofits, and government agencies are increasingly adopting implicit and explicit approaches to foster greater diversity in their ranks. In principle this is a good thing: diversity of thought improves the quality of decisions in most organizations. However, in recent years, many organizations have resorted exclusively to using genetic characteristics as a proxy for diversity of thought—relying on metrics such as race and gender as the exclusive barometers for measuring diversity in the leadership of an organization.

This approach is flawed on multiple levels. First, when institutions conflate racial and gender diversity metrics with diversity of thought in their organizations, they implicitly reinforce the incorrect assumption that genetic characteristics predict something important about the way that a person thinks—the most fundamental assumption underlying racism itself. Second, this approach empowers entrenched managers to create the visible appearance of diversity in their organizations while avoiding the need to engage with true diversity of thought, including challenges to their incumbency. Third, when a narrow conception of diversity is implemented through affirmative action or other quota-based systems, that fuels racism and sexism by fostering tokenism in the workplace and animus among communities that fail to benefit from these programs.

Notwithstanding these flaws, institutions are relying increasingly on racial and gender-related characteristics as the exclusive basis for measuring and implementing diversity in their organizations. Today leaders who fail to adopt this narrow approach are publicly vilified. However, these same leaders have also failed to offer alternative ways to measure and implement true diversity of thought in their organizations.

I propose a new movement to resist the enforcement of race- and gender-based diversity metrics across institutions by offering a new vision for achieving true diversity of thought in any organization. This new movement aims to more effectively achieve three essential objectives: (1) define what types of diversity of thought are important to an organization, (2) measure diversity of thought in an organization, and (3) select for diversity of thought when hiring leaders to scale an organization.

I call this "critical diversity theory" (or CDT) to reflect its critical perspective on the prevailing narrative of racial and gender diversity, in response to intellectual movements such as critical race theory and critical feminist theory, which spawned this narrow conception of diversity. Critical theory refers to an approach to inquiry that reveals and challenges power structures. CDT should follow this tradition by challenging the *new* power structure created by critical race and gender theory itself—one that has weaponized a narrow conception of diversity to implement a monolithic social agenda that is increasingly intolerant of dissent and agnostic to the institutional purpose of an organization.

CDT challenges this new power structure in a simple way. The first fundamental premise of CDT is that different organizations ought to approach diversity of thought in different ways depending on their institutional purpose—that is, by taking diverse approaches to the question of diversity itself. The second fundamental premise of CDT is that the most effective way to achieve diversity of thought in an organization is to screen candidates for the diversity of their thoughts, that the most effective way to achieve diversity of experience is to screen candidates for the diversity of their experiences, and that the most effective way to measure diversity of thought or experience in an organization is to measure the diversity of thoughts or experiences in that organization—without regard to genetically inherited characteristics such as race and gender.

CDT must become an interdisciplinary movement to succeed. As a starting point, this new movement will require leaders of companies, nonprofits, and government institutions to work together to create new methods of measuring and implementing true diversity of thought in their organizations. I propose a multidisciplinary collaboration between leaders of these organizations, working in conjunction with academic counterparts to develop measurable tools that any organization can implement to assess and advance diversity of thought in a way that is best suited to its own organizational purpose.

This will not be an easy undertaking: one reason that race and gender have become the predominant metrics for diversity is that they are simple to measure and implement. By contrast, true diversity of thought is difficult to achieve, especially when coupled with an organization's need for employees to align around its goals. A well-run organization requires not only diversity of thought but also an unwavering commitment to its mission and principles. These goals are necessarily in tension with one another, at least in some measure.

For example, one of Roivant's business principles is "be contrarian"—that is, challenge conventional wisdom when necessary.

It's impossible to create an environment where people challenge conventional wisdom if everyone thinks in the same way. So we value diversity in the ways people think—some who craft arguments, some who are expert at interpreting data, and so on. That's one form of diversity of thought.

But another of our business principles is to "climb the wall"—that is, to work hard to overcome obstacles. We *don't* want diverse attitudes with respect to their willingness to do that. Our main goal as a company is to develop medicines faster for patients who need them. We don't want diversity in our employees' commitments toward that goal. That's something that everyone at Roivant should be equally committed to. Applauding "diversity" *ad nauseum* is easy, but defining what type of diversity each organization should desire is much more important.

That's what CDT is all about: it forces institutions to define their true purpose. This new movement requires leaders of organizations to openly acknowledge the areas in which they seek diversity of thought while also defining the areas in which they prioritize *organizational alignment* over diversity of opinions. These are fundamental questions for any organization to answer. Diversity of thought is important, but only insofar as it helps an institution realize its true purpose.

Skin-deep diversity metrics like race and gender often subvert true institutional purpose in a woke world by supplanting that purpose with the activist goals espoused by critical race and critical gender theorists. By contrast, CDT invites leaders of organizations to actually *use* diversity—in particular, diversity of thought—to define the true essence of an organization by defining the areas in which diversity of thought is desirable and the areas in which it is not.

The answers to these questions will inevitably vary across organizations, and that's good. These are the very differences that allow
one institution to distinguish its purpose from that of another. Institutional pluralism is at the heart of American pluralism. Universities
educate students, pharma companies make medicines for patients,
banks lend money to borrowers, charities help people in need,
museums memorialize history, orchestras perform music, Congress
makes laws. They don't all do the same thing, and we shouldn't
want them to. That we have so many different institutions with distinct purposes is part of what makes our society vibrant. That's true
diversity. Regardless of our attitude toward woke values—whether
we love them or not—we should be dubious of dissolving true institutional diversity in favor of any homogeneous social agenda, even
if that agenda masquerades in the name of Diversity itself.

Here are five key principles that can serve as the foundation
of this new critical diversity theory movement across our
institutions. These principles are simple, not complicated;
implementing them will be hard, not easy.

Excellence, Opportunity, and Civility—an Alternative to "Diversity, Equity, and Inclusion"

1. **Excellence First**. Diversity is not an end in itself, but a
   means toward achieving excellence.
2. **Institutional Purpose**. Institutions should define their own
   unique purpose and define what kinds of diversity they
   seek—and do *not* seek—in order to pursue their purpose.

3. **Institutional Pluralism.** Nonprofit institutions may have conflicting perspectives on important social questions. That's a good thing: institutional pluralism is part of American pluralism.

4. **Separation of Corporation and State.** For-profit companies should focus exclusively on making products and providing services for profit, *not* on advancing unrelated social or political agendas.

5. **End Discrimination.** The best way to stop discrimination on the basis of race is to stop discriminating on the basis of race.[8] Same goes for gender and other inherited attributes.

M Y GRADUATION FROM Harvard in 2007 was a memorable one. I had the opportunity to see Bill Gates himself in the flesh at my graduation. I sat in the front row and shook his hand on stage.

Yet even today, I distinctly remember my disappointment in his speech at the time. It wasn't a bad speech. It just felt like the entire thing was about delivering an epilogue to the real story. He focused on the importance of giving back—but never really talked about how one goes about generating the things that one later gives back. That was the part I was most interested in learning from him that day, but I never did. His most memorable line of the speech, the one that stuck with me, was this: "Humanity's greatest advances are not in its discoveries, but in how those discoveries are applied to reduce inequity."

He concluded his speech by calling the students in the audience to action:

Be activists. Take on the big inequities. It will be one of the great experiences of your lives. You graduates are coming of age in an amazing time. As you leave Harvard, you have technology that members of my class never had. You have awareness of global inequity, which we did not have. And with that awareness, you likely also have an informed conscience that will torment you if you abandon these people whose lives you could change with very little effort. You have more than we had; you must start sooner, and carry on longer. Knowing what you know, how could you not?

As I listened to Gates, I looked on stage and saw Drew Gilpin Faust, the new president of the university, who had just replaced Larry Summers after he had been forced to resign for his now-infamous remarks. Despite being a student representative on the committee that selected her, I really had no idea how President Faust would actually lead the university. All I knew was that she was the first female president of Harvard, and that's what mattered most in the spring of 2007.

Things changed at Harvard after President Summers's departure. Under President Faust, in 2016 the university decided to change the title of certain academic posts that included the word "master" to "faculty dean" instead in response to protests from students who claimed the title had "echoes of slavery." The actual etymological root of the word was "magister" (Latin for "teacher"), but Harvard made the name change anyway.[9] A few years later, the university launched the Committee to Articulate Principles on Renaming, a sixteen-person body to explore the renaming of campus buildings, spaces, programs, professorships, and other objects "in view of their association with historical figures whose advocacy or support of activities would today be found abhorrent by members of the Harvard community."[10] Along the way, Harvard would banish the sinners too—notably in 2019, when the university pressured one of its law professors to step down as a faculty dean for serving as legal defense counsel to Harvey Weinstein.[11] I found it curious that Harvardians who vehemently advocated for the right to legal counsel for alleged terrorists in Guantanamo (which I too personally support) weren't also vocal about defending the same principle for Harvey Weinstein.

It was fitting that my commencement ceremony would prepare me for a decade ahead in a new world that looked very different from the one I knew as a kid in Ohio. In retrospect I witnessed the dawn of modern wokeism on display at graduation that day, a new culture that would soon spread across the country like a wildfire and eventually reach Ohio too. We were entering a new era obsessed with empowering those whom we label as "disempowered." Large corporations and universities goaded those same people to *self-identify* as disempowered too, leaving those very corporations and universities more empowered than ever.

It was the beginning of a long saga of sorting and then re-sorting ourselves into groups, of signifying our tribes to one another through the trivial things we say and wear. In this brave new era, the sinners of past epochs would face a stark choice: either self-flagellate on stage like Bill Gates or disappear like Larry Summers.

CHAPTER 13

Woke Consumerism and the Big Sort

N OW WOKENESS HAS GRADUATED FROM college and entered the corporate world. Modern corporations seize every opportunity to signal their virtuous identities to us so that as their customers, we can signal our own.

This mercenary corporate virtue-signaling was vividly on display after George Floyd was killed, when even fast-food companies fell all over themselves to align themselves with the Black Lives Matter movement. Pepsi had pioneered the effort to profit off the BLM movement years earlier with a commercial featuring Kendall Jenner abandoning a photo shoot to solve police brutality by offering soda to a cop. But this early effort to make money off of BLM was too crude. This time, corporations knew celebrities would not be enough. The situation called for socially conscious tweets.

Popeyes' Twitter account was one of the first to throw its weight behind the cause, tweeting, "We are nothing without Black lives. There's no room for injustice. We commit to strengthening every facet of our culture and policies to foster an environment where equality for Black people is a priority. We'll use our platform to support this movement. #BlackLivesMatter." Not to be outdone, a day later Wendy's Twitter account chimed in with "Our voice would be nothing without Black culture. Right now, a lot of people are hurting because of blatant racism against Black people. Their voices need to be heard. Period. #BlackLivesMatter."

The commitment was short-lived. Wendy's lost its voice a week later when Rayshard Brooks was killed outside one of its drive-throughs. It wasn't really Wendy's fault, but it decided to lie low just to be safe. Its Twitter account stayed silent for three weeks, resurfacing mainly to strenuously deny rumors that Wendy's had donated money to Donald Trump. It had leapt to associate itself with BLM at first, but the moment the association threatened its image, it shifted with the winds of profit. In the fight for justice, for-profit corporations make fickle friends.

Wokeness doomed itself when it became so mainstream that companies realized they could make money off it. Watching Wendy's Twitter account try to one-up Popeyes in social awareness is like hearing Hillary Clinton say, "Pokémon GO to the polls"[1]: both are signs that a trend has become too popular for its own good. There's something disingenuous about it, something condescending. Whenever this pandering occurs, whether it comes from politicians or corporations, you just know some slick PR guys brainstormed it up during a business lunch and then sat back and said, "They'll eat this shit up." They usually high-five each other afterward.

Make no mistake—that's what State Street was really thinking when it commissioned Fearless Girl, and it's what Goldman Sachs is really thinking when it institutes its boardroom diversity quota: *they'll eat this shit up.*

Part of what I'm saying is that bankers should shut up and bank. But I'm also making a broader point about America. At this point, anyone could see that something in this nation is broken. Maybe everyone sees it. We all want justice, we just disagree about what it is. We crave justice, but all Wendy's really has to offer is burgers, so it artificially ties the two together. Corporations have started feeding us aphorisms about equality because they know we hunger for more substantial fare.

Woke CEOs and investors trick consumers with the illusion that by engaging in normal acts of consumption we're fulfilling our social obligations. They tell us that by giving our money to the right companies (conveniently, *their* companies), we're making the world a better place. Maybe the idea is that it's strictly better to give our money to socially responsible companies than their near-identical competitors.

But we'd be strictly better off if companies and their customers ended the shared fiction that every capitalist transaction must also be part of some grand fight between good and evil. I was once at a New Year's party where a guy spent five minutes telling me how his handmade silk shirt was some kind of symbolic protest against the colonialism of the Dutch East India Company. All I remember is that I wasn't convinced he was doing as much good as he thought he was. He probably would've done more for the causes he cared about by giving the money to the first person who asked for it. But then he wouldn't have the silk shirt. Some company fed him some story about how he could make the world better by buying material things, and he eagerly ate it up.

Whatever justice is, surely it can't be attained so incidentally, by just picking the right shirts, the right burgers, and the right bankers. You can't get things you want anyway and order some equality on the side.

Sometimes a shirt is just a shirt. By making it part of some grand narrative about colonialism, corporations are appealing to our desire to be part of something greater than ourselves. Of course, brands have always tried to dress up ordinary goods and services as part of a lifestyle, part of an identity, but what's new is this widespread effort to convince consumers that buying these ordinary things is noble and virtuous. Corporations used to try to convince you that buying their stuff would make you cool; now they tell you buying it will make you good. The difference is subtle but important. What's cool is entirely subjective, but what's good is not. There's no real risk to letting the slick PR people define what's cool, but there's a lot of risk to letting them define what's good.

When I was young, it was cool to be rebellious, to act like you didn't care about anything. Now it's cool to be woke and act like you care about everything. So the stores in the mall that outfitted us as rebels when we were young dress us up like good people now that we're older.

By now we all know that woke shirts and woke tweets are often forms of virtue-signaling, but this obvious problem masks a more insidious one: corporate wokeness, and much of wokeness, in general, is fundamentally about *identity*-signaling. The main agenda, for both Wendy's and Popeyes, wasn't actually to send people the message that they were good; it was to send certain people the message that they were members of the same tribe—and by establishing membership in the tribe of their target consumers, they *automatically* establish themselves as good.

The two weren't actually trying to one-up each other at all, which explains why their statements were nearly identical. The true corporate competition was not between Wendy's and Popeyes, but between those two and Chick-fil-A, which had become a favorite target of liberal boycotts ever since it donated to religious organizations that opposed gay marriage. The tweets that Wendy's and Popeyes posted about BLM were obviously shallow. But shallow tweets are enough to sell a tribal association: if you want a fast-food chicken sandwich, you have to choose whether to open up a bag from Chick-fil-A in front of your friends or one from a chain that belongs to your tribe. You don't make the choice based on which sandwich tastes better.

How did we come to this farcical point where your politics chooses your sandwiches and your sandwich makers must choose their politics? I'm tempted to say that nothing is sacred anymore, but America's problem is actually the opposite: nothing is allowed to be ordinary anymore. Partisanship now infects everything and attaches sanctity to even the most mundane consumer decisions. In the American search for identity, to give our lives meaning, we make the ordinary sacred.

THE WAY WE use ordinary things to signal our tribal identities has dangerous consequences for our democracy. One of them is that this rampant identity-signaling has made it easier for us to unconsciously segregate ourselves.

Journalist Bill Bishop documented this new informal segregation in his 2004 book *The Big Sort: Why the Clustering of Likeminded America Is Tearing Us Apart*. He points out that as Americans have gained more economic freedom and technology has made travel easier over the decades, we've been more able than ever to move where we want to. He argues that when we choose a neighborhood, we choose it based on a lot of little factors that make it "just feel right"—things like whether there are parks, what kind of churches are around, whether you see neighbors walking their dogs and washing their trucks, whether there's a Starbucks on the corner. Whether there's a Chick-fil-A nearby.

It turns out that all these little factors that make a place feel right map onto partisan associations—it feels right to live among neighbors who share your values and beliefs. And so over the last few decades Americans have sorted themselves into red neighborhoods and blue ones. Bishop documents this self-sorting by examining the percentage of voters who lived in "landslide counties" during competitive presidential elections, counties where one party won by 20 percentage points or more. He found that the one point since World War II when Americans were most likely to live side by side with people who supported another political party was in 1976, at the time of the election between Gerald Ford and Jimmy Carter—at that time, during a close contest, only 26 percent of Americans lived in counties where the vote was a landslide.

Americans drifted apart over the next few decades. By 1992, during another competitive election, about 38 percent of Americans lived in landslide counties, and after that, like-minded Americans just kept flocking together. By the time Bishop was writing in 2004, "in one of the closest presidential contests in history, 48.3% of voters lived in communities where the election wasn't close at all."[2] David Wasserman, US House editor and senior election analyst for *The Cook Political Report*, investigated whether Bishop's thesis about the Big Sort has held up over the years and found that things have actually gotten even worse. By the time of the hard-fought 2016 election between Hillary Clinton and Donald Trump, a whopping 61 percent of American voters lived in counties that voted for one of the two by a 20-point margin or more. Wasserman concluded that purple America has all but disappeared; it's all red and blue now.[3]

The bottom line regarding these stats? Forty years ago it was completely normal to live alongside people who had different politics than you, but today it's strange. The country's been slowly but surely brought to a boil in a partisan pot. As we've gradually become more aware of our differences, we've increasingly chosen to surround ourselves with people who think the same way as us.

Corporate wokeness is an important enabler of this self-segregation because the things we buy dictate the places we go. They also determine whom we interact with once we get there. The things we buy and the merchants we buy those things from now signal which side we're on.

We don't just segregate ourselves geographically—the Big Sort has gone online too. Social media companies promised to bring people together, but instead they provide echo chambers where like-minded people reinforce each other's biases. Technology has made it easier than ever for us to travel where we want and talk to whom we want, but it turns out what most of us wanted was to reaffirm our beliefs. Back in 2004, Bishop noticed that we'd been sorting ourselves in physical space, and in the time since, we've done the same thing in cyberspace.

In 2020, when I joined Parler, the alternative social media site that became popular for its commitment to free speech in the wake of Silicon Valley's coordinated censorship crusade, I posted something that was critical of woke capitalism. One of the first responses I got was "Shut the fuck up, you fucking foreigner." Meanwhile, Twitter was no better. Users who self-identify as progressives routinely comment "shut up you right-wing Patel" in response to my tweets. My far-right friends gravitate to Parler. My liberal friends view Parler as untouchable and flock to Twitter. In reality they're both just echo chambers designed to allow different tribes to vent their frustrations.

The online sort only accelerates the Big Sort in the real world too. When corporations take sides in America's partisan culture war, they're not just signaling their tribe, they're selling you an easy way to signal yours. This kind of corporate wokeness can seem superficial, and it is, but there's something deviously sophisticated at its core. The clothes we wear, the food we eat, and the businesses we shop at have become our uniforms and weapons in America's tribal feud. If you're a liberal who likes coffee, you get it at Starbucks. If you're conservative, maybe you buy it from Black Rifle Coffee Company, which exists mostly to sell coffee to conservatives who hate Starbucks. It claims that if you love America, you ought to love its coffee, which sports names like "Freedom Fuel" but probably just tastes like coffee.

The taste was never really the point. Corporations are arming us with symbols that let us identify friends and foes so that we can sort ourselves to make us better consumers. History is littered with examples of young soldiers who fire someone else's gun from their shoulders. Today, capitalists are the gunsmiths of our culture war.

O UR INCREASING USE of ordinary goods to identify our tribal friends is just one side of the new trend of woke consumerism—it also demands that its disciples boycott those goods to punish political foes. Consumers commit a grave moral error when they give in to that demand. Money and morality weren't meant to mix.

Even refried beans have become weapons in the culture war. The growing trend of using companies as proxies to signal political identity was exemplified by the battle over Goya Foods, the largest Hispanic-owned food company in the US. Goya got into trouble when CEO Robert Unanue praised President Trump while attending a White House ceremony rolling out the administration's Hispanic Prosperity Initiative. Overnight, whether you ate Goya products or not was inseparably tied to whether you supported Trump.

Congresswoman Alexandria Ocasio-Cortez rallied the progressive troops by tweeting, "Oh look, it's the sound of me Googling 'how to make your own Adobo.'" Thousands of liberals joined her, posting pictures and videos of them banishing Goya from their pantries. On the other side, Ivanka Trump and the president himself both posted pictures smiling in front of Goya products. "If it's Goya, it has to be good," Ivanka wrote, parroting the company's motto as she proudly displayed a can of black beans. Not to be outdone, President Trump tweeted a picture of him giving a toothy grin and two thumbs up to a spread of Goya products laid out on his desk in the Oval Office. The president was partial to the chocolate wafers. Thousands of conservatives dutifully posted pictures of themselves stuffing shopping carts with Goya.

It's quickly becoming a given that boycotts are the first tool consumers will reach for to object to political statements they dislike. Witness, for instance, the fledgling boycott of Perdue Chicken. When Senator David Perdue deliberately mispronounced Kamala Harris's name, "#boycottperduechicken" immediately flooded Twitter. The problem? There was no actual connection between the Perdue who served in the Senate and the Perdue who founded the chicken company. After Perdue Chicken kept desperately pleading this fact, that boycott died a quiet death. But it confirmed the new woke policy: boycott first, ask questions later.[4]

In early 2021, activists in Georgia took this policy to its natural next step when they boycotted Coca-Cola, Delta Airlines, Home Depot, and UPS for the great sin of . . . not condemning Georgia's new voting law loudly enough.[5] Although vilified as "the new Jim Crow" over provisions like criminalizing gifts of food and drinks to voters and banning mobile voting sites, the law was in truth a mixed bag—it also expanded early voting opportunities and guaranteed a minimum number of drop boxes for ballots.[6]

The activists justified the boycotts by saying all these companies issued statements supporting BLM and were failing to follow through on them by being silent about Georgia's voting law. So it's a combo move. First the activists pressure companies to issue seemingly symbolic corporate platitudes in support of BLM, saying it's the least they could do; then they call for boycotts when those corporations don't side with substantive political policies. Get companies to give an inch, then take a mile. Protesters staged a "die-in" at Coca-Cola's museum in Atlanta and called for a boycott of Coke, while others gathered at the Delta terminal in Atlanta airport demanding that CEO Ed Bastian "kill the bill." The new group "Black Voters Matter" declared: "If you can't get involved in the business of fighting for democracy, then we're going to have to get involved in your business." The strategy worked like a charm; after holding out for a week, Coca-Cola and Delta folded and denounced Georgia's law.[7]

Major League Baseball then took the unprecedented step of moving its widely anticipated All-Star game out of Atlanta to Colorado instead, as a way of protesting Georgia's new voting law—ironically, in a year where the game was supposed to honor Hank

Aaron, the famed black baseball star who played for Atlanta.[8] Companies from American Express to PayPal to T. Rowe Price weighed in as well.[9] Now scarcely a week goes by without a new corporate-political declaration.

Conservatives like me will say this corporate politicking is just *Citizens United* on steroids and that liberals are hypocritical for rallying around the cry that corporations aren't people only to demand that corporations behave more like people. Liberals will say Coca-Cola's Georgia stand is just *Citizens United* applied consistently and that we conservatives are hypocrites for embracing mixing business with politics in *Citizens United* and then condemning it when companies take stands against Georgia's voting law.

As a moral matter, I don't like corporations influencing politics at all, whether through election spending or lobbying over voting laws. As a constitutional matter, I begrudgingly accept that both forms of corporate influence are legal. I'm also a bit more worried about Georgia-style lobbying than *Citizens United* because of an important asymmetry between the two: Coca-Cola doesn't stifle its employees' votes when it spends money on an election because people cast their votes *privately*, but when Coca-Cola announces an official corporate position against Georgia's voting law, that makes it more difficult for its employees to speak in favor of the law *publicly* without fear of retribution that might put their job security or upward economic mobility at risk. When corporate speech chills citizens' speech, that threatens democracy even more than when corporations simply write checks to political campaigns.

In Chapter 1, I talked about how corporations hide behind woke causes to disguise their greed and accumulate power. In Chapter 4, I focused on the inverse problem of woke executives, showing how America's rising managerial class uses the pretense of serving stakeholders to escape accountability and accrete power. Collectively, these represent examples of "woke capitalism"—a top-down phenomenon driven by elites who control capital and occupy seats of corporate power. By contrast, woke consumerism—consumer boycotts, buying sprees, and related identity-signaling—isn't a top-down problem driven by CEOs and influential investors. It comes from consumers themselves. This particular threat to democracy comes from within.

But once corporations discover the grassroots approach, they're quick to piggyback on it and turn it to their ends—witness Yelp's recent decision to encourage reviewers to tag restaurants they consider racist.[10] Yelp noticed that a lot of its users were warning people about racist behavior at businesses, and it decided to give them an official platform to make organizing boycotts easier. This was either a virtuous or vicious cycle, depending on how woke you are—the change started with woke consumers wanting to boycott, and then alert woke executives changed their business model to encourage the boycotts. This allows more woke consumers to vote with their dollars, placing more pressure on businesses to conform to woke values, whether they want to or not.

No matter what a CEO actually thinks, most of them will do anything to avoid being branded with the scarlet letter of racism. Best to tweet in support of Black Lives Matter and fire any employee who's even accused of racism. The moral of the Yelp story is this: once woke consumerism sparks a protest, woke capitalism can pour gasoline on it.

Using boycotts and buying sprees to mix capitalism and politics is harmful when it's always the first tool people reach for, but this impulse is actually the natural, inevitable, and understandable consequence of capitalism. If you think your barber's racist and you can't stand them, you go to a different one. You warn your friends not to go to the racist barber, and you tell them about the cool new one you found. It's built into the fabric of capitalism that consumers will choose whom to give business to based in part on whether they share social values. It's part of what allowed capitalism to tear down the caste system in India, for example.

But woke consumerism takes this too far. It's one thing for me to decide a barber's racist, go to a different one, and tell my friends about it. It's another if I don't even need a haircut, I hear about a racist barber in another city, and I drive over to stand outside his shop with a bullhorn, yelling at everyone not to go in. You can choose your barber based on whether you like his views on race or whether you like his wallpaper. But consumers start to cross a moral line when they move beyond making their own decisions and start making everyone else's. When I stand outside the barbershop with a bullhorn yelling about his racism, I'm not making my own decision about where to get my hair cut—I'm trying to starve the barber.

Wealth is a bullhorn. That's one of the biggest problems with woke consumerism. Playing politics through consumer boycotts is a rich man's game—the more money you have, the more impact your boycott has. In capitalism, each dollar is like a vote. It's perfectly fine for dollars to vote on which goods and services rise to the top. The capitalist principle of dollars being votes is embodied, for example, in the way companies select members of their board of directors. Shareholders elect the board of directors, but it's not that each shareholder has an equal voice—each *share* has equal weight, so the people who own the most shares have the biggest say. Since shares can straightforwardly be translated into dollars, dollars literally buy votes in the corporate context. And there's nothing wrong with that. In the marketplace of goods and services, one dollar, one vote is appropriate.

But the marketplace of ideas is supposed to follow the principle of one person, one vote. That's how we aggregate votes in a democracy. When we normalize using dollars to win battles over ideas, we're just handing the wealthy control over society's values. It's not that the rich are the only ones who get to play the game. In reality, many poorer Americans often participate in consumer boycotts too. But the cost of participation is higher for those with less money: using your buying power to signal your morality is a sort of luxury that implicitly costs more by mandating what you can buy and what you can't. To the extent that woke consumerism imposes a cost on consumers, it's one that's disproportionately borne by those who can least afford to bear it.

In theory, there are some potential advantages to having a market in votes, where they can be bought and sold. The biggest one is that one person, one vote doesn't allow voting results to reflect the intensity of voter preferences—a slight majority that has a weak preference for an outcome can overrule a sizable minority that strongly opposes it. In a vacuum, bringing dollars into the equation and letting people buy and sell votes to each other would allow votes to reflect the degree of a person's preference and not just the direction of it. The sizable minority with the stronger preference would be willing to buy some of the majority's votes, and the majority would be willing to sell. There's another, more basic argument for allowing a market of votes: all else being equal, if one person would rather have a certain amount of dollars than their vote and another would rather have that vote than their dollars, both people end up better off from their own perspective if you allow them to trade.

But although letting dollars buy votes is theoretically elegant, in the real world, voters don't all start out with equal resources—some are richer than others, and allowing votes to be bought and sold would just amount to letting the rich buy votes from the poor. Academics have overwhelmingly concluded that allowing a marketplace in votes would be tantamount to letting the rich disenfranchise the poor.*

Political philosopher Michael Sandel sums it up by saying that no one defends the outright purchase and sale of votes.[11] I took a course called Justice with him during my freshman year at Harvard. Admirably, he didn't even discuss his own theory until the end of the semester. Sandel is famous for his argument that over the last few decades capitalist thinking has infected and commodified other spheres of life. His big book on the topic is called *"What Money Can't Buy."* It turns out the answer is "less and less."

Sandel appeals to two kinds of values in arguing about the evils of market power: fairness and corruption. The first is straightforward—the more kinds of things dollars can buy, the more wealth inequality extends to inequality in other arenas of life.[12] This unfairness is the biggest problem with woke consumerism. When you think about it, consumer boycotts actually work the same way as shareholders electing members of a board of directors. The more shares you hold, the more of a voice you have—and the

---

* There are a few authors who make this point: Susan Rose-Ackerman, "Inalienability and the Theory of Property Rights," *Columbia Law Review* 85, no. 5 (June 1985): 931–969; Ben Holzer, Political Vote Buying Statues: Textual Limits, Enforcement Challenges, and the Need for Reform," *Legislation and Public Policy* 12 (2008): 211–223; Saul Levmore, "Precommitment Politics," *Virginia Law Review* 82, no. 4 (May 1996): 567–627; Debra Satz, *Why Some Things Should Not Be for Sale* (New York: Oxford University Press, 2010), and James Tobin, "On Limiting the Domain of Inequality," *Journal of Law and Economics* 13, no. 2 (October 1970): 263–277.

more buying power you have, the more weight your boycott holds. Boycotts can give the superficial illusion that they're a tool of mass mobilization, but they take political issues to territory that naturally favors the wealthy. If a hundred liberal households boycotted Goya, for instance, to come out ahead in the exchange it only needs one conservative who owns a restaurant chain to go on a Trump-fueled buying binge. The boycotters won't ever know how the dollars and cents ultimately shook out. But they'll feel good—maybe that's the real point.

Inviting withholding and spending money to be a primary tool in political argument is unfair to those who have less of it, but it also corrupts what democracy is supposed to be. This is the second kind of argument Sandel makes—fairness aside, he says that when we allow money to determine what happens in non-capitalist spheres like family, religion, or democracy, money inevitably corrupts those spheres and cheapens what they mean to everyone.[13]

When we use boycotts and buying sprees to determine political issues, we cheapen democracy. It doesn't just give the rich yet another advantage over the poor. It also makes those with buying power worse off, too, in subtle ways they don't recognize. It drags everyone down by making money, rather than open deliberation, the first tool of democracy. The image of citizens debating the issues of the day in the town square begins to sound like a laughable idealization, a naive fantasy, rather than the very foundation of democracy. When we use money to starve barbers we hear are racist, we're simply using raw power, the closest thing to physical violence we can legally get away with.

Here's the fundamental moral mistake woke consumerism makes: when punishment is the first tool we turn to rather than persuasion, we naturally start to see people who disagree with us as enemies, not fellow citizens. Sure, you might think it's the other way around—that we use punishment because we already think of our opponents as enemies. But I think the causation goes equally in both directions: as you turn to punish someone, you are naturally more prone to *see* them as your enemy than someone to whom you're committed to actually persuading. The beauty of democracy is its invitation to try to persuade the other side. The ugliness of woke consumerism is the way it replaces that invitation with a call to using brute force as punishment instead. It's a game in which all the players lose. And it leaves us divided as a people in the end.

All theoretical considerations aside, there's something obviously undemocratic about winning political arguments through censorship. Punishments for saying the wrong thing and associating with the wrong people are a special threat to the fundamentally American rights to freedom of speech and association. These rights are the bedrock of our democracy, which is why the First Amendment protects them from federal and state governments. But the Constitution can't protect us from ourselves. Only we can do that. When the citizens are banding together to stifle free speech and association, the solution can only be found in norms, not laws—we have to choose to stop employing these oppressive tools at the drop of the hat.

Maybe the left would be persuaded to stop boycotting and blacklisting its political opponents so wantonly if it just remembered that the last time blacklists were used so prominently as a political tool, the left was the target. Back in the '40s and '50s, Senator Joseph McCarthy brutalized his political enemies by framing them as communists, causing them to be blacklisted in their industries so that they'd lose their livelihoods. He didn't have to resort to reason or evidence. All he had to do was brand someone a communist or even a communist sympathizer, and fear of association with them would do his work for him. McCarthy's favorite targets for blacklisting were government employees, entertainers, academics, and labor union activists. The blacklist was a tool for stifling the left's ideas without actually having to debate them.

Now the blacklists are back, but this time the left is the one using them. Witness how right after Biden's victory Representative Ocasio-Cortez tweeted, "Is anyone archiving these Trump sycophants for when they try to downplay or deny their complicity in the future? I foresee decent probability of many deleted Tweets, writings, photos in the future." Immediately after her call to arms, a group calling itself the Trump Accountability Project sprang up, aiming to prevent people who'd worked for or donated to Trump from gaining future employment.[14] As an article in *Politico* drily noted, these types of enemy lists are "rarely a healthy sign in any democracy."[15] The *New York Post* made the reference to McCarthyism explicit. A columnist wrote, "Joseph Ocasio-McCarthy, your time is now. You've got a little list.[16]

The blacklist was wrong when McCarthy used it to target leftists in the '50s and it's wrong when AOC and her followers use it to target Trump supporters today. And it's wrong for the same reasons—this is not how a democracy is supposed to function. The target of the blacklists and boycotts doesn't matter, left or right. If speech is abhorrent, a democracy like ours is supposed to answer it with more speech, not censorship. That's one of the things that separates us from the Chinese Communist Party. Part of what it is to be American is to reason with those who disagree with you and beat them at the ballot box, not to attempt to legally deprive them of food and shelter. Citizens of a liberal democracy do not attempt to dominate their political opponents.

The spell of McCarthyism began to break when, in response to McCarthy's attempt to blacklist a young lawyer by branding him a communist, Joseph Welch famously asked McCarthy, "Have you no sense of decency, sir, at long last? Have you left no sense of decency?"[17] For all the valid theoretical considerations I've brought up against blacklisting and boycotting political opponents, I think Welch's way of putting it gets to the heart of things: it is unbecoming for one citizen to use the threat of starvation and homelessness to silence a fellow citizen. It lacks common decency.

THE FOUNDING FATHERS saw our Big Sort coming, as Bishop himself observes. One of their great fears was that the United States would be united in name only, that we'd sort ourselves into groups and be more loyal to those groups than to the nation itself. Whether the US would descend into partisan chaos or not was one of the main debates between the federalists, who wanted to ratify the Constitution, and the antifederalists, who wanted to keep the states independent. The two sides debated each other through articles in newspapers, trying to win the public over. The main voices for the federalists were James Madison, Alexander Hamilton, and John Jay. Their essays in support of the Constitution are now called the Federalist Papers, while the essays their opponents wrote are called the Antifederalist Papers.

The federalists won the day, so they got to write history, and as a result today civics classes teach that James Madison's tenth federalist paper brilliantly proved that the Constitution would prevent our nation from descending into squabbling between parties. He made the mistake of assuming that the only problem posed by factions would come from tyranny of the majority, arguing that the

Constitution's popular rule mechanisms would prevent a partisan minority from seizing power.[18]

In thinking that the problem of partisanship would come from an enduring partisan majority, Madison may have overlooked the importance of the possibility that we would have two similarly powerful factions continually striving with each other for dominance. This is the central problem of partisanship we face today—because Republicans and Democrats are closely matched in numbers and power, neither has a stable, enduring majority, so each constantly maneuvers to gain the slightest advantage over the other. When two rival factions are closely matched in political power, they have overwhelming incentives to place their own partisan interests above the country's whenever possible. John Adams actually saw this potential problem. Unfortunately, he didn't write any Federalist Papers or even play that large a role in drafting the Constitution— he was serving as an ambassador in London at the time.

Madison knew parties would be dangerous but didn't fully understand why. But we don't need to dig into all the details of his reasoning—present-day experience is all we need to prove that his theoretical arguments must've missed something important. Unfortunately, this dark prediction from an Antifederalist Paper written under the pen name Cato withstands the test of time better than any of the Founding Fathers' sunny assertions:

> But whoever seriously considers the immense extent of territory comprehended within the limits of the United States, together with the variety of its climates, productions, and commerce, the difference of extent, and number of inhabitants in all; the dissimilitude of interest, morals, and politics, in almost every one, will receive it as an intuitive truth, that a consolidated republican form

of government therein, can never form a perfect union . . . This unkindred legislature therefore, composed of interests opposite and dissimilar in their nature, will in its exercise, emphatically be like a house divided against itself.[19]

The antifederalists said that we couldn't have a shared nation without a shared identity and that we were just too big and too diverse to have a shared identity. They were even more right than they knew. In the time since then, we've gone from thirteen states to fifty, and the continental United States has stretched itself all the way to the West Coast. California and Alabama seem like different countries, but they live under the same federal roof.

As my old law professors Amy Chua and Jed Rubenfeld point out, the Constitution had some great successes in its attempts to forge one people out of many. Maybe the greatest of those was its guarantee of religious freedom, which allowed all kinds of religions to coexist—Protestants and Catholics and, later, Muslims, Hindus, Buddhists, atheists, agnostics, and many others. Thanks to the Constitution's protections, America was able to avoid the religious wars that had torn European countries apart for centuries. And in the Fourteenth Amendment, the Constitution gave America birthright citizenship, a unique and powerful force to guarantee that being American didn't require membership in any particular race or religion. Birthright citizenship is a powerful unifying statement—Chua and Rubenfeld note that no European or Asian country grants this right.[20]

But as with many things in life, one or two big mistakes can overwhelm many successes, and the Constitution allowed slavery. Now slavery is gone, but we're still paying the price for it today. While Madison and the other federalists thought economic class would be the main source of partisan division and turned all their efforts to arguing that the Constitution's checks and balances would deter class warfare, they were completely blind to the possibility that race, and gender, too, would be what divided us into factions. As liberals might say, these are blind spots you might expect from a document written by old white men, many of them slave owners.

The woke diagnosis of America's problems is that they can be attributed to lingering racism and sexism. My diagnosis is that we lack a shared national identity. We think of ourselves as black or white, male or female, Republican or Democrat; we don't think of ourselves as Americans. And so it becomes natural to make decisions based on what's good for our race, gender, or party rather than what's good for America. Wokeness flourishes in the absence of a shared national identity and then further divides us because we split ourselves into factions based on other commonalities. Corporate wokeness deepens that division by selling us symbols we can use to identify people who think like us.

The Founding Fathers thought our diversity would be our strength, while their opponents thought it would be our doom because it would divide us. Diversity itself is not the problem. But when diversity is all you have—when you have diversity without commonality—that diversity becomes a source of division because people sort themselves into tribes. Once that happens, the tribes start fighting each other over who gets what, the way humans always have.

CHAPTER 14

The Bastardization of Service

T HE ROOTS OF WOKE CAPITALISM begin with how we're
acculturated to think about the notion of service, starting from
a young age.

By my sophomore year at St. Xavier High School, it was clear
that I was going to get into a good college. I had the highest GPA,
and my résumé was studded with extracurricular accomplishments.
But as I sat down with my guidance counselor at our semesterly
catch-up, he suggested one final gap that I needed to fill: community service. It was the missing *coup de grace* on an otherwise perfect college application.

So I got to work, just as my other ambitious high school peers
were doing. We would dutifully troop to Bethesda North Hospital in Cincinnati on Saturday mornings and pretend to help people
there. The pretending was an important part of it. We all knew the
real point was to put some community service on our résumés to
look good to colleges. We figured the best of both worlds would be
to put service on our applications without *actually* having to serve.

We filed into the waiting room behind the hospital's front desk, where we'd ostensibly be on call to help wheel patients between rooms, fetch coffee, or do other odd jobs. Over time we developed an unofficial game about seeing who could take the fewest calls, who could do the least work.

They gave us these $5 pink vouchers for the hospital cafeteria, and people would pay each other with them to get out of work. It was a barter-based economy, like in prison. Those cafeteria vouchers were our packs of smokes.

We were an all-boys school, and there were a lot of other "volunteers" from the co-ed public schools in the area, so the popular guys would take it as a chance to talk to girls, shuffling off the calls to the less popular kids by paying them with cafeteria vouchers. A few kids actually helped patients from time to time. For my part, I didn't do very much of either—I used the time to study. From my perspective, I wasn't doing anything wrong. We all knew we were there to help us get into colleges, and I was just cutting out the middleman of service.

My college application essay was about my experience discharging one of the patients from the maternity ward. The woman had had a miscarriage, and it was my job to take a wheelchair to her floor and escort her out of the hospital to her car. The essay I wrote was dramatically titled "To Walk on Water." The last line waxed poetic: "The sun dared to meekly take a single peek over the gray clouds of one chill October morning."

I hadn't thought about that essay for many years, until 2019, when my wife Apoorva suffered a miscarriage. When I reread my essay seventeen years later, I was ashamed. It didn't read to me like the words of a kid who actually gave a damn about the woman's experience. Instead it was all about me—*my* feelings, *my* poetic turns of phrase, *my* experience of it. Cringeworthy or not, it worked: I applied to Harvard and MIT in the fall of 2002, and I was promptly accepted to both. They say you go to MIT to learn how the world works and you go to Harvard to learn how to run it. Naturally, I chose Harvard.

When I arrived on campus, I noticed a curious tradition: the Living-Wage Campaign. It turned out the Living-Wage Campaign at Harvard was like a Boston winter: you knew it was going to strike, but you could only wonder when and how hard.[1] Each fall when I arrived back at campus, it wasn't long before throngs of students and Cambridge activists marched, chanted, and protested outside the Holyoke Center and around Massachusetts Hall, believing that they were fighting an important battle in a larger war to achieve higher wages for Harvard's lowest-paid workers.

But that battle had already been fought and won years ago. The protests I witnessed in 2005 were just remnants of a campaign that had been held back in 2001, before I got there. The earlier campaign was successful enough that Harvard had already given in and created a commission to study the causes of low campus staff wages and implemented a number of its recommendations. By the time my classmates and I got there, Harvard's janitors were already being paid more than they had been, certainly more than janitors in the rest of the Boston area.

So it was strange seeing well-off students occasionally go on fasting protests in favor of raising the already-high wage for Harvard's janitors. Sometimes I wondered why that was the cause they chose. Why not go on a hunger strike to get Harvard to help the unemployed instead, or the city's vast homeless population? Those bitter Boston winters can be a death sentence if you spend them on the street. And thousands of men, women, and children were spending them there. Even today you can still see them on Harvard Square, sitting behind cardboard signs as the students' eyes pass over them, fixed on some higher cause only they can see.

What was it about Harvard janitorial pay that was so uniquely outrageous that it was what everyone rallied behind year after year? Out of all the evils in the world, why was this the one so many of my classmates agreed they couldn't abide?

I decided the answer was that fasting for the janitors had become something of a Harvard tradition, like the social justice equivalent of the big game versus Yale. The fact that this battle had been fought years ago wasn't a reason to stop; instead, it was a reason to keep going. Each fresh batch of protestors was nominally fasting for Harvard's janitors, but in reality they were hungering for a cause, in that they lacked any fundamental sense of personal purpose and filled that void by adopting the social cause that would give them the greatest sense of belonging with their peers. The bolder ones would storm into the office of Harvard's President in Massachusetts Hall, only to later argue that they shouldn't be punished—forgetting that one's willingness to bear punishment for breaking the rules is part of what makes civil disobedience heroic. And, of course, there's still that essay left to write for one's application to law school or business school or a master's program in public policy.

A few years later, I arrived as a first-year student at Yale Law School myself. Yale had its own traditions. The law school came together as a community every year to host something called the Public Interest Auction. They still do it today. Students and faculty offer some service, and people bid on it, and all the proceeds go to fund public interest work. You get the ex-McKinsey analysts offering to give you a professional assessment of your love life, including charts and graphs illustrating a cost-benefit analysis of whether to break up or not; you get people auctioning off a night of sweet guitar solos . . . it's fun. Of course, like any charity auction, you get something tangible in return for being "charitable."

But look past the fun, and you find that what consistently raised the most money was big-shot professors auctioning off dinners at their houses. These spots would go for hundreds of dollars. The bidding would just go up and up. Why? Because it was always the rich students gunning for prestigious judicial clerkships who would pay for those coveted dinner spots so they could have extra out-of-class time to charm the very professors who would be recommending them to judges. Sometimes I wondered if the professors knew what they were doing. Did they think everyone just wanted the pleasure of their company, or did they realize they were selling the wealthier kids access to future opportunities in the guise of serving the poor? I'd have preferred the model of professors just picking their favorite students from class.

And when it comes to protests, Yale law students expected the same special treatment as their Harvard College counterparts—and then some. In 2018, when Brett Kavanaugh was nominated to the Supreme Court and became ensnared in sexual allegations dating back to high school, many Yale law students decided to protest his nomination. A few of them wanted to attend a demonstration in Washington, D.C., but they didn't want to take the risk of falling behind in class—so they demanded that the school cancel classes to support their courageous acts of protest. Amazingly, nearly all of the school's professors acquiesced, but one corporate law professor chose to hold her class anyway. Yet her class that day was interrupted by protesters who entered the classroom and took down the names of any students who'd dared to show up to class that day—to shame them in front of their peers. So her class was effectively canceled by force.

You might expect the school's leadership to have condemned this form of bullying. Instead, the school took a different approach: they supported the "sit-in" students had organized at the law school itself. That way, students didn't have to take the risk of missing, say, Trusts & Estates or Bankruptcy class in order to protest social injustice in America. They could simply do both at the same time. To wit, the law school catered lunch for the event: no better way to prepare students for a future career as a seven-figure partner at Wachtell Lipton who also waxes eloquent about stakeholder capitalism.

So the story goes. Service is too often bundled with an ulterior motive in America. Only the best of us pursue it for its own sake. For the rest, including my younger self, it's frequently packaged with something self-serving to make it more appetizing. In high school we serve our communities so that we can get into nice colleges. Once we're at those nice colleges, we serve people so we can get nice jobs. As taxpayers we give to charity so that we can get a nice tax deduction in return. It's no wonder that once aspiring young capitalists get into those nice ESG investment jobs today, they turn around and serve people in a way that'll make them nice profits. Same goes for bushy-tailed startup CEOs in the Valley. Why should they think differently? We've always told them it was right and good for them to serve others by serving themselves.

Intentionally or not, it's how our society trains so many of our kids to think about service. That's why when they get older, they feel the need to repent—and to continue to make the mistake of mixing up their pursuit of profit with doing ancillary social service as well. We're too guilty now to nakedly pursue profit because we've never really done service for its own sake. At the same time, most of us don't really even know *how* to do service for its own sake—and so we simply regress into thinking about what we can get out of it.

A few years ago, I was working on a big deal with a large foreign company that was brokered by a banker. The banker introduced me to an investor in New York City who was close friends with the CEO of the foreign company. The banker thought building a relationship with this investor would in turn help build trust with the CEO, even if only indirectly. So we all met at this investor's Manhattan townhouse for dinner. My objective that night was to make a friend.

At the end of dinner, the investor's son came downstairs to say hello to the group. He was a senior in high school and was able to carry on a conversation with a group of adults in an unusually mature way. Once he discovered I was a Harvard alum, he asked me if he could follow up with me regarding advice on his college applications. I told him I was glad to help.

There was something sad about the fact that even when I took the time needed to help a high school kid with his college application, it turned out to be an instance where I derived an intangible business benefit too. I made friends with an influential investor, and I was able to give some advice to an ambitious kid. No one was the worse off for it. Like it or not, that's how modern American altruism works. A couple of months later, I got the big deal done.

Of course, I had to make good on my word to the kid. Mentors had helped me along the way, and a part of me wanted to do the same thing for this kid too. So I gave him some advice. I told him a secret I learned during my own time at Harvard. They say they want well-rounded college applicants, but in reality what they want is a well-rounded *class* of students, composed of people who were distinct in their own unique talents and interests. So I asked him what he could say that he did that no other high school kid in the country could say.

As it turned out, this kid—raised in a ritzy Manhattan townhouse and educated at New York's finest private schools—didn't need my help at all. He had his answer to my question ready. He had founded a nonprofit organization designed to combat sex slavery around the world. I nearly laughed. There was something amiss about an American minor founding a nonprofit to fight sexual assault in the third world. But it quickly became clear that this was a critical cornerstone of his college application.

As we continued the conversation, it became clear that he felt Harvard was the place for him. *Of course it was*. He needed to optimize his chance of landing a job in the investment world, just as his dad and his older brother had done. What's the best way to get into a place like Harvard? To found a nonprofit to fight sex slavery as a teenager. And it worked. *Of course it did*.

I stayed in touch with the kid over the years. Last time we spoke, he was shopping for internships at investment banks. I didn't hear much about the sex slavery nonprofit. But I'll bet he's doing his best now to fight for gender equality on Wall Street. Perhaps he'll become the leader of the "Diversity and Inclusion Committee" at a well-reputed investment bank one day. Maybe even Goldman Sachs.

There was something about that experience that bothered me, prompting a long overdue self-reflection. Why did I have such a sharp reaction to this kid and his sex slavery nonprofit? Why did it irritate me so much? If I'm being honest, it's because I saw myself in him: he reminded me of what I was like in high school. Maybe even what a small part of me is like today.

The trend of flaunting a woke résumé dates back to at least the early 2000s, when I'd applied to college. It's what I did. It's what my friends did too. But today that trend is on steroids: instead of half-heartedly helping patients at the local hospital, high school kids are founding elaborate nonprofits pretending to help sex slavery victims in the third world. Instead of going on hunger fasts for higher janitorial pay, college kids are storming the annual Harvard–Yale football game and calling for both endowments to divest from fossil fuels and cancel Puerto Rican debt holdings—snapping selfies for social media along the way.[2]

Woke culture today is like a supercharged version of the faux performative service that I first saw as a high school student. Now it's no longer just fulfilling a psychological gap in the minds of misguided adolescents. Today it serves to legitimize and whitewash the naked self-interested pursuit of profits and power by Wall Street, Silicon Valley, and the rest of corporate America.

Committed liberals should be concerned about what woke capitalism does to pure ideals like service, altruism, and social good. Anyone who sincerely cares about important causes like female empowerment, racial equality, and environmentalism ought to be offended when these causes are cheapened by corporations that pawn them off to advance their own goals.

For example, are black communities really going to be better off if we "defund the police"? Or if we "clear the jails"? Or if we "dismantle the nuclear family structure"? Or do these slogans simply make those who utter them feel more noble? Satisfying our own moral hunger is just another form of self-indulgence.

Sure, maybe in the short run, some progressives will be happy that there are more women or black people on boards because Goldman Sachs and Nasdaq decided to mandate it for companies that go public. Maybe the people who run Goldman Sachs and Nasdaq truly couldn't care less about that social goal and are simply using it to distract the public from seeing their other business practices, like bribing Malaysian officials and making slush funds for them. I certainly think that's a big part of what's happening. A lot of progressives probably agree with that. But the difference is that they're still fine with it because it advances the goal they care more about achieving, irrespective of the intentions of powerful corporations that make it happen.

But in the long run, when you ask someone to take care of your baby who doesn't actually care about your baby, the baby ends up worse off too. It reminds me of why it was so difficult for us to find a nanny to take care of our baby boy, Karthik. Apoorva and I both work full-time jobs, so it was impossible for us to take care of Karthik without one. Our first nanny—let's call her Sylvie— was completely proficient in taking care of him. She was competent and fast at doing all the tasks associated with caring for a baby: mixing the milk, getting him dressed, putting him to sleep, and changing his diaper. But she was also incredibly fast to get a pacifier in his mouth every time he made the earliest sound that suggested he *might* cry, quick to finish reading his baby books to him, quick to wrap up the time set aside to help him practice crawling and walking.

There was something about the way she did her job that made it clear she didn't particularly love it. She was just doing it for a paycheck. That's perfectly fine in most contexts. But not for the person who takes care of our baby. For that, we wanted someone who loved not only doing the job but who might grow to actually love Karthik too. Eventually we hired a new nanny—let's call her Katie—who like me had grown up in Ohio. She was trained to take care of kids who were slightly older than Karthik, but it was clear that she loved what she did and was open to learning. Pretty soon, she was able to do all of the same tasks that Sylvie had done, and just as adeptly, but with a warmth and buoyancy that only comes from actually enjoying what you're doing.

Goldman Sachs and Nasdaq, or Volkswagen and Unilever for

that matter, remind me of Sylvie more than Katie. Feminists, racial justice advocates, and environmentalists today effectively entrust large corporations to be good stewards of their values. Yet when a steward doesn't know much about, let alone actually care much about, the values they're safeguarding, bad things happen. For one thing, social currents in the world change from time to time. If it were for some reason more profitable or otherwise beneficial for any of those companies to take up the exact opposite social cause at some point in the future—say, misogynist, racist, or pollutive causes—there's little doubt in my mind that many of them would. Right now the winds for progressives favor latching themselves onto the powerful train of woke capitalism. But as the saying goes, he who marries the times will be a widower tomorrow.

Worse still, inauthentic corporate stewards often change the purpose of the underlying social cause itself due to a combination of ignorance and indifference toward it. For example, the goal of feminism isn't actually to put more women on corporate boards. That's just a tactic. The real goal is to live in a world where men and women regard one another with genuinely held mutual respect as co-equals. The same goes for racial equality and the regard that people of different races ought to have for one another. Yet without actually taking up those *deeper* causes and instead confining themselves to the narrow tactic of, say, implementing tokenism in the boardroom, they may actually undermine the longer-run goal.

In the real world, there are of course a certain number of fixed slots on a corporate board or on an executive team or on a speakers' dais at a conference or in a medical school class. When we say that a certain number of those slots need to be filled by women or black people or gay people, we will achieve the narrow goal of achieving greater representation of those groups. But it's questionable whether achieving representation in this way *actually* advances the goal of achieving equality in the deeper sense of fostering genuinely held mutual respect for all people, whether it's neutral with respect to that goal, or whether it's downright *harmful* to that goal. But they don't care because by achieving the visible tableau of "diversity," they will have already satisfied their own private purpose of satisfying their corporate "stakeholders."

Do these quotas advance the goals of social activists who care deeply about achieving racial equality or female empowerment? Personally, I don't think so. Even if yes, at the very least it comes at a cost. As for the corporations that practice these norms, they couldn't care less, as long as they've achieved the goal of reputationally laundering themselves by doing the woke thing.

But when corporations use social causes as pawns, they defile the integrity of the causes themselves. Call it a Kantian argument of sorts. Kant argued that you shouldn't use people merely as a means to an end. I feel the same way about ideals—you shouldn't use them as a means to an end either. We shouldn't take a sincerely held value and then prostitute it for private gain. Many principled progressives probably feel the same way too. The dilemma for them is that corporations help them advance their own social agendas in the near term, even as they bastardize the agendas in the long run.

So how did we get here? I believe it's this: as Americans, we're trained from a young age to think about service to others as being about something that we do to advance our own self-interest. I certainly was. It's an unfortunate feature of modern American culture. There's no such thing as doing service for the sake of service—just as there's no such thing as pursuing *profit* just for the sake of pursuing profit either. They're two sides of the same coin: in America we simply can't do anything just for its own sake anymore. It's like we're constantly mixing earth and water. Each one is just fine on its own. But when you mix them up, you're left with mud.

The romantic in me says that we should all just do service for its own sake, period. It's certainly an idealistic notion. Michael Sandel, my former professor at Harvard, points to an example in Sweden of a town that happened to be a great site for nuclear waste disposal. When residents of that town were asked if they were okay with taking on that burden for their country, 50 percent of the citizens said yes. But when asked if they'd do it in exchange for $8,000 each, only 25 percent said yes. From a coldly rational point of view, you might expect that if 50 percent would do it for free, even more would do it for $8,000. But the citizens were thinking like citizens doing service for their country, not money-maximizing consumers. They thought taking on the burden of hosting a nuclear waste disposal facility was a civic duty, not something that should be commodified. Offering money to get them to do their duty was an insult, not a bonus. A beautiful Swedish story.[3]

But we all know that America doesn't work that way. And that's okay. At the end of the day, I have no problem with the existence of tax deductions to foster charitable giving, for example. Yes, there's a lot of game-playing that needs to be fixed, but there's nothing inherently wrong with the basic principle of incentivizing people to be charitable by giving them back a few cents on the dollar in tax savings. It's a big part of why America's great tradition of philanthropy simply doesn't exist in places like China, where billionaires get neither the tax deduction nor the cultural cachet associated with philanthropy in America—and as a consequence bequeath their wealth to their children at a disproportionately higher rate than they do in America. Our nation is, at least on the net, better off for it.

Yet here's where it all goes awry. Teaching our kids to use acts of service to distinguish themselves from one another or to pad their college applications doesn't teach them to become better citizens. Instead, it breeds cynicism. Anyone who's had a kid will tell you that young kids sometimes *will* just do things for other people. They'll do it even if you don't give them a reward or a round of applause. Yet as adults we take that native instinct and bastardize it in the minds of America's next generation by mixing it up with the idea of how to get ahead in the world.

So it's no surprise that those kids later grow up to be woke capitalists. It's rooted in a guilt complex for never genuinely having helped other people. So once they're in cushy positions, they try to mix up their profit-oriented pursuits with making up for their past. Yet they don't even know exactly how to pursue service for its own sake because they never developed the muscle memory for how to do real service in the first place. It was always something used to develop a competitive advantage rather than something done for its own sake.

That's what woke capitalism is all about: companies performatively one-upping each other to show that they're the good guys, and consumers falling for their tricks because they're simply hungry for a cause. So part of the solution has to be to fill that void, that hunger, starting at a young age, so companies and others can't exploit it later on.

I have a radical yet simple proposal for how to do that: mandate civic service for high school summer break, and make it universal. In my view, this will create not only better citizens but less flimsy capitalists later in life as well. Equally importantly, at a time when we've become obsessed with our differences from one another, national service creates a sense of shared purpose and experience.

When we have no shared identity to take pride in, we take pride in unshared ones, which then puts us at odds with each other. But by creating shared solidarity through shared experiences when our kids are young, we make wokeness superfluous as they get older.

Young Americans will then enter the workforce with a greater appreciation for what makes their country great. If they go to college, they'll be less likely to be swayed by faculty-lounge Marxists who want to paint America as an evil oppressor. Those who become the next generation of capitalist leaders will have been exposed to normal Americans, bursting elitist bubbles before they even have a chance to form. For most of the book I've made the case for erecting firm boundaries between *institutions* like capitalism and democracy to prevent each from polluting the other. But I also believe that dissolving boundaries between different types of *people* will ultimately strengthen our country.

The heart of the case for mandatory civic service is that a national identity requires shared values, and shared values require shared experiences. In the time since *Brown v. Board of Education*, America has replaced formal segregation by race with informal segregation by race, class, and party. Universal civic service would bring us back together.

There's a surprising amount of support for requiring young Americans to serve their nation in some way. A 2017 Gallup poll found that 49 percent of all Americans were in favor of mandatory civic service for young men and women.[4]

The idea's had bipartisan support for a long time, it's just never really been at the forefront of the national consciousness. Its time may have finally arrived. A few summer breaks spent serving their fellow citizens would teach young Americans the important lesson that all rights come with duties attached. It would teach them that respecting and serving others isn't an infringement on freedom— it's a necessary part of what allows it to flourish. Not only that, civic service would teach them that freedom is worth protecting. You value things more when you've put some effort into them. Putting time into building the nation would give young adults a sense of ownership over it, and for the rest of their lives they'd want to fight harder to preserve it. Americans should feel like America belongs to them, and to do that they need to build it, not just inherit it.

The idea of universal civil service has been proposed by a wide range of American luminaries. Far from a mere theory, it has been applied effectively by a variety of other nations.

The most famous articulation of the idea that Americans needed to remember their debt to their country—and not just its debt to them—probably comes from John F. Kennedy. In his 2020 presidential campaign, Pete Buttigieg echoed JFK's call to national service and pointed out how serving in the military allowed him to meet Americans from many different races, education levels, and income levels.[5] Buttigieg was trying to continue a tradition that goes back not only to JFK, but even further, to Franklin Delano Roosevelt's Civilian Conservation Corps, which helped the country dig its way out of the Great Depression by putting millions of young men to work rebuilding the country, giving them food, shelter, jobs, money, and, most important, a shared sense of purpose. The Civilian Conservation Corps was the most popular of the New Deal programs. Nearly a century later, as we grapple with our own economic and civil crises, this may yet again prove to be the way forward.

Universal civic service isn't just a liberal idea. Conservative icon William F. Buckley, Jr., proposed a civilian analogue to military service, one that focused on rebuilding our country instead of making war with others. Buckley emphasized that the main value of the service would be that it was a collective expression of thanks. He argued that a year of national service would remind Americans that they owed their freedoms to previous generations and would strengthen ties between new generations.[6]

General Stanley McChrystal (Retired), a political nonpartisan, has been publicly pushing for universal civic service since 2012. Like Buckley, McChrystal argues that Americans have a strange presumption that the main way to serve their nation is to join its military.[7] They're right. We seem to have settled on a bizarre system in which a few people, often poor, serve the country by joining the army, and the rest of us fulfill our duty by fervently saying "Thank you for your service" whenever we see them—as if service to country is a heroic burden that a few shoulder so that the rest don't have to.

But McChrystal points out that we have it backward: we should view national service as ordinary, not extraordinary, and to make that shift, it has to become universal, commonplace. National service should be a part of every citizen's life, part of what it *means* to be a citizen. In Buckley's view, to think of civic service as a burden would be like thinking of giving a gift as a burden. Receiving gifts and giving them in return isn't supposed to be like a capitalist transaction in which each party calculates the costs and benefits. Instead, it's supposed to be a mutual expression of respect. When people show their respect and appreciation for each other, the pie of respect grows, and there's more to go around.

This is the common thread that binds these American thinkers from different eras and ideologies. They're all pointing out that there's an enormous difference between *working off* a debt and *repaying* one. Working off debt has its place in our capitalist tradition, but it belongs in the realm of zero-sum games about the efficient division of resources. Civic service belongs to an entirely different tradition, our democratic one. In this realm, our task is not to divide scarce material resources but to grow a shared spiritual one. In our democratic tradition, like our gift-giving one, when we show others that we value them, we become better ourselves.

In spite of its bipartisan appeal and roots in American history, truly universal civic service has never quite had its day in our nation. However, in other countries, national service has proven to be an effective glue uniting disparate communities. Since its independence in 1967, Singapore, a small but incredibly diverse multicultural state, has required its male citizens to serve for two years in the military, police, or civil defense forces—helping to establish a shared national identity.[8] In a 2017 survey, 84 percent of Singaporeans stated that their national identity was either greater or equal to their ethnic identity.[9]

Rwanda had an especially pressing need to unite different ethnicities to forge a common national identity. In 1994, the country's Hutu ethnic majority systematically slaughtered the Tutsi minority, killing a million people in the course of a hundred days. Tutsi rebels ultimately overthrew the Hutu government. In the aftermath, Rwanda turned to national service to bind the country's wounds. On the last Saturday of every month, all able-bodied Rwandans come together for mandatory community service called umuganda, where they clean streets, cut grass, build roads, and repair houses.[10] The government estimates that more than 90 percent of the population participates.[11]

In Israel, mandatory military service brought together disparate Ashkenazi, Sephardi, and Mizrahi Jews from the Diaspora with Druze citizens and forged a new national identity. Unfortunately, this identity isn't universally shared because two groups are exempt from conscription, ultra-Orthodox Haredi Jews and Arab Israelis. Together, the exempt groups currently make up more than 30 percent of Israel's population—a figure expected to rise to 60 percent by 2050 given higher proportional birth rates.[12] The religious exemption from military service for ultra-Orthodox Haredi Jews has become a source of national strife. When the state of Israel was created in 1948, the exemption only affected 400 people—Haredi Jews now constitute about 10 percent of Israel's Jewish population.[13] Israel is still divided over the exemption of Haredi Jews: currently, as a matter of law, they are no longer exempt from the draft, but as a matter of fact, they're still exempt.[14]

Having large and growing segments of its population exempt from national service causes resentment between Israel's secular and religious citizens, along with intensifying the divide between its Arab and Jewish ones. As the population of people who are exempt from the draft grows, those who are subject to it are increasingly dodging it. The enlistment rate among Israelis who are legally obliged to serve has dropped from 75 percent to below 50 percent over the last twenty years.[15]

Here's a biotech guy's take on social science: when you want to see what effect one thing has on another, you not only look at what happens when you add them together, you study what happens when you separate them. If you want to show that a chemical causes cancer, for instance, one way to do it is by injecting it into cells and seeing if they proliferate uncontrollably. But to get even more proof, you'd also want to remove the chemical and see if that reverses the effect. The same principle can apply to policies. There's the positive case where implementing mandatory national service can bind a nation together. But there's also the negative case where it can deepen divisions in a society, when national service is mandatory but not universal. When only part of a society is expected to serve it, what should be an expression of gratitude can instead look like a burden that's unequally shared.

The truth is that American thinkers have proposed the idea of universal national service without proposing how to make it happen because universal service sounds like a military draft. Ever since the Vietnam War it's been political suicide to suggest anything that even remotely resembles the draft. There are at least a couple of ways to get around this mental block. First, we need to emphasize the non-military nature of mandatory national service. It's easy to rally against war, but if we require young Americans to pick a cause they're passionate about and spend a few months on it, are they really going to rally by the thousands to object to fighting hunger, poverty, pollution, illiteracy, and homelessness? What slogans would they chant? These are, after all, causes that most of them care about. Better yet, we'd be providing them money and structure to help them do things they want to do anyway.

A second way to get past our mental block is to require national service of teenagers, not legal adults. Because, according to my proposal, national service must be universal in order to create a shared national identity and it also has to be mandatory. And to make it mandatory, we should frame it as just another part of the mandatory education that we already require of adolescents.

Taking this approach would counter the argument that such service is an infringement on freedom and would support the idea that it is a society's duty to teach its young virtue. We can present national service, as France is doing, as a simple extension of schooling. France is currently implementing a mandatory civic service program for its own teenagers. The plan is for all French citizens to perform mandatory service for a month when they're sixteen, doing things like "teaching, working with charities, and working with the police, fire service, or army," followed up by voluntary placement to spend another three to twelve months on one of those causes.[16]

For an American version of this idea, I propose requiring high school students to serve the nation each year during a portion of their summer break—so they'd do four summers of national service, adding up to about a year's worth of experience. This would both create unity and get rid of a troubling source of inequality. At almost three months on average, our summer breaks are staggeringly long by international standards with well-documented deleterious effects on children. Research suggests that students, on average, forget about 25 to 30 percent of what they learned during the school year over summer breaks.[17] This burden is felt more by the poor, who can't pay thousands of dollars for fancy summer schools and camps. American parents spend $16.6 billion annually providing summer enrichment activities for their kids.[18]

Since racial minorities are disproportionately poor, our summers-off system disadvantages them further—a prime example of systemic inequality. The same study that reports 25 to 30 percent summer learning loss also suggests that Black and Latino students lose more knowledge over the summer than white students.[19] This is how systemic inequality works—first myriad causes make minorities poorer than average, and then policies like extended summer breaks compound the harm.

My problem with woke complaints about "systemic racism" isn't that it doesn't exist. It's that too often it's used as a vague, judgmental catchall phrase for all of America's woes. Woke activists fail to focus on more tangible examples of truly *systemic* inequality just because they aren't quite as fashionable to talk about. The existence of summer break as an institution is probably one of the greatest systematic inequalities in our educational system. But there's something about going out and chanting "End Summer Break" that doesn't quite have the same moral ring to it as "Defund the police."

It's boring to campaign against long summer breaks. It's much easier and more satisfying to say that we should just end structural racism and then everything else will follow. Liberals complain about trickle-down economics, but they believe in trickle-down politics—don't worry about boring little policy fixes, just raise your voice against racism instead.

My problem with complaints of systemic racism isn't that they're *wrong*, it's that they're *lazy*. Saying that the root problem is pervasive and overwhelming racism can perversely make it seem as if someone's missing the big picture when they focus on narrow policy solutions rather than fighting all the evil racists. It's more viscerally satisfying to fight bad people than bad policies.

Presumably, data-driven progressives would agree with me that America's extended summer breaks have the effect of widening the education and income gap between different races and classes. Whether we call this structural inequality "systemic racism" or not matters much less than what we do about it. We can remedy this inequality and help create a shared American identity in one stroke by having high school students spend a couple of months in structured national service programs.

I want our youth to love America, but I don't think indoctrinating them about its greatness is enough. I want to put them in a position to discover its greatness by working together to build it. Learning about diversity and loving your country don't have to be at odds with each other. The way to do both is to have Americans from all walks of life meet each other and make things together.

Achieving this won't be easy. For starters, building the political consensus required to implement an ambitious proposal like universal civic service will require reminding Americans of what it actually means to be an American—to be an individualist in our economy while still owing a civic duty to our democracy. As poet John Donne reminded us, no man is an island. Every man is a piece of a continent, a part of the main. As for America, we're a nation of individuals. And that's a good thing, as long as we still see ourselves as a nation in the end.

CHAPTER 15

Who Are We?

WHEN OUR BABY KARTHIK WAS born, he taught me a lot. He came into the world on February 23, 2020, during the lead-up to the first major wave of COVID-19 in the US. Things were still uncertain in those first few months. The World Health Organization and the Chinese government both stated that there was no human-to-human transmission of the virus. Public health leaders in the US discouraged the use of masks and encouraged Americans to go about living their normal lives. Yet it didn't make sense that Chinese state police were forcibly evacuating individuals from their home to be quarantined, if that was all there was to the story.

We had already moved to Ohio in late 2019, but my wife Apoorva was still finishing the final few months of her training as an airway surgeon at New York Presbyterian Hospital. By the middle of March the city was preparing for the health catastrophe of a generation. The city's hospitals were scrambling to make space for a tidal wave of patients in need of ventilators. The Navy sent large ships to the Hudson River to serve as makeshift hospitals. The two-million-square-foot Jacob K. Javits Convention Center became a field hospital.

Meanwhile, we had a two-week-old infant, and Apoorva faced a difficult decision: whether to head to the frontlines to treat patients or take her maternity leave with our baby as she had planned. On the one hand, her colleagues really needed her help. On the other, there were many doctors in the city, but only one mom for our newborn son.

Ultimately, Apoorva decided that it was her duty to treat patients during the city's hour of need, and I decided that it was my duty to become the principal caretaker of our son at our home in Ohio. It was the exact opposite of what we had envisioned only a few months before, when we thought that I would be fielding the busy travel schedule of a CEO while Apoorva took maternity leave. But we made that decision together.

The decision seemed easier at first since we assumed that it would only result in a couple of weeks' separation. But things got worse quickly. Apoorva stayed sequestered in her parents' apartment along with her father, himself a doctor, who had also volunteered to treat hospitalized ICU patients on the frontline. We still don't know exactly who got infected when, but after a few weeks, both Apoorva and her father were infected in the line of duty.

Both suffered initially, but her father got progressively worse. His pulse oxygen levels dropped after a few days, and he landed in the ICU as a patient, hospitalized for nearly two weeks. As a doctor herself, Apoorva scoured the scant but emerging literature on how to treat severe COVID-19 patients. We had multi-hour discussions late into the evening each night to discuss which investigational therapies he should take and the wisdom of receiving steroids or not at a time when there was minimal clinical data to support any decision. Even worse, Apoorva's brother became ill as well, ending up in the same hospital at the same time. That spring quickly became hell.

A couple of weeks turned into a couple of months. It crushed Apoorva to be separated from our baby son, to see him on Face-Time instead of holding him in her arms. She'd looked forward to giving Karthik his first bath. Instead I was the one who did it, as she looked after her father and other COVID-19 patients at her hospital when she returned to work within days of her own recovery. Even after we reunited at the end of May, it took most of the summer before Apoorva's normally jubilant attitude came back. We didn't know whether to attribute it to post-COVID fatigue, postpartum depression, or her just having been through a rough few months.

In retrospect, we were lucky. Thousands of health-care workers and millions of American families went through far worse. Now that things are finally back to normal, we often reflect on those painful months. Apoorva recovered from COVID-19, and so did her father. Thankfully her brother is doing well too. The long-term effects of COVID-19 infection are still unknown. They say it permanently scars the lungs of some patients. The biggest scar it left on our family was an emotional one. I know that Apoorva would make the same decision again if she had to do it all over. But she still sorely misses those few months of Karthik's early life, and she will never get them back.

She would've been a good doctor even if she made the opposite choice; she was a good mother even in making the choice that she did. I hope the same was true for my choices as a father and a CEO. I probably accomplished less as Roivant's CEO last spring than I otherwise might have. I don't think Roivant is any worse off today as a result. Apoorva spent less time with her newborn son soon after he was born. He'll never know the difference, even though she does.

So what's the moral of the story? It's that we are each more than just one thing. And that's what true pluralism is all about: the pluralism of identities *within* each of us.

That vision of pluralism stands in stark contrast to the woke version of identity. According to wokeness, we are each defined by a small handful of characteristics that we inherit on the day we're born. In a woke world, we are each defined by the innate and the immutable, by the visible and the skin-deep. This narrative now permeates our social consciousness in America. It's reinforced by not only the people who lead our government but the people who lead the companies where we work and the schools where our children learn.

This rigid vision was summed up neatly by Congresswoman Ayanna Pressley when she effectively declared that we are each a prisoner of our skin color.[1] It was on display in late 2020 when states from California to New York to Tennessee explicitly decided to take "racial equity" into account when deciding who would receive the vaccines first. Or when states like Oregon set aside funds for COVID-19 relief explicitly on the basis of the race of their recipients.

According to this worldview, you are simply a fault line at the intersection of the tectonic plates of group identity. You aren't really a free agent in the world, but simply a member of your "group" who is supposed to advance your group's interests. Your race isn't just the color your skin happens to be. It's essential to your voice, your ideas, and your identity. This is what woke essentialism is all about: it posits that your genetically inherited attributes are the true essence of who you are.

I reject that narrative, and I think every American should too. I'm not just a man. I'm a proud father, a loyal husband, and a grateful son. I'm not just a person of color. I'm a Hindu, a child of immigrants, an American citizen, and a proud native of Ohio. I'm not just a former CEO, but a scientist and an entrepreneur. I'm the author of my own destiny, sometimes for the better and sometimes for the worse, but always unlimited by what someone else thinks I should be. I'm not defined by any single one of those things. Rather, I am all of those things at once and a great deal more. Each of those identities is part of my personal mosaic—the mosaic that *together* comprises who I am as an American. That's what true American pluralism is all about.

In contrast, the woke version of pluralism is to get a bunch of different-looking people together in the same room and celebrate that visible tableau of diversity. But that's just putting lipstick on essentialism. True pluralism isn't about celebrating the differences *between* us as people. It's about the diversity of identities *within* each of us—rich mosaics that go beyond the color of our skin or the number of our X chromosomes. Pluralism means rising above the narrow demands of woke culture to discover that there's more to each of us than our immutable characteristics.

The fundamental problem with wokeness isn't just that it offers the wrong answer to the question of who we are. The deeper problem is that it forecloses the possibility of shared solidarity as Americans. If we see each other as nothing more than the color of our skin, our gender, our sexual orientation, or the number of digits in our bank accounts, then it becomes impossibly difficult to find commonality with those who don't share those characteristics. Yet if we define ourselves on a *plurality* of attributes, then we find our path to true solidarity as a people.

For example, I'm brown, conservative, and Hindu. The person I recently elevated to the position of CEO of my company is white, liberal, and Jewish. He's progressive. I'm not. But we both share a passion for discovering new drugs for patients who need them.

My neighbor is black, progressive, and Christian. I'm none of those things. But we are both fathers of children who I hope will one day play sports together, go to class together, and learn from one another. We don't need to have everything in common with one another. We only need a few things that bind us together as a people.

So—who are we as a people? I can't remember a time in my life when we more badly needed an answer to that question.

America is like each of us: our country isn't just one thing either. That's what makes America unique. Historically, most countries were defined on the basis of a single attribute—a single ethnicity, a single language, a single religion, a single monarch. Not America. We were the first and greatest country defined exclusively on the basis of a set of ideas, enshrined under a single Constitution. America wasn't just a place. It was a vision of what a place could be. America was about democracy. Capitalism. Reason, science, and enlightenment. Faith and purpose. Freedom. Individualism. Solidarity through a commitment to something greater than ourselves.

These are quintessentially American values and ideals. We should care about preserving each of them. But sometimes that means leaving each of them alone and keeping them separate from one another. That's part of what it means to reject essentialism and to embrace true American pluralism.

That's what bothers me about fashionable modern ideas like woke capitalism. On its face, the idea that corporations shouldn't just make products and provide services for profit but should also address other social and cultural issues sounds pretty benign. But on deeper inspection, it demands that we blur the lines between our two most fundamental institutions: capitalism and democracy. It demands that companies concern themselves with the moral questions that America is supposed to adjudicate through its democracy—racial justice, gender equality, whether and how to fight climate change. And in doing so, it gives capitalist leaders an outsized role in our democracy.

That's also what bothers me about the influence of woke culture over other institutions. A scientist's application for an NIH grant or a doctor's proposal for a poster presentation at a medical conference should be judged on the basis of scientific merit, not on the basis of the race or gender of the applicant. Yet that's what we increasingly see in the demand for "diversity" in science. The list goes on.

In contrast, real pluralism means separating different institutions from one another and keeping their respective purposes intact and distinct. That pluralistic vision is part of what makes America great. It's what makes America itself.

That leaves us with a paradox, a uniquely American puzzle. On the one hand, America is plural in nature: there are many Americas and many ways to be American. There are many different values to which we aspire and many institutions that comprise our nation. On the other hand, our diversity is meaningless if there's nothing greater that binds us together across those differences. That's the quandary at the heart of America itself.

I can't promise an answer to the puzzle, but here's what I know. At our core, there are and always have been two distinctive ideals that define us as a nation. The first is the American Dream. The second is *E Pluribus Unum*—the idea that from many, we Americans become one.

The American Dream is a dream of prosperity, freedom, and opportunity. It's the idea that no matter who your parents are, you can achieve your dreams through hard work, commitment, and ingenuity. It's the dream my father had when he came to America from Vadakanchery in the late 1970s. It didn't matter if he were a Brahmin or a Shudra, brown or white. It didn't matter if he had a thick Indian accent or a southern drawl; ten bucks in his pocket, as he did then, or a million in his bank account, as he does today. My parents never woke up from the dream that brought them here. Instead they passed it on to me, and now I pass it on to my son.

E Pluribus Unum is etched on every American coin, down to the penny. "From many, one." It's the idea that all of us as individuals, freely pursuing our own dreams, from a limitless variety of backgrounds, can unite into a single nation and pledge allegiance to the same flag and freely speak to one another even if they disagree about their politics.

Individualism and unity. Contradictory as these might seem, they are each in America's heart. Most of us surely feel these two aspirations within ourselves. The desire for individual freedom and opportunity on the one hand and the desire to be part of something transcending our individual selves on the other. America isn't just one of those things. It's both of them.

Our best shot at making the American Dream real is through capitalism. Our best shot at making *E Pluribus Unum* real is through democracy. That's why capitalism and democracy are the mother and father of America. The year 1776 wasn't just an accident. It was the year of the Declaration of Independence and *The Wealth of Nations*. It was the year America was *born*.

Yet these two ideals are in tension with one another. A creative, productive tension, but a tension all the same. It reminds me of the feeling that I sometimes had as a kid when I heard my parents in the depth of a heated argument and worried they might get divorced. It was my worst nightmare as a kid, but in reality they remain happily married to this day. I am who I am because of both of them, and the same goes for America and her parents too.

Our prosperity and individual freedom depend on the integrity of capitalism. Our unity and political freedoms depend on the integrity of democracy. With the birth of woke capitalism, we lose both and are left with neither. Wokeness turns *E Pluribus Unum* on its head—"from many, one" to "from one, many." It perverts the American Dream into an American nightmare in which the characteristics you inherit at birth determine who you are and what you can achieve.

My woke friends argue that they don't actually *want* America to work that way, but that it's simply how America *does* work—an ugly reality that we have to accept before we change it. They mean that earnestly. But they miss the most important point: *the way we as citizens choose to describe America changes the way America actually works*.

In the end, America isn't a place at all. It's an idea. We call it the American *Dream* for a reason. It's not a destination that we reach; it's a vision we aspire to, one that we'll always fall short of but keep pursuing anyway. That's part of what it means to have a dream. But over the last decade, something scary happened: *we woke up*. And once you wake up from a dream, you forget what it was all about. That's the real danger of wokeness.

We still have time to get this right. If the 2010s were about celebrating our diversity as individuals, then the 2020s should be about celebrating what we still share in common as a people. They should be about reviving the ideals that bind us together as a nation. The American Dream. *E Pluribus Unum*. From many, one. We shouldn't let self-interested corporations and politicians exploit us with skin-deep identities and cheap social causes that they sell us to advance their own agendas. That's just their trick: divide and conquer America by making our shared ideals disappear. Our shared identity has disappeared right along with it.

Yet as Michael Caine's character says in the movie, it's not enough to make something disappear. You have to bring it back.[2] That's the defining challenge of our time, and it's the most important work we'll ever do as Americans.

NOTES

INTRODUCTION: THE WOKE-INDUSTRIAL COMPLEX

1. *The Prestige*. Directed by Christopher Nolan, Touchstone Pictures, Warner Bros, Newmarket Productions, Syncopy, 2006.

2. When using the terms "black" and "white" as racial adjectives, I use lowercase for both for consistency.

3. Romano, Aja. "A History of 'Wokeness.' " *Vox*, 9 Oct. 2020, www.vox.com /culture/21437879/stay-woke-wokeness-history-origin-evolution-controversy.

4. Ramaswamy, Vivek, and Rubenfeld, Jed. "Save the Constitution from Big Tech." *The Wall Street Journal*, 11 Jan. 2021, www.wsj.com/articles/save-the -constitution-from-big-tech-11610387105.

CHAPTER 1

1. "Asspen." *South Park: Season 6, Episode 2*, directed and written by Trey Parker, featuring Trey Parker and Matt Stone, aired March 12, 2002. southpark.cc .com/episodes/y0ffuc/south-park-asspen-season-6-ep-2.

2. "Goldman Sachs to Pay $3bn over 1MDB Corruption Scandal." *BBC News*, BBC, 22 Oct. 2020, www.bbc.com/news/business-54597256.

3. Hope, Bradley, et al. "The Secret Money Behind 'The Wolf of Wall Street.' " *The Wall Street Journal*, 1 Apr. 2016, www.wsj.com/articles/malaysias-1mdb-the-secret -money-behind-the-wolf-of-wall-street-1459531987.

4. "r/Wallstreetbets—Goldman Sachs Alludes to GME & WSB." *Reddit*, www.reddit.com/r/wallstreetbets/comments/l3ucyv/goldman_sachs_alludes_to _gme_wsb/.

5. Chappell, Bill. "Malaysia's Former PM Najib Razak Begins Trial on 1MDB Slush-Fund Charges." *NPR*, 3 Apr. 2019, www.npr.org/2019/04/03/709388200/malaysias-former-pm-najib-razak-begins-trial-on-1mdb-slush-fund-charges.

6. "One Year Later: Purpose of a Corporation." *Business Roundtable—Purpose of a Corporation*, http://purpose.businessroundtable.org/.

7. "In the Round: Business Roundtable CEOs on Leadership and the Purpose of a Corporation." *Politico*, www.politico.com/sponsored-content/2020/09/in-the-round?cid=202009hp#/.

8. Duffy, Evita. "Whistleblower: Coca-Cola Tells Employees 'Try to Be Less White.'" *The Federalist*, 20 Feb. 2021, thefederalist.com/2021/02/20/whistleblower-coca-cola-uses-antiracist-training-that-tells-employees-try-to-be-less-white/.

9. Bastian, Ed. "Ed Bastian Memo: Your Right to Vote." *Delta News Hub*, Delta Airlines, 31 Mar. 2021, news.delta.com/ed-bastian-memo-your-right-vote.

10. "Statement from James Quincey on Georgia Voting Legislation: Company Statement." *The Coca-Cola Company: Refresh the World. Make a Difference*, The Coca-Cola Company, 1 Apr. 2021, www.coca-colacompany.com/media-center/georgia-voting-legislation.

11. "The Right to Vote Is Fundamental—a Letter from Biotechnology Industry Leaders." *Endpoints News*, 15 Apr. 2021, endpts.com/the-right-to-vote-is-fundamental-a-letter-from-biotechnology-industry-leaders/.

12. Gore, Al, and David Blood. "Capitalism after the Coronavirus." *The Wall Street Journal*, 29 June 2020, www.wsj.com/articles/capitalism-after-the-coronavirus-11593470102.

13. Benioff, Marc. "Marc Benioff: We Need a New Capitalism." *The New York Times*, 14 Oct. 2019, www.nytimes.com/2019/10/14/opinion/benioff-salesforce-capitalism.html.

14. Douthat, Ross. "The Rise of Woke Capital." *The New York Times*, 28 Feb. 2018, www.nytimes.com/2018/02/28/opinion/corporate-america-activism.html.

15. Mankiw, N. Gregory. "C.E.O.s Are Qualified to Make Profits, Not Lead Society." *The New York Times*, 24 July 2020, www.nytimes.com/2020/07/24/business/ceos-profits-shareholders.html.

16. Kaplan, Steven. "The Enduring Wisdom of Milton Friedman." *ProMarket*, 29 Sept. 2020, promarket.org/2020/09/14/the-enduring-wisdom-of-milton-friedman/.

17. Schmidt, Christine. "Al Gore Talks Climate Change, the Role of Money in Politics at the IOP." *The Chicago Maroon*, 13 May 2014, chicagomaroon.com/article/2014/5/13/al-gore-talks-climate-change-the-role-of-money-in-politics-at-the-iop/.

18. Blankenship, Kyle. "Merck CEO Calls on Private Industry to 'Stabilize Society' amid Racial Injustice, Economic Downturn." *FiercePharma*, 16 Oct. 2020,

www.fiercepharma.com/pharma/merck-ceo-calls-private-industry-to-stabilize
-society-amid-racial-injustice-economic.

19. Stankiewicz, Kevin. "'There Is No Middle Ground'—Black CEOs Urge Companies to Oppose Restrictive Voting Laws." *CNBC*, 31 Mar. 2021, www.cnbc .com/2021/03/31/ken-frazier-black-ceos-urge-firms-to-oppose-restrictive-voting -laws.html.

20. Kelly, Jack. "Pope Francis Partners with Corporate Titans to Make Capitalism More Inclusive and Fair: Is This for Real or Just Corporate Virtue Signaling?" *Forbes*, 9 Dec. 2020, www.forbes.com/sites/jackkelly/2020/12/09/pope-francis -partners-with-corporate-titans-to-make-capitalism-more-inclusive-and-fair-is-this -for-real-or-just-corporate-virtue-signaling/?sh=2d317e704c7b.

21. "About Us." *Council for Inclusive Capitalism*, 4 Mar. 2021, www.inclusive capitalism.com/about/.

22. "Ex-Tyco CEO Dennis Kozlowski Found Guilty." *NBCNews*, 17 June 2005, www.nbcnews.com/id/wbna8258729.

23. "Decacorn" is Silicon Valley's term of art for a venture-backed company that is worth more than $10 billion on paper prior to its IPO. It's a play on the older term "unicorn," which refers to a pre-IPO company that's worth more than $1 billion on paper.

24. "Amazon Donates $10 Million to Organizations Supporting Justice and Equity." About Amazon, Amazon, 9 Nov. 2020, www.aboutamazon.com/news /policy-news-views/amazon-donates-10-million-to-organizations-supporting -justice-and-equity?utm_medium=sp&utm_source=gateway&utm _term=blmdonate.

25. Blest, Paul. "Leaked Amazon Memo Details Plan to Smear Fired Warehouse Organizer: 'He's Not Smart or Articulate.'" VICE, 2 Apr. 2020, www.vice.com/en /article/5dm8bx/leaked-amazon-memo-details-plan-to-smear-fired-warehouse -organizer-hes-not-smart-or-articulate.

26. "NIKE, Inc. Statement on Commitment to the Black Community." *Nike News*, Nike, 5 June 2020, news.nike.com/news/nike-commitment-to-black-community.

27. Miller, Tim. "After White House Meeting with Trump, Mike Lindell Calls for Military Coup on Facebook." *The Bulwark*, 17 Jan. 2021, thebulwark.com/after -white-house-meeting-with-trump-mike-lindell-calls-for-military-coup-on -facebook/?amp&__twitter_impression=true.

CHAPTER 3

1. "How We're Supporting Communities & Recovery." *Uber.com*, Uber, 2020, www.uber.com/us/en/coronavirus/community-recovery/.

2. Strine, Leo. "The Dangers of Denial: The Need for a Clear-Eyed Understanding of the Power and Accountability Structure Established by the

Delaware General Corporation Law (2015). *Wake Forest Law Review*, Vol. 50, 761, 2015, *U of Penn*, *Inst for Law & Econ* Research Paper No. 15-08, ssrn.com/abstract =2576389

3. "Don't Limit the Revolution." *The Economist*, 29 Sept. 2016, www.economist .com/business/2016/09/29/dont-limit-the-revolution.

4. Davoudi, L., McKenna, C., and Olegario, R. "The Historical Role of the Corporation in Society." *Journal of the British Academy*, Vol. 6(s1), 17–47, 2018, www.thebritishacademy.ac.uk/documents/976/JBA-6s1-Davoudi-McKenna -Olegario.pdf.

5. Davoudi, L., McKenna, C., and Olegario, R. "The Historical Role of the Corporation in Society." *Journal of the British Academy*, 6(s1): 17–47. 2018. www .thebritishacademy.ac.uk/documents/976/JBA-6s1-Davoudi-McKenna-Olegario .pdf.

6. fee.org/articles/do-corporations-have-social-responsibilities/.

7. Coy, Peter. "Revisiting Milton Friedman's Critique of Stakeholderism." *Bloomberg*, 11 Sept. 2020, www.bloomberg.com/news/articles/2020-09-11/milton -friedman-s-attacked-stakeholder-capitalism-before-it-was-popular.

8. Hood, John. "Do Corporations Have Social Responsibilities?: John Hood." *Do Corporations Have Social Responsibilities?*, Foundation for Economic Education, 1 Nov. 1998, fee.org/articles/do-corporations-have-social-responsibilities/#:~:text =Jones%20of%20the%20University%20of,firms%20rarely%20receive%20an %20invoice.%E2%80%9D.

9. Sorkin, Andrew Ross. "A Free Market Manifesto That Changed the World, Reconsidered." *The New York Times*, 11 Sept. 2020, www.nytimes.com/2020/09/11 /business/dealbook/milton-friedman-doctrine-social-responsibility-of-business .html.

10. Tyler Halloran, "A Brief History of the Corporate Form and Why It Matters," *Fordham Journal of Corporate & Financial Law*. news.law.ford ham.edu/jcfl/2018/11/18/a-brief-history-of-the-corporate-form-and-why-it-matters /#_edn26.

11. Wells, Harwell. "The Modernization of Corporation Law, 1920–1940 (January 27, 2009). *University of Pennsylvania Journal of Business Law*, Vol. 11, 2009, Temple University Legal Studies Research Paper No. 2009-10. ssrn.com/abstract =1333675.

CHAPTER 4

1. McGinley, Laurie. "Former FDA Commissioners Say Right-to-Try Bills Could Endanger 'Vulnerable Patients.'" *The Washington Post*, 22 Aug. 2019, www .washingtonpost.com/news/to-your-health/wp/2018/03/18/former- fda-commissioners-say-right-to-try-bills-could-endanger-vulnerable -patients/.

2. Chotiner, Isaac. "Michael Lind on Populism, Racism, and Restoring Democracy." *The New Yorker*, 6 Feb. 2020, www.newyorker.com/news/q-and-a /michael-lind-on-populism-racism-and-restoring-democracy.

3. Lind, Michael. "The New Class War." *American Affairs Journal*, 6 Aug. 2017, americanaffairsjournal.org/2017/05/new-class-war/.

4. Fama, Eugene F., and Jensen, Michael C. "Separation of Ownership and Control." *Foundations of Organizational Strategy*, Harvard University Press, 1998, and *Journal of Law and Economics*, Vol. 26, June 1983, ssrn.com/abstract=94034 or dx.doi .org/10.2139/ssrn.94034.

5. Lind, Michael. "The New Class War." *American Affairs Journal*, 6 Aug. 2017, americanaffairsjournal.org/2017/05/new-class-war/.

6. Lind, Michael. "The New Class War." *American Affairs Journal*, 6 Aug. 2017, americanaffairsjournal.org/2017/05/new-class-war/

7. "The VW Emissions Scandal: A Failure of ESG Investing?" *Investment and Wealth Management Insights*, Rock Point Advisors, www.rockpointadvisors.com /insights-the-vw-emissions-scandal-a-failure-of-esg-investing.php.

8. Ewing, Jack. "Engineering a Deception: What Led to Volkswagen's Diesel Scandal." *The New York Times*, 16 Mar. 2017, www.nytimes.com/interactive/2017 /business/volkswagen-diesel-emissions-timeline.html.

9. "Volkswagen Is World's Most Sustainable Automotive Group." *Volkswagen US Media Site*, Volkswagen, 11 Sept. 2015, media.vw.com/en-us/releases/566.

10. Winterkorn, Martin. "Letter to Our Shareholders." *Volkswagen Group Annual Report 2014*, 2014, annualreport2014.volkswagenag.com/strategy/letter-to-our-share holders.html.

11. "Learn about Volkswagen Violations." *EPA*, Environmental Protection Agency, 27 Sept. 2019, www.epa.gov/vw/learn-about-volkswagen-violations.

12. La Monica, Paul R. "Volkswagen Stock Has Plunged 50%. Will It Ever Recover?" *CNNMoney*, money.cnn.com/2015/09/24/investing/volkswagen-vw -emissions-scandal-stock/.

13. Makortoff, Kalyeena. "Volkswagen Cut from Top Sustainability Index." *CNBC*, 30 Sept. 2015, www.cnbc.com/2015/09/29/volkswagen-cut-from-dow-jones -sustainability-ranking.html.

14. Parloff, Roger. "How VW Paid $25 Billion for 'Dieselgate' and Got Off Easy." *Fortune*, 6 Feb. 2018, fortune.com/2018/02/06/volkswagen-vw-emissions -scandal-penalties/.

15. Cremer, Andreas. "Ex-Volkswagen CEO Denies Early Knowledge of Diesel Emissions Cheating." *Reuters*, 19 Jan. 2017, www.reuters.com/article/us -volkswagen-emissions-winterkorn/ex-volkswagen-ceo-denies-early-knowledge -of-diesel-emissions-cheating-idUSKBN15318J.

16. Boston, William. "Volkswagen's Ex-CEO Is Ordered to Stand Trial over Emissions Scandal." *The Wall Street Journal*, 9 Sept. 2020, www.wsj.com/articles

/volkswagens-ex-ceo-is-ordered-to-stand-trial-over-emissions-scandal
-11599654843.

17. Clinton, Hillary. "Price Gouging like This in the Specialty Drug Market Is Outrageous. Tomorrow I'll Lay out a Plan to Take It on. -H." *Twitter*, 21 Sept. 2015, twitter.com/HillaryClinton/status/645974772275408896?s=20.

18. Pollack, Andrew. "Drug Goes from $13.50 a Tablet to $750, Overnight." *The New York Times*, 20 Sept. 2015, www.nytimes.com/2015/09/21/business/a-huge
-overnight-increase-in-a-drugs-price-raises-protests.html.

19. Crow, David. "Clinton Pledge on Drug Prices Knocks $15bn Off Biotechs." *Financial Times*, 21 Sept. 2015, www.ft.com/content/82af1c82-6083-11e5-9846
-de406ccb37f2.

20. Tirrell, Meg. "Martin Shkreli's Legacy: Putting a 'Fine Point' on the Drug Pricing Debate." *CNBC*, 9 Mar. 2018, www.cnbc.com/2018/03/09/martin-shkrelis
-legacy-shaping-the-drug-pricing-debate.html.

21. Thomas, Katie. "How to Protect a Drug Patent? Give It to a Native American Tribe." *The New York Times*, 8 Sept. 2017, www.nytimes.com/2017/09/08/health
/allergan-patent-tribe.html.

22. Hurley, Lawrence. "U.S. Supreme Court Rejects Allergan Bid to Use Tribe to Shield Drug Patents." *Reuters*, 15 Apr. 2019, www.reuters.com/article/us-usa
-court-allergan/u-s-supreme-court-rejects-allergan-bid-to-use-tribe-to-shield
-drug-patents-idUSKCN1RR1FD.

23. Sharfman, Bernard S. "The Importance of the Business Judgment Rule" (December 29, 2017). *New York University Journal of Law and Business*, 27 (Fall 2017), https://ssrn.com/abstract=2888052.

24. Hamburger, Philip. "Stop Feeding College Bureaucratic Bloat." *The Wall Street Journal*, 2 June 2019, www.wsj.com/articles/stop-feeding-college-bureaucratic
-bloat-11559507310.

25. Vedder, Richard K. *Restoring the Promise: Higher Education in America*. Independent Institute, 2019.

26. Abrams, Samuel J. "Think Professors Are Liberal? Try School Administrators." *The New York Times*, 16 Oct. 2018, www.nytimes.com/2018/10/16/opinion
/liberal-college-administrators.html.

27. Perry, Mark J. "Diversity and Administrative Bloat in Higher Education." *American Enterprise Institute*, 24 July 2018, www.aei.org/carpe-diem/diversity-and
-other-administrative-monstrosities-in-higher-education/.

CHAPTER 5

1. Asness, Cliff. "Virtue Is Its Own Reward: Or, One Man's Ceiling Is Another Man's Floor." *Cliff's Perspectives*, AQR Capital Management, 18 May 2017, www.aqr
.com/Insights/Perspectives/Virtue-is-its-Own-Reward-Or-One-Mans-Ceiling-is
-Another-Mans-Floor.

2. Asness, Cliff. "Virtue Is Its Own Reward: Or, One Man's Ceiling Is Another Man's Floor." *Cliff's Perspectives*, AQR Capital Management, 18 May 2017, www .aqr.com/Insights/Perspectives/Virtue-is-its-Own-Reward-Or-One-Mans-Ceiling -is-Another-Mans-Floor.

3. Schwab, Klaus, and Peter Vanham. *Stakeholder Capitalism: A Global Economy That Works for Progress, People and Planet.* John Wiley & Sons, Inc., 2021.

4. Gore, Al, and David Blood. "Capitalism after the Coronavirus." *The Wall Street Journal*, 29 June 2020, www.wsj.com/articles/capitalism-after-the-coronavirus -11593470102.

5. Fink, Larry. "A Fundamental Reshaping of Finance." *BlackRock*, 14 Jan. 2020, www.blackrock.com/ch/individual/en/larry-fink-ceo-letter#:~:text=Our%20 investment%20conviction%20is%20that,for%20client%20portfolios%20going%20 forward.

6. GuruFocus.com. "Can ESG Investing Beat the Market? Part 1." *Yahoo! News*, Yahoo!, 5 July 2020, www.yahoo.com/news/esg-investing-beat-market-part -194405037.html.

7. www.statestreet.com/content/dam/statestreet/documents/ss_associates /Corporate%20Resilience%20and%20Response%20During%20Covid19_Exec _2020April_3049915.GBL.pdf

8. Hale, Jon. "Sustainable Funds Weather the First Quarter Better Than Conventional Funds." *Morningstar, Inc.*, 3 Apr. 2020, www.morningstar.com/articles/976361 /sustainable-funds-weather-the-first-quarter-better-than-conventional-funds.

9. "ESG Investing: a Social Uprising." *(US) Federated Hermes*, 5 Nov. 2018, www.hermes-investment.com/us/insight/equities/esg-investing-a-social -uprising/.

10. Segal, Julie. "ESG Has Failed to Outperform for Years. Is This a Fix?" *Institutional Investor*, 13 May 2020, www.institutionalinvestor.com/article/b1lm2j93 w09cv9/ESG-Has-Failed-to-Outperform-for-Years-Is-this-a-Fix.

11. Hale, Jon. "3 Momentous Events Highlight the Impact of Investing in 2020." *Morningstar, Inc.*, 21 Dec. 2020, www.morningstar.com/articles/1015649/3 -momentous-events-highlight-the-impact-of-investing-in-2020.

12. "2020 Report On US Sustainable, Responsible and Impact Investing Trends." *USSIF.org*, The Forum for Sustainable and Responsible Investing, 2021, www.ussif .org/store_product.asp?prodid=42.

13. Collins, Sean, and Kristen Sullivan. "Advancing Environmental, Social, and Governance Investing." *Deloitte Insights*, Deloitte, 20 Feb. 2020, www2.deloitte .com/us/en/insights/industry/financial-services/esg-investing-performance .html#new-esg-fund-launches-to-acceler.

14. Biden, Joe. "Plan for Climate Change and Environmental Justice: Joe Biden." *Joe Biden for President: Official Campaign Website*, Joe Biden, 29 Oct. 2020, joebiden .com/climate-plan/.

15. Choi, Matthew. "Kerry Leans on Wall Street." *POLITICO*, 12 Mar. 2021, www.politico.com/newsletters/morning-energy/2021/03/12/kerry-leans-on-wall-street-793946.

16. "Real Meat. No Compromise." *Memphis Meats*, 2021, www.memphismeats.com/.

17. "About." *Beyond Meat—Go Beyond®*, Beyond Meat, 2021, www.beyondmeat.com/about/.

18. Heller, Martin C., and Keoleian, Gregory A. "Beyond Meat's Beyond Burger Life Cycle Assessment: A Detailed Comparison between a Plant-Based and an Animal-Based Protein Source." 2018 CSS Report, University of Michigan: Ann Arbor 1-38.

CHAPTER 6

1. Friedman, Milton. "A Friedman Doctrine—The Social Responsibility of Business Is to Increase Its Profits." *The New York Times*, 13 Sept. 1970, www.nytimes.com/1970/09/13/archives/a-friedman-doctrine-the-social-responsibility-of-business-is-to.html.

2. Schwab, Klaus. "Davos Manifesto 1973: A Code of Ethics for Business Leaders." World Economic Forum, 1973, www.weforum.org/agenda/2019/12/davos-manifesto-1973-a-code-of-ethics-for-business-leaders/.

3. Schwab, Klaus, and Peter Vanham. *Stakeholder Capitalism: A Global Economy That Works for Progress, People and Planet*, 185–186. John Wiley & Sons, Inc., 2021.

4. OccupyRichmond2011. "Occupy Richmond 10/6/11 Intro to 'Progressive Stack.'" *YouTube*, 8 Oct. 2011, www.youtube.com/watch?v=SCwhlZtHhWs.

5. von Mises, Ludwig. "The Anti-Capitalistic Mentality." *Mises Institute*, 1956, mises.org/library/anti-capitalistic-mentality.

CHAPTER 7

1. Hengeveld, Maria. "The Corporate Parent: The Collapse of Corporate Social Responsibility at Unilever." *Plough*, 15 Dec. 2020, www.plough.com/en/topics/justice/social-justice/the-corporate-parent.

2. "Every U Helps Empower Women and Girls." *Unilever*, 2021, www.unilever.com/brands/every-u-does-good/female-empowerment/.

3. "Business and Philanthropic Partners: Partnerships: Businesses and Philanthropies." *UN Women*, United Nations, 2021, www.unwomen.org/en/partnerships/businesses-and-foundations/major-partners#unilever.

4. Hengeveld, Maria. "The Corporate Parent: The Collapse of Corporate Social Responsibility at Unilever." *Plough*, 15 Dec. 2020, www.plough.com/en/topics/justice/social-justice/the-corporate-parent.

5. aidsfreeworld.org/statements/2020/6/23.

6. Koenig, Andy. "Look Who's Getting That Bank Settlement Cash." *The Wall Street Journal*, 28 Aug. 2016, www.wsj.com/articles/look-whos-getting-that-bank -settlement-cash-1472421204.

7. United States Constitution, Article I, Section 9, Clause 7.

8. Frank, Ted. "For Some Class-Action Lawyers, Charity Begins and Ends at Home." *The Wall Street Journal*, 22 Mar. 2018, www.wsj.com/articles/for-some -class-action-lawyers-charity-begins-and-ends-at-home-1521760032.

9. Yeatman, William. "Obama's Electric Car Money Grab." *The Wall Street Journal*, 2 Nov. 2016, www.wsj.com/articles/obamas-electric-car-money-grab-1478041904.

10. Pollack, Andrew. "Drug Goes from $13.50 a Tablet to $750, Overnight." *The New York Times*, 20 Sept. 2015, www.nytimes.com/2015/09/21/business/a-huge -overnight-increase-in-a-drugs-price-raises-protests.html#:~:text=The%20drug %2C%20called%20Daraprim%2C%20was,hundreds%20of%20thousands%20of%20 dollars.

11. Copeland, Rob, et al. "Turing Pharmaceuticals Replaces Martin Shkreli as CEO." *The Wall Street Journal*, 19 Dec. 2015, www.wsj.com/articles/turing -pharmaceuticals-close-to-replacing-martin-shkreli-as-ceo-1450454741.

12. Farberov, Snejana. "Martin Shkreli Hurls Sexist Comment at Taylor Swift in HipHopDx Interview." *Daily Mail Online*, 16 Dec. 2015, www.dailymail.co.uk /news/article-3363202/Martin-Shkreli-hurls-sexist-comment-Taylor-Swift-saying -play-2million-Wu-Tang-Clan-album-exchange-sexual-favor.html.

13. "Martin Shkreli Headed to Jail after Bail Revoked over Hillary Clinton Post." *The Guardian*, 13 Sept. 2017, www.theguardian.com/us-news/2017/sep/13 /martin-shkreli-jail-securities-fraud-hillary-clinton.

14. Mangan, Dan. " 'Pharma Bro' Martin Shkreli Found Guilty of 3 of 8 Charges, Including Securities Fraud." *CNBC*, 4 Aug. 2017, www.cnbc.com/2017/08/04 /pharma-bro-martin-shkreli-convicted-in-federal-fraud-case.html#:~:text=Bio tech%20and%20Pharma-,'Pharma%20bro'%20Martin%20Shkreli%20found%20 guilty%20of%203%20of,8%20charges%2C%20including%20securities%20fraud& text=Martin%20Shkreli%20was%20accused%20of,years%20in%20prison%20 when%20sentenced.

CHAPTER 8

1. al-Qadi, Fadi. "Do Not Forget the Jailed Saudi Women's Rights Activists." *Human Rights News | Al Jazeera*, Al Jazeera, 8 Mar. 2020, www.aljazeera.com/opinions /2020/3/8/do-not-forget-the-jailed-saudi-womens-rights-activists.

2. Hubbard, Ben. "Saudi Arabia Says Jamal Khashoggi Was Killed in Consulate Fight." *The New York Times*, 19 Oct. 2018, www.nytimes.com/2018/10/19/world /middleeast/jamal-khashoggi-dead-saudi-arabia.html.

3. Coskun, Orhan. "Exclusive: Turkish Police Believe Saudi Journalist Khashoggi Was Killed in Consulate—Sources." *Reuters*, 6 Oct. 2018, www.reuters.com/article

/us-saudi-politics-dissident/exclusive-turkish-police-believe-saudi-journalist -khashoggi-was-killed-in-consulate-sources-idUSKCN1MG0HU.

4. "Arab Source: Khashoggi Murdered by Ex-Spokesman of Saudi-Led Coalition in War on Yemen." *Farsnews*, 10 Oct. 2018, web.archive.org/web/20181011053539 /en.farsnews.com/newstext.aspx?nn=13970718000686.

5. Hearst, David. "EXCLUSIVE: Seven of Bin Salman's Bodyguards among Khashoggi Suspects." *Middle East Eye*, 18 Oct. 2018, www.middleeasteye.net/news /exclusive-seven-bin-salmans-bodyguards-among-khashoggi-suspects.

6. O'Keeffe, Kate, and Aruna Viswanatha. "China Warns U.S. It May Detain Americans in Response to Prosecutions of Chinese Scholars." *The Wall Street Journal*, 17 Oct. 2020, www.wsj.com/articles/china-warns-u-s-it-may-detain-americans -in-response-to-prosecutions-of-chinese-scholars-11602960959.

7. Yang, Jing, and Lingling Wei. "China's President Xi Jinping Personally Scuttled Jack Ma's Ant IPO." *The Wall Street Journal*, 12 Nov. 2020, www.wsj.com /articles/china-president-xi-jinping-halted-jack-ma-ant-ipo-11605203556.

8. Qiuyan, Qu. "Chinese Derogatory Social Media Term for 'White Left' Western Elites Spreads." *Global Times*, 21 May 2017, www.globaltimes.cn/content /1047989.shtml.

9. "An Update on Our Work to Serve All Stakeholders." *Airbnb Newsroom*, 28 Jan. 2020, news.airbnb.com/serving-all-stakeholders/.

10. Volz, Dustin, and Kirsten Grind. "Airbnb Executive Resigned Last Year over Chinese Request for More Data Sharing." *The Wall Street Journal*, 20 Nov. 2020, www.wsj.com/articles/airbnb-executive-resigned-last-year-over-chinese-request -for-more-data-sharing-11605896753?mod=mhp.

11. Volz, Dustin, and Kirsten Grind. "Airbnb Executive Resigned Last Year over Chinese Request for More Data Sharing." *The Wall Street Journal*, 20 Nov. 2020, www.wsj.com/articles/airbnb-executive-resigned-last-year-over-chinese-request -for-more-data-sharing-11605896753?mod=mhp.

12. Buckley, Chris. "China Is Detaining Muslims in Vast Numbers. The Goal: 'Transformation.'" *The New York Times*, 8 Sept. 2018, www.nytimes.com /2018/09/08/world/asia/china-uighur-muslim-detention-camp.html.

13. Zenz, Adrian. "Sterilizations, IUDs, and Mandatory Birth Control: The CCP's Campaign to Suppress Uyghur Birthrates in Xinjiang." *The Jamestown Foundation*, June 2020, jamestown.org/wp-content/uploads/2020/06/Zenz-Sterilizations -IUDs-and-Mandatory-Birth-Control-FINAL-27June.pdf?x60014.

14. Shukla, Ajai. "How China and India Came to Lethal Blows." *The New York Times*, 19 June 2020, www.nytimes.com/2020/06/19/opinion/China-India-conflict .html.

15. Chen, Frank. "PLA's New Assault Ships 'Most Detrimental' to Taiwan." *Asia Times*, 30 Apr. 2020, asiatimes.com/2020/04/plas-new-assault-ships-pose-a-threat -to-taiwan/.

16. Makichuk, Dave. "Cold War Quandary: China Builds a Third Assault Carrier." *Asia Times*, 11 Aug. 2020, asiatimes.com/2020/08/cold-war-quandary-china-builds-a-third-assault-carrier/.

17. Feng, Emily. "China Enacts Security Law, Asserting Control over Hong Kong." *NPR*, 30 June 2020, www.npr.org/2020/06/30/885127007/china-enacts-security-law-asserting-control-over-hong-kong.

18. Yglesias, Matthew. "The Raging Controversy over the NBA, China, and the Hong Kong Protests, Explained." *Vox*, 7 Oct. 2019, www.vox.com/2019/10/7/20902700/daryl-morey-tweet-china-nba-hong-kong.

19. Yglesias, Matthew. "The Raging Controversy over the NBA, China, and the Hong Kong Protests, Explained." *Vox*, 7 Oct. 2019, www.vox.com/2019/10/7/20902700/daryl-morey-tweet-china-nba-hong-kong.

20. Perper, Rosie. "China and the NBA Are Coming to Blows over a pro-Hong Kong Tweet. Here's Why." *Business Insider*, 22 Oct. 2019, www.businessinsider.com/nba-china-feud-timeline-daryl-morey-tweet-hong-kong-protests-2019-10#on-october-8-california-based-game-company-blizzard-banned-a-professional-esports-player-and-confiscated-his-prize-money-after-he-voiced-support-for-hong-kong-protesters-11.

21. "LeBron Addresses Backlash to Hong Kong Comments." *Reuters*, 16 Oct. 2019, www.reuters.com/article/us-basketball-nba-lal-lebron-backlash/lebron-addresses-backlash-to-hong-kong-comments-idUSKBN1WV01F.

22. Davis, Scott. "LeBron James Says He Doesn't Think Daryl Morey Was 'Educated' before Sending pro-Hong Kong Tweet, Says There Are Ramifications to Free Speech." *Business Insider*, 14 Oct. 2019, www.businessinsider.com/lebron-james-daryl-morey-uneducated-china-hong-kong-free-speech-2019-10.

23. Herndon, Astead W. "LeBron James on Black Voter Participation, Misinformation and Trump." *The New York Times*, 21 Oct. 2020, www.nytimes.com/2020/10/21/us/politics/lebron-james-trump-black-voters.html.

24. Herndon, Astead W. "LeBron James on Black Voter Participation, Misinformation and Trump." *The New York Times*, 21 Oct. 2020, www.nytimes.com/2020/10/21/us/politics/lebron-james-trump-black-voters.html.

25. "Disney Criticised for Filming Mulan in China's Xinjiang Province." *BBC News*, BBC, 7 Sept. 2020, www.bbc.com/news/world-54064654.

26. Richwine, Lisa. "Disney CEO Says It Will Be 'Difficult' to Film in Georgia If Abortion Law Takes Effect." *Reuters*, 30 May 2019, www.reuters.com/article/us-usa-abortion-walt-disney-exclusive/disney-ceo-says-it-will-be-difficult-to-film-in-georgia-if-abortion-law-takes-effect-idUSKCN1T003X.

27. Rosenberg, Alyssa. " 'Doctor Strange' Shows Why Diversity Advocates Should Take Chinese Censorship Seriously." *The Washington Post*, 28 Apr. 2019, www.washingtonpost.com/news/act-four/wp/2016/04/28/doctor-strange-shows-why-diversity-advocates-should-take-chinese-censorship-seriously/.

28. Hinshaw, Drew, et al. "Pushback on Xi's Vision for China Spreads Beyond U.S." *The Wall Street Journal*, 28 Dec. 2020, www.wsj.com/articles/pushback-xi -china-europe-germany-beyond-u-s-11609176287.

29. Magnier, Mark. "US-China Summit in Alaska Turns Civil after Fiery Start, but No Room for Hosted Dinner." *Yahoo! News*, *South China Morning Post*, 18 Mar. 2021, sg.news.yahoo.com/no-way-treat-guests-wang-221113353.html

30. "Secretary Antony J. Blinken, National Security Advisor Jake Sullivan, Director Yang and State Councilor Wang at the Top of Their Meeting." U.S. Department of State, 23 Mar. 2021, www.state.gov/secretary-antony-j-blinken-national -security-advisor-jake-sullivan-chinese-director-of-the-office-of-the-central -commission-for-foreign-affairs-yang-jiechi-and-chinese-state-councilor -wang-yi-at-th/.

31. Conger, Kate. "Google Removes 'Don't Be Evil' Clause from Its Code of Conduct." *Gizmodo*, 18 May 2018, gizmodo.com/google-removes-nearly-all -mentions-of-dont-be-evil-from-1826153393.

32. Helft, Miguel, and David Barboza. "Google Shuts China Site in Dispute over Censorship." *The New York Times*, 22 Mar. 2010, www.nytimes.com/2010 /03/23/technology/23google.html.

33. Lohr, Steve. "Interview: Sergey Brin on Google's China Move." *The New York Times*, 22 Mar. 2010, bits.blogs.nytimes.com/2010/03/22/interview-sergey -brin-on-googles-china-gambit/.

34. Gallagher, Ryan, and Lee Fang. "Google Suppresses Memo Revealing Plans to Closely Track Search Users in China." *The Intercept*, 21 Sept. 2018, theintercept .com/2018/09/21/google-suppresses-memo-revealing-plans-to-closely-track -search-users-in-china/.

35. Wei, Lingling, et al. "China Has One Powerful Friend Left in the U.S.: Wall Street." *The Wall Street Journal*, 2 Dec. 2020, www.wsj.com/articles/china -has-one-powerful-friend-left-in-the-u-s-wall-street-11606924454.

36. Schwab, Klaus, and Peter Vanham. *Stakeholder Capitalism: a Global Economy That Works for Progress, People and Planet*, p. 209. John Wiley & Sons, Inc., 2021.

37. Fink, Larry. "A Sense of Purpose." *BlackRock*, 17 Jan. 2018, www.blackrock .com/corporate/investor-relations/2018-larry-fink-ceo-letter.

38. Fink, Larry. "Larry Fink's Chairman's Letter to Shareholders." *BlackRock*, 29 Mar. 2020, www.blackrock.com/au/individual/larry-fink-chairmans-letter.

39. Wei, Lingling, et al. "China Has One Powerful Friend Left in the U.S.: Wall Street." *The Wall Street Journal*, 2 Dec. 2020, www.wsj.com/articles/china -has-one-powerful-friend-left-in-the-u-s-wall-street-11606924454.

40. "Netflix Comedy Show Censored in Saudi Arabia." *Amnesty International*, 2 Jan. 2019, www.amnesty.org/en/latest/news/2019/01/saudi-arabia-censorship-of -netflix-is-latest-proof-of-crackdown-on-freedom-of-expression/.

41. "Social Responsibility." *McKinsey & Company*, 2021, www.mckinsey.com /about-us/social-responsibility#.

42. Kolhatkar, Sheelah. "McKinsey's Work for Saudi Arabia Highlights Its History of Unsavory Entanglements." *The New Yorker*, 1 Nov. 2018, www.newyorker .com/news/news-desk/mckinseys-work-for-saudi-arabia-highlights-its-history -of-unsavory-entanglements.

43. Rose, Shelby, and Jessie Yeung. "Tencent-Backed 'Top Gun' Cuts Taiwan Flag from Tom Cruise's Jacket." *CNN*, 22 July 2019, www.cnn.com/2019/07/22 /media/top-gun-flags-intl-hnk/index.html.

44. Whitten, Sarah. "Disney under Fire for 'Mulan' Credits That Thank Chinese Groups Linked to Detention Camps." *CNBC*, 8 Sept. 2020, www.cnbc .com/2020/09/08/disney-thanked-groups-linked-to-china-detention-camps-in -mulan-credits.html.

45. "2020 Corporate Social Responsibility Report." *Social Responsibility Reporting*, The Walt Disney Company, Feb. 2021, thewaltdisneycompany.com/app/uploads /2021/02/2020-CSR-Report.pdf.

46. Craymer, Lucy. "WSJ News Exclusive | China's National-Security Law Reaches Into Harvard, Princeton Classrooms." *The Wall Street Journal*, 19 Aug. 2020, www.wsj.com/articles/chinas-national-security-law-reaches-into-harvard -princeton-classrooms-11597829402?st=ttbel6s769ksa0q&reflink=article_imessage _share.

47. Beschizza, Rob. "Uber CEO on Saudi Murder of Journalist: 'We've Made Mistakes Too.'" Boing Boing, 11 Nov. 2019, boingboing.net/2019/11/11/uber-ceo -on-saudi-murder-of-jo.html.

CHAPTER 9

1. "Ex-Facebook Executive Chamath Palihapitiya: Social Media Is 'Ripping Apart' Society | CNBC." *YouTube*, CNBC, 12 Dec. 2017, www.youtube.com/watch ?v=MakEIlvlyfE.

2. "Coronavirus: YouTube Bans 'Medically Unsubstantiated' Content." *BBC News*, BBC, 22 Apr. 2020, www.bbc.com/news/technology-52388586.

3. "Fact-Checking on Facebook." *Facebook Business Help Center*, Facebook, 2021, www.facebook.com/business/help/2593586717571940?id=673052479947730.

4. Ahmari, Sohrab. "Meet Your (Chinese) Facebook Censors." *New York Post*, 21 Oct. 2020, nypost.com/2020/10/20/meet-your-chinese-facebook-censors/.

5. Loesch, Dana. "Mailchimp Deplatforming a Local Tea Party Is a Hallmark of Fascism." *The Federalist*, 16 Nov. 2020, thefederalist.com/2020/11/16 /mailchimp-deplatforming-a-local-tea-party-is-a-hallmark-of-fascism/.

6. Montgomery, Blake. "PayPal, GoFundMe, and Patreon Banned a Bunch of People Associated with the Alt-Right. Here's Why." BuzzFeed News, 2 Aug.

2017, www.buzzfeednews.com/article/blakemontgomery/the-alt-right-has-a-payment-processor-problem.

7. Henney, Elliot. "Airbnb Cancels Reservation for Self-Proclaimed 'Proud Boy' ahead of MAGA March in DC." *WJLA*, ABC 7 News, 12 Nov. 2020, wjla.com/news/local/airbnb-reservations-proud-boys-hate-groups.

8. Oliver, Blake. "At the Expense of Its Partners' Neutrality, Expensify Boosts Biden." *Accounting Today*, 29 Oct. 2020, www.accountingtoday.com/opinion/at-the-expense-of-its-partners-neutrality-expensify-boosts-biden.

9. Bokhari, Allum. "Google Is Still Erasing Breitbart Stories About Joe Biden from Search." *Breitbart*, 3 Nov. 2020, www.breitbart.com/tech/2020/11/03/google-is-still-erasing-breitbart-stories-about-joe-biden-from-search/.

10. Alexander, Harriet. "Ex-Engineer at Google Says Glitch Which Blocked Conservative Websites Exposed Secret Internal List." *Daily Mail Online*, 22 July 2020, www.dailymail.co.uk/news/article-8547049/Ex-engineer-Google-says-glitch-blocked-conservative-websites-exposed-secret-internal-list.html.

11. Perlroth, Nicole. "One Man's Fight with Google over a Security Warning." *The New York Times*, 5 Jan. 2012, bits.blogs.nytimes.com/2012/01/05/one-mans-fight-with-google-over-a-security-warning/.

12. Epstein, Robert. "Why Google Poses a Serious Threat to Democracy, and How to End That Threat." *Senate Committee on the Judiciary*, American Institute for Behavioral Research and Technology, 16 June 2019, www.judiciary.senate.gov/imo/media/doc/Epstein%20Testimony.pdf.

13. Lee, Michael. " 'Strongly Biased in Favor of Liberals': Psychologist Says Google Manipulated Content ahead of Election That Swayed Votes." *Washington Examiner*, 25 Nov. 2020, www.washingtonexaminer.com/news/strongly-biased-in-favor-of-liberals-psychologist-says-google-manipulated-content-ahead-of-election-that-swayed-votes.

14. "Tucker Exclusive: Tony Bobulinski, Ex-Hunter Biden Associate, Speaks out on Joe Biden." *YouTube*, Fox News, 27 Oct. 2020, www.youtube.com/watch?v=2zLfBRgeFFo.

15. Schreckinger, Ben. "Justice Department's Interest in Hunter Biden Covered More Than Taxes." *POLITICO*, 10 Dec. 2020, www.politico.com/news/2020/12/09/justice-department-interest-hunter-biden-taxes-444139.

16. Blitzer, Ronn. "Facebook, Twitter Take Heat over Hunter Biden Story during Hearing; Dorsey Admits 'This Action Was Wrong'." *Fox News*, 17 Nov. 2020, www.foxnews.com/politics/facebook-twitter-grilled-hunter-biden-story-hearing-dorsey.

17. Rohde, Gregory Lewis. *Minority Broadcast Ownership*. Novinka Books, 2002. books.google.com/books?id=JcGgubA29MgC&pg=PA20&dq=hoover+%22cannot+be+thought%22+%22single+person+or+group%22&hl=en&newbks=1&newbks_redir=0&sa=X&ved=2ahUKEwjc58e787LlAhVopVkKHQD

_AIgQ6AEwAXoECAUQAg#v=onepage&q=hoover%20%22cannot%20be
%20thought%22%20%22single%20person%20or%20group%22&f=false.

18. Needleman, Sarah E. "Facebook Suspends Trump Indefinitely amid Pressure on Social Media to Clamp Down." *The Wall Street Journal*, 8 Jan. 2021, www.wsj
.com/articles/president-trump-to-regain-ability-to-tweet-from-his-personal-twitter
-account-11610032898.

19. Needleman, Sarah E. "Twitter Bans President Trump's Personal Account
Permanently." *The Wall Street Journal*, 9 Jan. 2021, www.wsj.com/articles/twitter
-says-it-is-permanently-suspending-account-of-president-trump-11610148903.

20. "Oversight Board Accepts Case on Former US President Trump's Indefinite Suspension from Facebook and Instagram." *Oversight Board*, Jan. 2021, over
sightboard.com/news/236821561313092-oversight-board-accepts-case-on-former
-us-president-trump-s-indefinite-suspension-from-facebook-and-instagram/.

21. "Facebook Bans 'Voice of Trump' from Platform." *BBC News*, BBC, 1 Apr.
2021, www.bbc.com/news/world-us-canada-56598862.

22. Thorbecke, Catherine. "Social Media Companies Restricting Trump
Accounts Cite Risk for Violence." *ABC News*, ABC News Network, 13 Jan. 2021, abc
news.go.com/Technology/social-media-companies-restricting-trump-accounts-cite
-risk/story?id=75176327.

23. Manskar, Noah. "Jack Dorsey Says Blocking Post's Hunter Biden Story Was
'Total Mistake'—but Won't Say Who Made It." *New York Post*, 25 Mar. 2021, nypost
.com/2021/03/25/dorsey-says-blocking-posts-hunter-biden-story-was-total
-mistake/?utm_campaign=iphone_nyp&utm_source=message_app.

24. Leonard, Ben. "Twitter Says Marjorie Taylor Greene Was Locked out of
Her Account by Mistake." *POLITICO*, 19 Mar. 2021, www.politico.com/news
/2021/03/19/twitter-lock-marjorie-taylor-greene-account-477161%C2%A0.

25. "Twitter Mistakenly Suspends Marjorie Taylor Greene, Again." *AP NEWS*,
Associated Press, 5 Apr. 2021, apnews.com/article/twitter-mistakenly-suspends
-majorie-taylor-greene-again-9ae8cb2aa4a2094ee1d6c9dc7a56e74b.

26. Hutzler, Alexandra. "Ron Paul Blocked from Accessing Facebook Page over
Violating 'Community Standards.'" *Newsweek*, 11 Jan. 2021, www.newsweek.com/ron
-paul-blocked-accessing-facebook-page-over-violating-community-standards-1560639.

27. My term of art for someone who is almost certainly a billionaire but whose
exact net worth is unknown.

28. Porter, Jon. "Today I Learned about Intel's AI Sliders That Filter Online
Gaming Abuse." *The Verge*, 8 Apr. 2021, www.theverge.com/2021/4/8/22373290
/intel-bleep-ai-powered-abuse-toxicity-gaming-filters.

29. Peters, Jay. "Discord Bans the r/WallStreetBets Server, but New Ones Have
Sprung to Life." *The Verge*, 27 Jan. 2021, www.theverge.com/2021/1/27/22253251
/discord-bans-the-r-wallstreetbets-server.

30. Stanley, Alyse. "Facebook Bans Popular Stock Trading Group amid Game-Stop Stock Price Chaos." *Gizmodo*, 29 Jan. 2021, gizmodo.com/facebook-bans-popular-stock-trading-group-amid-gamestop-1846156731.

31. "Psaki: Treasury Secretary Yellen 'Monitoring' GameStop Stock Situation." *Fox Business*, 27 Jan. 2021, video.foxbusiness.com/v/6226782689001#sp=show-clips.

32. "47 U.S. Code § 230—Protection for Private Blocking and Screening of Offensive Material." *Legal Information Institute*, Cornell Law School, 2021, www.law.cornell.edu/uscode/text/47/230.

33. jolt.richmond.edu/2020/08/27/the-origins-and-original-intent-of-section-230-of-the-communications-decency-act/.

34. Allyn, Bobby. "As Trump Targets Twitter's Legal Shield, Experts Have a Warning." *NPR*, 30 May 2020, www.npr.org/2020/05/30/865813960/as-trump-targets-twitters-legal-shield-experts-have-a-warning.

35. "Joe Biden Says Age Is Just a Number." *The New York Times*, 17 Jan. 2020, www.nytimes.com/interactive/2020/01/17/opinion/joe-biden-nytimes-interview.html?smid=nytcore-ios-share.

36. Shepardson, David, and Nandita Bose. "Tech Chief Executives to Defend Key Law in Front of U.S. Senate Panel on Wednesday." *Reuters*, Thomson Reuters, 27 Oct. 2020, www.reuters.com/article/us-usa-tech-senate/tech-chief-executives-to-defend-key-law-in-front-of-u-s-senate-panel-on-wednesday-idUSKBN27C2M9.

37. Norwood v. Harrison, 413 U.S. 455, 93 S. Ct. 2804 (1973). casetext.com/case/norwood-v-harrison?.

38. *Railway Employees' Dept. v. Hanson*, 351 U.S. 225, 76 S. Ct. 714 (1956). casetext.com/case/railway-employes-dept-v-hanson?.

39. *Skinner v. Railway Labor Executives' Assn*, 489 U.S. 602, 109 S. Ct. 1402 (1989). casetext.com/case/skinner-v-railway-labor-executives-assn?.

40. Romm, Tony. "The Technology 202: Lawmakers Plan to Ratchet Up Pressure on Tech Companies' Content Moderation Practices." *The Washington Post*, 17 July 2020, www.washingtonpost.com/news/powerpost/paloma/the-technology-202/2019/04/09/the-technology-202-lawmakers-plan-to-ratchet-up-pressure-on-tech-companies-content-moderation-practices/5cabee50a7a0a475985bd372/.

41. Blumenthal, Richard. "No Private Company Is Obligated to Provide a Megaphone for Malicious Campaigns to Incite Violence. It Took Blood & Glass in the Halls of Congress—& a Change in the Political Winds—for the Most Powerful Tech Companies to Recognize, at the Last Possible Moment, the Threat of Trump. T.co/td1qIMPteW." *Twitter*, 9 Jan. 2021, twitter.com/SenBlumenthal/status/1347720813076733954?s=20.

42. *Bantam Books, Inc. v. Sullivan*, 372 U.S. 58, 83 S. Ct. 631 (1963). casetext.com/case/bantam-books-inc-v-sullivan.

43. *Carlin Communications, Inc. v. Mountain States Telephone & Telegraph Co.*, 827 F.2d 1291 (9th Cir. 1987). casetext.com/case/carlin-comm-v-mountain-st-tel-tel.

44. *Hammerhead Enterprises, Inc. v. Brezenoff*, 707 F.2d 33 (2d Cir. 1983). casetext .com/case/hammerhead-enterprises-inc-v-brezenoff?.

45. *Carlin Communications, Inc. v. Mountain States Telephone & Telegraph Co.*, 827 F.2d 1291 (9th Cir. 1987). casetext.com/case/carlin-comm-v-mountain-st-tel-tel.

46. Barrett, Paul M., and J. Grant Sims. *False Accusation: The Unfounded Claim That Social Media Companies Censor Conservatives.* NYU Stern Center for Business and Human Rights, Feb. 2021, staticl.squarespace.com/static/5b6df958f8370af3217 d4178/t/60187b5f45762e708708c8e9/1612217185240/NYU%20False%20 Accusation_2.pdf.

47. Roose, Kevin. "How the Biden Administration Can Help Solve Our Reality Crisis." *The New York Times*, 2 Feb. 2021, www.nytimes.com/2021/02/02 /technology/biden-reality-crisis-misinformation.html.

CHAPTER 10

1. McWhorter, John. "The Virtue Signalers Won't Change the World." *The Atlantic*, 27 July 2020, www.theatlantic.com/ideas/archive/2018/12/why-third-wave -anti-racism-dead-end/578764/.

2. www.washingtonpost.com/outlook/2020/06/18/white-fragility-is-real -white-fragility-is-flawed/.

3. www.washingtonpost.com/entertainment/museums/african-american -museum-site-removes-whiteness-chart-after-criticism-from-trump-jr-and-conservative -media/2020/07/17/4ef6e6f2-c831-11ea-8ffe-372be8d82298_story.html.

4. Bergner, Daniel. "'White Fragility' Is Everywhere. But Does Antiracism Training Work?" *The New York Times*, 15 July 2020, www.nytimes.com/2020/07/15 /magazine/white-fragility-robin-diangelo.html?searchResultPosition=1.

5. Enloe, Chris. " 'Try to Be Less White': Coca-Cola Hit with Backlash over 'Confronting Racism' Training Course." *TheBlaze*, 21 Feb. 2021, www.theblaze.com /news/coca-cola-backlash-racism-training.

6. Borysenko, Karlyn. "Oh, What's This? Is It Talking Points That @LinkedIn Is Providing Their Employees, Provided by an Internal Whistleblower? I Do Believe It Is! Pic.twitter.com/jC8srcZUNz." *Twitter*, 23 Feb. 2021, twitter.com/DrKarlynB /status/1364275780260409348?s=20.

7. Doyle, Andrew. "The 'Anti-Racism' Movement Is Sowing Deeper Divisions." *The Spectator*, 5 Dec. 2020, www.spectator.co.uk/article/the-anti-racism -movement-is-sowing-deeper-divisions.

8. Folkenflik, David. "2 Prominent 'New York Times' Journalists Depart over Past Behavior." *NPR*, 6 Feb. 2021, www.npr.org/2021/02/06/964618301 /two-prominent-new-york-times-journalists-depart-over-past-behavior.

9. Pedersen, Courtney. "Alumna Releases Video of Journalism Department Chair Using Racial Slur in Lecture." *Central Michigan Life*, 7 July 2020, www.cm-life.com/article/2020/07/journalism-department-chair-on-paid-administrative-leave.

10. Flaherty, Colleen. *Professor Suspended for Saying Chinese Word That Sounds like an English Slur*, 8 Sept. 2020, www.insidehighered.com/news/2020/09/08/professor-suspended-saying-chinese-word-sounds-english-slur.

11. Lewis, Story by Helen. "How Capitalism Drives Cancel Culture." *The Atlantic*, 15 July 2020, www.theatlantic.com/international/archive/2020/07/cancel-culture-and-problem-woke-capitalism/614086/.

12. Jivani, Jamil. "Jamil Jivani: No One Gets to Tell Me What Kind of Black Man to Be." *National Post*, 20 July 2020, nationalpost.com/opinion/jamil-jivani-no-one-gets-to-tell-me-what-kind-of-black-man-to-be.

13. Shahrooz, Kaveh. "The Woke Want to Hear from People of Colour. Just Not All of Us." *Macdonald*, 4 Aug. 2020, www.macdonaldlaurier.ca/woke-want-hear-people-colour-just-not-us/.

14. *University of California Regents v. Bakke*, 438 U.S. 265, 98 S. Ct. 2733 (1978). casetext.com/case/regents-of-university-of-california-v-bakke?.

15. Unz, Ron. "The Myth of American Meritocracy." *The American Conservative*, 28 Nov. 2012, www.theamericanconservative.com/articles/the-myth-of-american-meritocracy/.

16. Walsh, Joe. "Biden DOJ Drops Lawsuit Claiming Yale Discriminates against White and Asian Students." *Forbes*, 3 Feb. 2021, www.forbes.com/sites/joewalsh/2021/02/03/biden-doj-drops-lawsuit-claiming-yale-discriminates-against-white-and-asian-students/?sh=6a4a912d24d2.

17. Hartocollis, Anemona. "Harvard Rated Asian-American Applicants Lower on Personality Traits, Suit Says." *The New York Times*, 15 June 2018, www.nytimes.com/2018/06/15/us/harvard-asian-enrollment-applicants.html.

18. "BIOEquality Agenda." *BIO*, 2021, www.bio.org/bioequality-agenda.

19. "Ensuring Scientific Justice by Building Bridges to Minority Communities Is Centerpiece of BIOEquality Agenda." *BIO*, 6 Aug. 2020, www.bio.org/press-release/ensuring-scientific-justice-building-bridges-minority-communities-centerpiece.

20. deMeza, William. "'Hey, Take It Outside!'—Politics in the Workplace." *JD Supra*, Holland & Knight, www.jdsupra.com/post/contentViewerEmbed.aspx?fid=8bd8d8d9-58b5-431f-b44c-349576d99129.

21. "Code of Ethics and Business Conduct: Ethics & Compliance." *Huntington Ingalls*, Huntington Ingalls Industries, Oct. 2014, www.huntingtoningalls.com/wp-content/uploads/2016/06/huntington-ingalls-code-of-ethics.pdf.

22. Ruiz, Michael. "Virginia Shipyard Worker Fired for Refusing to Remove 'Trump 2020' Hat: Report." *Fox News*, 3 Sept. 2020, www.foxnews.com/us/virginia-shipyard-worker-fired-trump-hat.

23. Kokalitcheva, Kia. "Behind the Scenes of Coinbase's Internal Fight over Black Lives Matter." *Axios*, 1 Oct. 2020, www.axios.com/coinbase-controversy-b707973c-0f24-4d1e-9690-78ac5fdb94e7.html.

24. Armstrong, Brian. "Coinbase Is a Mission Focused Company." *Medium*, The Coinbase Blog, 8 Oct. 2020, blog.coinbase.com/coinbase-is-a-mission-focused-company-af882df8804.

25. DiCamillo, Nate. "5% of Coinbase Employees Take Severance Offer over 'Apolitical' Stance." *CoinDesk*, 8 Oct. 2020, www.coindesk.com/60-coinbase-employees-take-apolitical-severance-package.

26. Brown, Abram. "Some Business Leaders Should Face a Firing Squad, Former Twitter CEO Dick Costolo Suggests in Angry Tweet." *Forbes*, Forbes Magazine, 1 Oct. 2020, www.forbes.com/sites/abrambrown/2020/10/01/some-business-leader-should-face-a-firing-squad-former-twitter-ceo-dick-costolo-suggests-in-angry-tweet/?sh=6c7d07f77b94.

27. Hess, Abigail Johnson. "60% of Employees Say Discussing Politics at Work Is Unacceptable—57% Do It Anyway." *CNBC*, 10 Feb. 2020, www.cnbc.com/2020/02/10/60percent-of-workers-say-political-talk-at-work-is-unacceptable-but-57percent-do.html.

28. Lewis, Paul. "'I See Things Differently': James Damore on His Autism and the Google Memo." *The Guardian*, 17 Nov. 2017, www.theguardian.com/technology/2017/nov/16/james-damore-google-memo-interview-autism-regrets.

29. Feinberg, Ashley. "Internal Messages Show Some Google Employees Supported James Damore's Manifesto." *Wired*, 8 Aug. 2017, www.wired.com/story/internal-messages-james-damore-google-memo/.

30. Pichai, Sundar. "Note to Employees from CEO Sundar Pichai." *Google*, 8 Aug. 2017, www.blog.google/topics/diversity/note-employees-ceo-sundar-pichai.

31. Copeland, Rob. "Fired by Google, a Republican Engineer Hits Back: 'There's Been a Lot of Bullying.'" *The Wall Street Journal*, 1 Aug. 2019, www.wsj.com/articles/fired-by-google-a-republican-engineer-hits-back-theres-been-a-lot-of-bullying-11564651801.

32. Soave, Robby. "Remember When a Democratic Polling Firm Fired the Guy Who Thought Violent Protests Could Backfire Politically?" *Reason*, 27 Aug. 2020, reason.com/2020/08/27/protests-violence-david-shor-kenosha-biden-trump/.

33. Perse, Erin. "Young Woman Sacked from Literary Agency for Standing Up for Women and Girls." *The Post Millennial*, 28 Aug. 2020, thepostmillennial.com/young-woman-sacked-from-literary-agency-for-standing-up-for-women-and-girls.

34. Hinsliff, Gaby. "Maya Forstater's Case Was about Protected Beliefs, Not Trans Rights | Gaby Hinsliff." *The Guardian*, 22 Dec. 2019, www.theguardian.com/commentisfree/2019/dec/22/maya-forstater-case-about-protected-beliefs-not-trans-rights.

35. Baculi, Spencer. "Literary Assistant Agent Sasha White Fired by the Tobias Literary Agency for 'Anti-Trans Sentiments.'" *Bounding Into Comics*, 25 Aug. 2020,

boundingintocomics.com/2020/08/25/literary-assistant-sasha-white-fired-by-the-tobias-literary-agency-for-anti-trans-sentiments/.

36. Romano, Aja. "Harry Potter and the Author Who Failed Us." *Vox*, 11 June 2020, www.vox.com/culture/21285396/jk-rowling-transphobic-backlash-harry-potter.

37. Ramaswamy, Vivek. "Vivek Ramaswamy: Election 2020—Are We Witnessing the Beginning of the End of Wokeism?" *Fox News*, 14 Nov. 2020, www.foxnews.com/opinion/affirmative-action-race-income-vivek-ramaswamy.

38. Jarvis, Jacob. "Donald Trump Made Gains in Every Demographic except for White Men." *Newsweek*, 5 Nov. 2020, www.newsweek.com/donald-trump-support-demographics-white-men-exit-poll-1545144.

CHAPTER 11

1. *Bostock v. Clayton County*, 140 S. Ct. 1731, 207 L. Ed. 2d 218 (2020). casetext.com/case/bostock-v-clayton-county?.

2. "Questions and Answers: Religious Discrimination in the Workplace." EEOC, U.S. Equal Employment Opportunity Commission, www.eeoc.gov/laws/guidance/questions-and-answers-religious-discrimination-workplace.

3. Peterson v. Wilmur Comms., 205 F. Supp. 1014 (E.D. Wisc. 2002).

4. Hooks, Kristopher. "Grant Napear Fired from Radio, Resigns from Sacramento Kings Days after Tweeting 'All Lives Matter'." *abc10.Com*, KXTV, 2 June 2020, www.abc10.com/article/sports/nba/sacramento-kings/grant-napear-fired-from-radio-resigns-from-sacramento-kings/103-65df8a48-8cc8-4bf4-af6e-59e97db66200.

5. "What You Should Know: Workplace Religious Accommodation." EEOC, U.S. Equal Employment Opportunity Commission, www.eeoc.gov/laws/guidance/what-you-should-know-workplace-religious-accommodation#:~:text=Title%20VII%20of%20the%20Civil,on%20operation%20of%20the%20business).

6. "Section 12: Religious Discrimination." *EEOC*, U.S. Equal Employment Opportunity Commission, www.eeoc.gov/laws/guidance/section-12-religious-discrimination#_ftnref25.

7. United States v. Seeger, 380 U.S. 163 (1965).

8. Welsh v. United States, 398 U.S. 333 (1970).

9. *Venters v. City of Delphi*, 123 F.3d 956 (7th Cir. 1997). casetext.com/case/venters-v-city-of-delphi?.

10. *Venters v. City of Delphi*, 123 F.3d 956 (7th Cir. 1997). casetext.com/case/venters-v-city-of-delphi?.

11. *Peterson v. Wilmur Communication, Inc.*, 205 F. Supp. 2d 1014 (E.D. Wis. 2002). casetext.com/case/peterson-v-wilmur-communication-inc?.

12. *EEOC v. United Health Programs of America, 350 F.Supp.3d 199 (E.D. NY. 2018).* scholar.google.com/scholar_case?case=1243300210889432963&hl=en&as_sdt=6,45&as_vis=1.

13. Mitchell, Joshua. "Dead Conservative Memes Can't Defeat the Identity Politics Clerisy." *The American Mind*, 3 Nov. 2020, americanmind.org/essays/dead -conservative-memes-cant-defeat-the-identity-politics-clerisy/.

CHAPTER 12

1. Summers, Lawrence H. *Remarks at NBER Conference on Diversifying the Science & Engineering Workforce*, Harvard College, 14 Jan. 2005, web.archive .org/web/20080130023006/www.president.harvard.edu/speeches/2005/nber .html.

2. Summers, Lawrence H. *Remarks at NBER Conference on Diversifying the Science & Engineering Workforce*, Harvard College, 14 Jan. 2005, web.archive.org /web/20080130023006/www.president.harvard.edu/speeches/2005/nber.html.

3. Bolton, Robert. "The Academic Hoax with a Serious Purpose." *Australian Financial Review*, 7 June 2019, www.afr.com/policy/health-and-education/sex-lies -and-manuscripts-the-academic-hoax-with-a-serious-purpose-20190606-p51v0m.

4. Sokal, Alan D. "Transgressing the Boundaries: Toward a Transformative Hermeneutics of Quantum Gravity." *JSTOR*, Duke University Press, 1996, www .jstor.org/stable/466856?seq=1.

5. Powell, Michael. "Inside a Battle over Race, Class and Power at Smith College." *The New York Times*, 24 Feb. 2021, www.nytimes.com/2021/02/24/us /smith-college-race.html.

6. Weiss, Bari. "Whistleblower at Smith College Resigns over Racism." *Common Sense with Bari Weiss*, 19 Feb. 2021, bariweiss.substack.com/p/whistleblower -at-smith-college-resigns.

7. Kaufmann, Eric. "Academic Freedom in Crisis: Punishment, Political Discrimination, and Self-Censorship." *CSPI Center*, 1 Mar. 2021, cspicenter.org/reports /academicfreedom/.

8. Note that this is an allusion to a well-known quote from Supreme Court Justice John Roberts: en.wikipedia.org/wiki/Parents_Involved_in_Community _Schools_v._Seattle_School_District_No._1

9. Coughlan, Sean. "Harvard Abolishes 'Master' in Titles in Slavery Row." *BBC News*, BBC, 25 Feb. 2016, www.bbc.com/news/education-35659685

10. Walsh, Colleen. "Harvard Announces Committee to Articulate Principles on Renaming." *Harvard Gazette*, 4 Mar. 2021, news.harvard.edu/gazette/story /2020/10/harvard-announces-committee-to-articulate-principles-on-renaming/.

11. Taylor, Kate. "Harvard's First Black Faculty Deans Let Go amid Uproar over Harvey Weinstein Defense." *The New York Times*, 11 May 2019, www.nytimes .com/2019/05/11/us/ronald-sullivan-harvard.html?referringSource=articleShare.

CHAPTER 13

1. "Clinton Drops a Pokemon Go Reference at Rally." *YouTube*, CNN, 14 July 2016, www.youtube.com/watch?v=jt6riM2aDLk.

2. Bishop, Bill, and Robert G. Cushing. *The Big Sort: Why the Clustering of like-Minded America Is Tearing Us Apart*. Mariner Books, 2009.

3. Wasserman, David. "Purple America Has All but Disappeared." *FiveThirtyEight*, 8 Mar. 2017, fivethirtyeight.com/features/purple-america-has-all-but-disappeared/.

4. Prensky, Matthew. "GOP Sen. Perdue and Perdue Chicken? Company Firmly Says No Link after Threat of Boycott." *The Daily Times*, Salisbury Daily Times, 19 Oct. 2020, www.delmarvanow.com/story/news/local/maryland/2020/10/18/georgia-sen-david-perdue-chicken-boycott-not-affiliated-kamala-harri/3702195001/.

5. Levine, Sam. "Georgia Activists Call for Coca-Cola Boycott over 'Deafening Silence' on Voting Rights." *The Guardian*, Guardian News and Media, 25 Mar.2021,www.theguardian.com/us-news/2021/mar/25/georgia-activists-coca-cola-boycott-voting-rights?CMP=Share_iOSApp_Other.

6. Bailey, Phillip M. "Trump Blasts Georgia Election Law as 'Too Weak,' Continuing Attacks on Kemp, Raffensperger as 'RINOS.'" *USA Today*, 7 Apr. 2021, www.usatoday.com/story/news/2021/04/07/trump-georgia-election-law-too-weak-attacks-kemp-raffensperger/7123560002/

7. Gelles, David. "Delta and Coca-Cola Reverse Course on Georgia Voting Law, Stating 'Crystal Clear' Opposition." *The New York Times*, 31 Mar. 2021, www.nytimes.com/2021/03/31/business/delta-coca-cola-georgia-voting-law.html.

8. Chappell, Bill. "MLB Moves All-Star Game to Colorado amid Uproar over Georgia Voting Law." *NPR*, 6 Apr. 2021, www.npr.org/2021/04/06/984711881/mlb-moves-all-star-game-to-colorado-amid-uproar-over-georgia-voting-law#:~:text=Sports-,MLB%20Moves%20All%2DStar%20Game%20To%20Colorado,Uproar%20Over%20Georgia%20Voting%20Law&text=Kirkland%2FGetty%20Images-,Major%20League%20Baseball%20has%20taken%20the%202021%20All%2DStar%20Game,stadium%20during%20the%20midsummer%20game.

9. Glazer, Emily, et al. "CEOs Plan New Push on Voting Legislation." *The Wall Street Journal*, 11 Apr. 2021, www.wsj.com/articles/ceos-plan-new-push-on-voting-legislation-11618161134.

10. Malik, Noorie. "New Consumer Alert on Yelp Takes Firm Stance against Racism." Yelp, 14 Oct. 2020, blog.yelp.com/2020/10/new-consumer-alert-on-yelp-takes-firm-stance-against-racism.

11. Sandel, Michael J. "What Money Shouldn't Buy." *The Hedgehog Review* 5, 2003: 77–97.

12. Sandel, Michael J. *What Money Can't Buy: The Moral Limits of Markets*. Penguin, 2013.

13. Sandel, Michael J. *What Money Can't Buy: The Moral Limits of Markets*. Penguin, 2013.

14. "Trump Accountability Project: Meet New Group Seeking to Blacklist Staff Who Worked for Trump Administration." *Firstpost*, 12 Nov. 2020, www.firstpost.com/world/trump-accountability-project-meet-new-group-seeking-to-blacklist-staff-who-worked-for-trump-administration-9007641.html.

15. Lizza, Ryan, et al. "AOC Wants to Cancel Those Who Worked for Trump. Good Luck with That, They Say." *POLITICO*, 9 Nov. 2020, www.politico.com/news/2020/11/09/aoc-cancel-worked-for-trump-435293.

16. Podhoretz, John. "AOC & Co.'s Loathsome Plan to Keep Lists of Pro-Trumpies." *New York Post*, 12 Nov. 2020, nypost.com/2020/11/11/aoc-co-s-loathsome-plan-to-keep-lists-of-pro-trumpies/.

17. "Joseph McCarthy: United States Senator." *Encyclopædia Britannica*, 2021, www.britannica.com/biography/Joseph-McCarthy#ref1041884.

18. Madison, James. "Federalist Papers No. 10 (1787)." *Bill of Rights Institute*, 1787, billofrightsinstitute.org/founding-documents/primary-source-documents/the-federalist-papers/federalist-papers-no-10/.

19. Cato. "Cato III." Teaching American History, 25 Oct. 1787, teachingamericanhistory.org/library/document/cato-iii/.

20. Chua, Amy, and Jed Rubenfeld. "The Threat of Tribalism." *The Atlantic*, 14 Sept. 2018, www.theatlantic.com/magazine/archive/2018/10/the-threat-of-tribalism/568342/.

CHAPTER 14

1. Ramaswamy, Vivek. "Uncounted Costs of a Living Wage." *The Harvard Crimson*, 12 Oct. 2005, dev.thecrimson.com/article/2005/10/12/uncounted-costs-of-a-living-wage/.

2. Foote, Dustin. "Student Activists on the Harvard-Yale Protest, One Year Later." *Deadspin*, 23 Nov. 2020, deadspin.com/student-activists-on-the-harvard-yale-protest-one-year-1845742949.

3. Sandel, Michael J. *What Money Can't Buy: The Moral Limits of Markets*. Penguin, 2013.

4. Norman, Jim. "Half of Americans Favor Mandatory National Service." *Gallup*, 5 Apr. 2021, news.gallup.com/poll/221921/half-americans-favor-mandatory-national-service.aspx.

5. Choi, Matthew. "Pete Buttigieg Suggests National Service Program." *POLITICO*, 16 Apr. 2019, www.politico.com/story/2019/04/15/pete-buttigieg-national-service-program-1277274.

6. Buckley, William F. *Gratitude; Reflections on What We Owe to Our Country*. Random, 1990.

7. McChrystal, Stanley A. "'You Don't Have to Wear a Military Uniform to Serve Your Country.'" *The Atlantic*, 20 July 2016, www.theatlantic.com/politics /archive/2016/07/you-dont-have-to-wear-a-military-uniform-to-serve-your -country/491765/.

8. "National Service (Amendment) Bill." Singapore Statutes Online, 27 Feb. 1967, sso.agc.gov.sg/Bills-Supp/3-1967/Published/19670301?DocDate=19670301.

9. Mathews, Mathew, et al. "CNA-IPS Survey on Ethnic Diversity in Singapore." *Lee Kuan Yew School of Public Policy*, Nov. 2017, lkyspp.nus.edu.sg/docs /default-source/ips/wp-28_cna-ips-survey-on-ethnic-identity-in-singapore.pdf ?sfvrsn=4952600a_2.

10. Yee, Amy. "How Rwanda Tidied Up Its Streets (and the Rest of the Country, Too)." *NPR*, 18 July 2018, www.npr.org/sections/goatsandsoda/2018/07 /18/628364015/how-rwanda-tidied-up-its-streets-and-the-rest-of-the-country-too.

11. "Impact Assessment of Umuganda 2007–2016." *Rwanda Governance Board*, Oct. 2017, rgb.rw/fileadmin/Key_documents/HGS/Impact_Assessment_of_Umuganda _2007-2016.pdf.

12. Jager, Avi. "The Myth of Compulsory Military Service in Israel." *The Jerusalem Post*, 18 Oct. 2018, www.jpost.com/opinion/the-myth-of-compulsory -military-service-in-israel-569779.

13. "Israel Ends Ultra-Orthodox Military Service Exemptions." *BBC News*, BBC, 12 Mar. 2014, www.bbc.com/news/world-middle-east-26542316.

14. Ari Gross, Judah. "IDF Exemption for Haredim Expires but Nothing's Likely to Change, for Now." *The Times of Israel*, Feb. 2021, www.timesofisrael .com/idf-exemption-for-haredim-expires-but-nothings-likely-to-change-for-now/.

15. Jager, Avi. "The Myth of Compulsory Military Service in Israel." *The Jerusalem Post*, 18 Oct. 2018, www.jpost.com/opinion/the-myth-of-compulsory -military-service-in-israel-569779.

16. Neuman, Scott. "France Plans Revival of Compulsory National Service." *NPR*, 28 June 2018, www.npr.org/2018/06/28/624173544/france-plans-revival-of -compulsory-national-service.

17. Atteberry, A., and A. McEachin. "School's Out: Summer Learning Loss across Grade Levels and School Contexts in the United States Today." In K. Alexander, S. Pitcock, and M. Boulay (Eds). *Summer Learning and Summer Learning Loss* and A. New York: Teachers College Press, 2016.

18. "American Express Spending & Saving Tracker: June 2012 Cost of Keeping Kids Busy in Summer." *Thenewsmarket*, American Express and Echo, 25 June 2012, preview.thenewsmarket.com/Previews/AEXP/DocumentAssets/244035_v2.pdf.

19. Atteberry, A., and A. McEachin, "School's Out: Summer Learning Loss across Grade Levels and School Contexts in the United States Today. In K. Alexander, S. Pitcock, and M. Boulay (Eds). *Summer Learning and Summer Learning Loss* and A. pp35-54. New York: Teachers College Press, 2016.

CHAPTER 15

1. Klar, Rebecca. "Pressley: Democrats Don't Need 'Any More Black Faces That Don't Want to Be a Black Voice.'" *The Hill*, 16 July 2019, thehill.com/home news/house/453007-pressley-democrats-need-any-more-black-voices-that-dont -want-to-be-a-black.

2. *The Prestige*. Directed by Christoper Nolan, Touchstone Pictures, Warner Bros, Newmarket Productions, Syncopy, 2006.

ACKNOWLEDGMENTS

I would like to thank my friends, family members, and colleagues, without whose love and support I could have never succeeded, including in writing this book. Though I will not name each of you individually, I thank you from the bottom of my heart.

In particular, I would like to thank Chris Nicholson for his intellectual partnership in writing this book. I am grateful to him for always pushing me not to simply please those who agree with me, but to be empathetic to those who don't.

I would like to thank Jed Rubenfeld for his brilliance and intellectual generosity, and Ben Pham for his loyal and tireless support. I am also grateful to my colleagues including Josephine, Kevin, Paul, Matt, Eric, Mayukh, Frank, Jo, and Ben, who helped me create the professional space to write this book.

I thank my parents for reminding me where I came from; my mother Geetha for the sacrifices that she made to allow me to get to where I am; and my father V.G. for teaching me humility through the example that he sets.

I thank my brother Shankar for his faith in me, and for always giving me strength when I need it, and my sister-in-law Nikita for being an incredible teammate. I thank my father-in-law Ash for his inspiration through excellence; my mother-in-law Mamta for her energetic support of my pursuits; and my brother-in-law Akash for his impassioned engagement with my ideas.

I thank my wife and the love of my life Apoorva, who inspires me every day to be the best version of myself. Thank you, Apoorva, for supporting all my crazy adventures, and for being the best mom in the world to our son!

Lastly, just for fun, I thank Lynn Chu. Without her special form of encouragement, I would have never completed this book.

ABOUT THE AUTHOR

Vivek Ramaswamy is an entrepreneur who has founded multiple successful enterprises. A first-generation American, he is the founder and Executive Chairman of Roivant Sciences, a new type of biopharmaceutical company focused on the application of technology to drug development. He founded Roivant in 2014 and led the largest biotech IPOs of 2015 and 2016, eventually culminating in successful clinical trials in multiple disease areas that led to FDA-approved products.

Mr. Ramaswamy was born and raised in southwest Ohio. He graduated summa cum laude in biology from Harvard in 2007 and began his career as a biotech investor at a prominent hedge fund. Mr. Ramaswamy continued to work as an investor while earning his law degree at Yale, where he was a recipient of the Paul and Daisy Soros Fellowship for New Americans.

Mr. Ramaswamy was featured on the cover of *Forbes* magazine in 2015 for his work in drug development. In 2020 he emerged as a prominent national commentator on stakeholder capitalism, free speech, and woke culture. He has authored numerous articles and op-eds, which have appeared in the *Wall Street Journal*, *National Review*, *Newsweek*, and *Harvard Business Review*.

Mr. Ramaswamy serves on the board of directors of the Philanthropy Roundtable and the Foundation for Research on Equal Opportunity.